ADVERSITY & JUSTICE

ADVERSITY & JUSTICE

A HISTORY OF THE
UNITED STATES BANKRUPTCY COURT
FOR THE EASTERN DISTRICT
OF MICHIGAN

KEVIN M. BALL

Wayne State University Press
Detroit

20 19 18 17 16   5 4 3 2 1

ISBN 978-0-8143-3607-6 (cloth)
ISBN 978-0-8143-3609-0 (ebook)

Library of Congress Cataloging Number: 2016934127

∞

Designed and typeset by Bryce Schimanski
Composed in Adobe Caslon Pro

This book is dedicated to the
Honorable Walter Shapero,
United States Bankruptcy Judge
for the Eastern District of Michigan,
whose vision, guidance, and patience
made it possible.

CONTENTS

FOREWORD

Bankruptcy, with its courts, judges, and practitioners, along with debtors, small and large, individual and corporate, and all those devoid of means but not hope, has come to occupy a more and more significant place in the national economy and the body politic. In doing so, acting together, they represent the embodiment, effectuation, and fulfillment of the age-old principle of affording the possibility of a second chance and a fair way of dealing with financial hardship and economic adversity. The evolution of the law and the attendant increase in the awareness, role, and stature of bankruptcy courts and their judges and practitioners in the personal and economic life of our country are worthy of being chronicled. In so doing, that process not only informs us of and preserves the past but also provides food for thought for further development and improvement.

In recent years, more and more courts have been documenting their histories in various ways. In the Eastern District of Michigan, David Chardavoyne has led the way with his excellent history of our district court, published in 2012. Believing that our bankruptcy court has likewise played and continues to play an important and sometimes unique role in our district, with the encouragement of United States District Judge Avern Cohn and the approval and support of my bankruptcy judge colleagues, we ascertained from our bankruptcy community a sufficient depth of interest in such a project to make it worthwhile and feasible. That led to the formation of a steering committee to develop its nature and scope. The committee originally consisted of Barbara Rom, Judith Christie, Paula Hall, John Mayer, Rita Wallace, Wallace Handler, William

Cohen (the latter two of whom have been the principal contributing and ongoing participants in the effort), and me. It soon became obvious that the road to financial and editorial success included developing a relationship with the Historical Society of the United States District Court for the Eastern District of Michigan, with which we agreed upon a protocol allowing the project to come under its umbrella. Its participation has been most helpful. Moving forward, we solicited and received the much-appreciated and adequate financial support from the bankruptcy community, chose Kevin Ball to be the researcher and author, and obtained the commitment of Wayne State University Press to be the publisher. A part of the ongoing project has been taking a number of oral histories, which in and of themselves are valuable parts of an institution's history. To be sure, completion and publication have taken longer than originally anticipated. That said, and somewhat fortuitously, the passage of time led to the inclusion of the final chapter on the city of Detroit bankruptcy, an event of such significance that the project could not have been deemed complete without it.

As must be noted, support and sponsorship of the project do not constitute an endorsement of the contents of the work or its author's expressed opinions, which are his own. The bankruptcy community and those interested and who will benefit from works such as this thank him for his authorship and his enormous contribution to what we believe is a significant and worthwhile endeavor.

Walter Shapero
United States Bankruptcy Judge
Eastern District of Michigan

ACKNOWLEDGMENTS

This book was a long time in the making. I must first acknowledge and thank the Bankruptcy Committee of the Historical Society of the United States District Court for the Eastern District of Michigan, which commissioned this book. In particular, I must single out the contributions of Judge Walter Shapero, I. William Cohen, and Wallace Handler. Judge Shapero conceived of this project and patiently led it to its conclusion. Moreover, Judge Shapero, together with Bill and Wally, were my editors, reviewing drafts, making comments, and providing encouragement (and much needed prodding) throughout the process. I have known all three of them and worked closely with them for many years, and their contributions, guidance, and friendship have been invaluable. Judy Christie of the Historical Society was also of much help, especially in getting the project off the ground, as was Elise Keller of the Eastern District of Michigan's law library.

The staff at Wayne State University Press, particularly Kathy Wildfong and Annie Martin, are due many thanks, both for their patience and their help bringing this project to a successful conclusion.

I owe a debt of gratitude to the many people who allowed me to interview them about the court. They include David Sherwood, the Hon. Avern Cohen, the Hon. Steven W. Rhodes, David Ruskin, the Hon. Walter Shapero, I. William Cohen, Robert Joslyn, Jonathan Katcher, and Martin Reisig. Ira Jaffe, the late Stuart Hertzberg, and the late Irving Boigon all sat for interviews with Judy Christie of the Historical Society. Their recollections were very useful and their cooperation much appreciated. David Chardavoyne, author of a history of the Eastern District of Michigan's district court, provided several useful suggestions that helped make this a much better book. Katherine Gullo, clerk of the bankruptcy court, and her staff were very helpful and provided me with much useful information.

The following people and firms made financial contributions to this project. I am grateful for their generous support, which has been essential to the project's success. (To the best of my knowledge this is a complete list. If by chance anyone was inadvertently omitted, I apologize and also thank them for their participation in the project.)

AlixPartners

BBK

Stanley Bershad

Bodman PLC

Buckstad & Associates

Carson Fischer, PLC

Clark Hill PLC

Couzens, Lansky, Fealk, Ellis, Roeder & Lazar

Dickinson Wright

Robert Diehl

Dykema Gossett PLLC

Erman, Teicher, Zucker and Friedman

Foley & Lardner LLP

Law Office of Jerome Frank

Gold, Lange & Majoros, PC

Goldstein, Bershad & Fried PC

Dennis Haley

Jacob & Weingarten

Jaffe, Rait, Heuer & Weiss

Dennis Kayes

Kemp Klein Law Firm

Kostopoulos and Associates

McDonald Hopkins, PLC

Ralph McDowell

Miller, Canfield, Paddock and Stone, PLC

Pepper Hamilton, LLP

Plante & Moran, PLLC

Schafer & Weiner, PC

Seyburn Kahn, PC

Hon. Walter Shapero

Silverman & Morris, PLLC

Sullivan, Ward, Asher & Patton, PC

Charles J. Taunt

Kurt Thornbladh

Nathan Zousmer

Finally, but certainly not least, I owe a great deal of thanks to my family. My oldest son, Steve, spent one summer providing invaluable assistance to me examining microfilmed copies of old issues of the *Detroit News* and *Free Press*, seeking information about the court's earliest days. My son Brian and daughter Lauren provided much-needed emotional balance throughout the project. My wife, Krispen Carroll, was as always my greatest source of support and inspiration.

INTRODUCTION

On July 18, 2013, lawyers representing an emergency manager appointed by Michigan's governor to supervise Detroit's financial affairs filed a petition for bankruptcy for the city in the United States Bankruptcy Court for the Eastern District of Michigan. In the mid-twentieth century, Detroit was the center of America's automobile industry, a manufacturing powerhouse with 1.8 million residents. By 2014, however, it had shrunk to barely more than a third that size and was buried under more than $18 billion in debt with no obvious way out. The filing made Detroit the largest city ever to seek relief under a theretofore obscure and relatively unused provision of the Bankruptcy Code known as Chapter 9, and it rocketed the Eastern District of Michigan's bankruptcy court to the forefront of national attention. Every filing, every reply, and every proceeding in the case drew attention, and news reports about the case were reported daily in both the local media and national outlets like the *New York Times* and the *Wall Street Journal*. Every statement and decision from Steven W. Rhodes, the longtime Detroit jurist assigned to the case, was scrutinized for hints on how he might rule on the most critical issues. (Rhodes himself refused to be interviewed or provide statements to the media.)

The Eastern District of Michigan's bankruptcy court was unaccustomed to such attention. With few exceptions, bankruptcy courts go about their business in relative obscurity. Bankruptcy cases are like other legal matters; they are of vital and intense interest to the participants but only very rarely gain the attention of the general public. Moreover, bankruptcy law is very complex, and its provisions to eliminate debts and set aside otherwise valid transactions often run contrary to commonly understood legal principles and widely accepted notions of fairness. The combined effect is that it is a rare occurrence for bankruptcy courts to receive more than brief mention in the media.

As a result, the bankruptcy courts are a mystery to many people, including some lawyers and perhaps especially those people who have found a need to seek relief or redress there. And yet bankruptcy is exceedingly popular among Americans, at least in practice. More than a million individuals and thousands of businesses sought relief in the bankruptcy courts in 2014, statistics that had become commonplace in the preceding two decades notwithstanding efforts by Congress to limit the number of bankruptcy filers.

If, as is sometimes said, a well-functioning democracy depends on an informed public, an understanding of an institution that directly affects the lives of so many people seems essential. This book is an effort to meet that challenge. It is a history of one of those courts, the United States Bankruptcy Court for the Eastern District of Michigan. That court is in many ways indistinguishable from most of the other ninety-three U.S. bankruptcy courts. The Bankruptcy Code and Rules are national laws that (with some local variation) govern the cases in each of those districts. Bankruptcy judges tend to be selected from each jurisdiction's local legal establishment and serve for renewable fourteen-year terms. The lawyers who practice before those judges usually come from a small, highly specialized subset of the general bar.

These characteristics are as true in the Eastern District of Michigan as they are in the other federal districts. Nevertheless, the bankruptcy court for the Eastern District of Michigan can with good reason be considered distinctive. It has a heritage tied closely to the fortunes of its region that at the same time has placed it within and sometimes at the head of major developments in bankruptcy administration. The court was created following the enactment of the Bankruptcy Act of 1898, America's first permanent national insolvency law. The automobile industry was just coming into being at that time, and the Eastern District would play an important role in shaping Detroit's burgeoning car business in the ensuing decades.[1] Perhaps because of the rapid changes the city experienced in that era (which included business failures as well as great successes), the court became a national leader in improving the bankruptcy laws and their administration. Most readers will learn here for the first time about Paul H. King, a referee[2] on the court from 1919 until his untimely death in 1942. King is now almost entirely forgotten, but he was one of Detroit's most prominent citizens, a leader in both local and national civic and charitable organizations. He was also the foremost advocate in the 1920s and 1930s for bankruptcy reform and was responsible for the founding of two of the field's most prominent professional organizations, the National Bankruptcy Conference and the National Association of Referees in Bankruptcy (now the National Conference of Bankruptcy Judges).[3] In later decades, many of the court's judges and attorneys would take leading roles in these organizations, further shaping the practice and administration of bankruptcy law.

The title of this book, *Adversity and Justice*, reflects both the nature of bankruptcy and the story of the court. Adversity is at the heart of bankruptcy. No person or business gladly files bankruptcy; they are usually forced to do so because of an otherwise insurmountable financial challenge or adverse event. Conversely, creditors want to be paid and not wait years to recover little if anything on their claims.

But justice is part of bankruptcy law, too. Ultimately, American bankruptcy law is an attempt to rationally deal with the effects of economic displacement or failure. It is based on two principles. The first is the idea of the "fresh start," that is, the debtor's ability to exit bankruptcy free from the burdens of his/her/its past financial misfortunes and mistakes. Supreme Court Justice George Sutherland explained the rationale of the fresh start in his 1934 decision in *Local Loan Co. v. Hunt*:

> The power of the individual to earn a living for himself and those dependent upon him is in the nature of a personal liberty quite as much if not more than it is a property right. To preserve its free exercise is of the utmost importance, not only because it is a fundamental private necessity, but because it is a matter of great public concern. From the viewpoint of the wage-earner there is little difference between not earning at all and earning wholly for a creditor. Pauperism may be the necessary result of either. The amount of the indebtedness, or the proportion of wages assigned, may here be small, but the principle, once established, will equally apply where both are very great. The new opportunity

in life and the clear field for future effort, which it is the purpose of the Bankruptcy Act to afford the emancipated debtor, would be of little value to the wage-earner if he were obliged to face the necessity of devoting the whole or a considerable portion of his earnings for an indefinite time in the future to the payment of indebtedness incurred prior to his bankruptcy.[4]

The other policy supporting American bankruptcy law's emphasis on justice is the principle of equitable distribution to creditors, that is, that a debtor's creditors should be treated according to predetermined, universally applied rules and not benefit from heavy-handed efforts or preferential treatment by the debtor. Taken together, these principles mark a departure from the state court free-for-alls, debtors' prisons, and widespread foreclosures and seizures that characterized pre–Bankruptcy Act debtor-creditor law. Today the American bankruptcy system is widely considered to be the world's foremost institution dealing with insolvency, with parts of it informing the laws of other countries.

However, the concepts of adversity and justice have special meaning for the bankruptcy court for the Eastern District of Michigan. Justice has certainly been part of the court's history; as detailed in these pages, its bench has been the home of several well-respected jurists, many with national reputations. However, adversity has also been part of the court's story. It has twice coped with court scandals. One of those incidents occurred nearly a hundred years ago. District Judge Arthur Tuttle, who had supervisory authority over the bankruptcy court, dealt with the problem in a very private yet effective way. Those events are publicly recounted here for the first time. The other scandal occurred in the early 1980s. Unlike the earlier one, it played out in public. The court was the subject of intense scrutiny for months, both in the media and from federal investigators. Ultimately the court's chief clerk, a deputy clerk, and one of its most prominent lawyers went to prison; a judge resigned in disgrace. The effect on the court was traumatic, and its recovery took years.[5]

Ultimately, then, for whatever civic merit this project might have, it is also a story about people. As already stated, bankruptcy courts are mostly structurally alike. Bankruptcy cases tend to be indistinguishable from one another, except to the participants themselves or on those relatively rare occasions when they are of some great public importance, such as when they are filed by a major corporation (or a major city) or when they define areas of law. What distinguishes one bankruptcy court from another, what mostly makes them worthy of our unique attention, are the people who inhabit them: the referees and judges in particular, and also the attorneys, debtors, and other parties who appear before them. This is the story of one such place, the United States Bankruptcy Court for the Eastern District of Michigan.

This book is intended for a general as well as a legal audience. The next section contains a general primer on American bankruptcy law. It is not exhaustive but is meant to help the nonspecialist understand the basic legal concepts discussed throughout the book. Those already versed in the field can safely move ahead to chapter 1.

A BRIEF OVERVIEW OF U.S. BANKRUPTCY LAW

Like most comprehensive legislation, American bankruptcy law is complex. The following overview is not intended to provide a comprehensive summary of bankruptcy law and practice. Rather, it provides an explanation of the basic provisions of bankruptcy law and is intended to be useful to lay readers and nonspecialists to aid their understanding of the events described in this book.[6]

Some portions of bankruptcy law are applicable to all bankruptcy filers (called debtors) and all kinds of cases. However, for purposes of a basic understanding of bankruptcy law, it is useful to categorize the different types of bankruptcy cases, first by the nature of the debtor and then by the kind of relief sought. Hence, there are personal liquidations (Chapter 7) and repayment plans (Chapter 13), corporate liquidations (also Chapter 7 but with significant differences from personal cases), and business reorganizations (Chapter 11).[7]

Personal Bankruptcy: Chapter 7

The ultimate goal of individual debtors (also called consumer or personal debtors) who file bankruptcy is that at the end of their case they receive a discharge from, with few exceptions, all of their financial obligations that exist as of the time their case is filed. Those obligations are voided, and creditors are barred from seeking collection of those debts.

A debtor may be denied discharge for certain kinds of serious wrong-doing, such as failing to obey bankruptcy court orders or concealing assets. Specific debts may also be excepted from discharge. These include certain classes of debt, such as student loans, most tax debts, and family support obligations. Other excepted debts are the result of particular acts of misconduct, such as fraud committed by the debtor while acting in a fiduciary capacity or injuries and losses caused by the debtor's willful and malicious actions. Such actions are uncommon. In the vast majority of consumer Chapter 7 cases, the debtor is relieved of all of his obligations to repay his debts owed at the time his case was filed, and creditors are barred by the discharge from seeking repayment.

Personal bankruptcy may be one of two types, Chapter 7 or Chapter 13 (see next section). In a Chapter 7, or straight liquidation case, the debtor turns all of his assets over to the bankruptcy court to be sold by a bankruptcy trustee. The sale proceeds are used first to pay the trustee's fees and costs associated with liquidation and distribution, and then are distributed to the debtor's creditors. Federal bankruptcy law establishes the order of payment. Secured creditors, that is, those who have liens on particular assets, are paid first from the sale proceeds of those particular assets. The remaining proceeds are distributed to certain claimants designated by law as holding "priority" claims, including certain claims for wages and employment benefits, taxing authorities, and unpaid spousal and child support. Remaining funds, if any, are distributed pro rata to the debtor's remaining creditors (known in bankruptcy parlance as unsecured creditors).

In fact, relatively few personal Chapter 7 cases result in any distribution to creditors. This is because bankruptcy law allows debtors to retain a specified portion of their real and personal property (determined by value), notwithstanding their bankruptcy filing. These are known as exemptions. Exemptions are allowed on items provided by federal or state law, such as household goods, professional tools, motor vehicles, pension and other retirement benefits, and at least a portion of the equity in the debtor's residence. Although the exemptions are mostly limited in amount, that limit usually exceeds the actual value of the debtor's property. As a result, no property is liquidated, and no distribution is made to creditors. These are called "no-asset" cases and account for the bulk of personal Chapter 7 filings.

Most Chapter 7 cases are resolved fairly quickly. A "first meeting of creditors" is held approximately thirty days after a new case is filed. The meeting has some of the characteristics of a formal judicial hearing but is held outside of the court and is presided over by a case trustee. The case trustee is a private attorney or other insolvency professional appointed by the Department of Justice to investigate the debtor's financial affairs, collect and liquidate non-exempt property, and supervise the claims process. Because of case volumes, most first meetings are over within minutes. In nearly all consumer Chapter 7 cases, the first meeting is the only formal contact the debtor will have with the bankruptcy system. In most cases, an order discharging the debtor from all of his financial obligations incurred prior to filing bankruptcy is entered about sixty days after the first meeting. The median duration of a consumer bankruptcy case in 2010, from filing to formal closing by the court clerk, was 120 days.[8]

Aside from discharge, the other, and most immediate, benefit to the debtor is the automatic stay of proceedings. The automatic stay goes into effect immediately when a new bankruptcy case is filed, without notice to any creditor, and halts any kind of action by a creditor to enforce or collect a debt or other financial obligation. A creditor or collector who knowingly violates the stay may be subject to sanctions, and actions taken in violation of the stay are void or voidable.[9] Creditors may seek an order from the court modifying the automatic stay in certain circumstances.

Therefore, once the debtor files bankruptcy, the only remedy available to most unsecured creditors is to file a proof of claim with the bankruptcy court and share in any distribution that might be made in the case.

Personal Bankruptcy: Chapter 13

Chapter 13 bankruptcy is available to debtors with regular income. Debtors agree to use a portion of their ongoing income to repay all or a portion of the debts over a three- to five-year period, during which time their financial affairs remain under the supervision of a case trustee (known as a Chapter 13 standing trustee).

In return, Chapter 13 debtors obtain the benefit of the automatic stay and retain all of their property, even if it has a higher value than the exempt amounts allowed under the law. Therefore, Chapter 13 is sometimes an attractive option for debtors with substantial equity in their property, particularly their personal residences.

Payments are made according to a Chapter 13 Plan that is subject to review by the standing trustee and creditors and that must be approved by the court. Debtors receive a discharge when they make all of the payments required under the approved plan. Debtors who fail to comply with the plan have their cases either dismissed or converted to Chapter 7. In 2013, 31.1 percent of the individual bankruptcy cases filed nationally were Chapter 13 cases.[10]

Business Bankruptcy: Chapter 7

For businesses like corporations and limited liability companies, Chapter 7 remains the basic form of bankruptcy. However, unlike individuals, business organizations neither receive a discharge nor may claim a portion of their property as exempt from liquidation. This is because bankruptcy law permits corporations and other business entities to either reorganize under Chapter 11 (see next section) or liquidate under Chapter 7. In a Chapter 7 liquidation, the operations of the business cease when the bankruptcy case is filed. The bankrupt business's property is turned over to the court and is liquidated by the trustee. In addition, the trustee may seek recovery of certain pre-filing payments made by the debtor to its creditors (known as avoidance actions in the Bankruptcy Code but often described in media reports as "claw-back" actions). Any recoveries from those actions are added to the liquidation proceeds and are distributed to creditors according to the priorities established by bankruptcy law.

Business Bankruptcy: Chapter 11

Financially troubled businesses that do not wish to liquidate may seek relief under Chapter 11. Chapter 11 bankruptcy, known as reorganization, is the most complicated form of bankruptcy. Cases often stretch out for years before they are finally resolved.

Under Chapter 11, the automatic stay provides companies with breathing space from their creditors while their managers develop a plan of reorganization. The contents of the plan are regulated by statute and subject to approval by the court and acceptance of a majority of the debtor's creditors. Creditor acceptance is key. Therefore, much of management's efforts in a Chapter 11 case are directed toward negotiations with creditors. A plan of reorganization agreed to by a majority of creditors is likely to be approved by the court, sometimes even if it does not meet all of the statutory requirements. Alternatively, the court has the authority to approve a plan even when creditors do not accept it under a procedure known as "cram-down."

Chapter 11 provides major benefits to a reorganizing company besides debt reduction. Provisions of the bankruptcy code allow the courts to terminate the debtor's long-term contracts and obligations, including real estate and equipment leases, purchase contracts, and collective bargaining agreements. Hence, Chapter 11 has become a favorite restructuring tool of retailers and airlines.

As noted, businesses in Chapter 11 are usually run by their pre-bankruptcy managers. However, creditors may organize into formal committees with some oversight powers. Additional oversight is provided by the Office of the United States Trustee, a division of the Department of Justice (and different than Chapter 7 case trustees or Chapter 13 standing trustees). Despite the attention given to prominent Chapter 11 cases like those involving Lehman Brothers, Enron, and General Motors, they account for a small number of bankruptcy case filings. According to the Administrative Office of the United States Courts, Chapter 11 cases accounted for less than 1 percent of all bankruptcy cases filed in the United States in 2013 and 2014.[11]

1

BANKRUPTCY IN THE
NINETEENTH CENTURY

Although bankruptcy law is now entrenched within the American legal system, this was not always so. Indeed, although Article I, Section 6 of the Constitution gives Congress the authority to establish uniform bankruptcy laws, it did so only fitfully and over great opposition until 1898. However, an examination of the evolution of American bankruptcy law before 1898 is helpful to understanding how it was practiced thereafter. This chapter provides a short overview of nineteenth-century bankruptcy law and describes the events leading to the passage of the 1898 Bankruptcy Act, with special attention, where applicable, to the state of Michigan and more particularly to the Eastern District.

AMERICAN BANKRUPTCY BEFORE 1898

Although the Constitution authorizes Congress to enact uniform bankruptcy laws, congressional efforts to pass such laws throughout the nineteenth century were controversial and the resulting statutes were widely unpopular and only briefly in force. National financial troubles in the late eighteenth century led Congress to narrowly pass the first national bankruptcy law in 1800. The statute was administered by the federal courts and was more of a collection device than a bankruptcy law in the modern sense, although it did provide discharges for debtors. Jurisdiction under the law was limited to those cases filed by creditors against "merchant" debtors, that is, small businessmen with trade debts. The 1800 act was very unpopular and was repealed in 1803. Presaging criticism leveled at later bankruptcy laws, its opponents claimed among other things that the law mostly benefited auctioneers, bailiffs, attorneys, and the like while creditors saw little real financial gain.

Despite the frequent economic downturns in the U.S. economy in the early decades of the nineteenth century, Congress did not enact another bankruptcy law until 1841, four years after Michigan gained statehood. Like many other issues of the antebellum period, bankruptcy legislation was caught up in the growing divide between the North and South and their conflicting concepts of national power. Uniform bankruptcy laws were favored on the whole by northern merchant and manufacturing interests but opposed in the southern agrarian states. However, the U.S. economy frequently swayed between periods of boom and bust in the earlier nineteenth century, giving rise to multiple financial crises and spurring support for federal bankruptcy legislation. Speculative investing was rampant in the early 1830s. By the middle of 1837, the economic bubble it caused burst, pushing the country into another crisis.

Michigan had only just become a state, but it played something of an unwitting role in the events leading to the adoption of a new bankruptcy law. Because of its rapid growth as settlers moved to the state from more established places in the East, and in part because of its impending statehood, Michigan in the 1830s was the site of unchecked land speculation. One very heavily invested speculator was U.S. senator Daniel Webster of Massachusetts. An ardent nationalist and a fervent advocate for national bankruptcy legislation, Webster traveled to Detroit in July 1837 to visit his son Fletcher, a lawyer in the city, and to view investment property he held in the area. He used his visit to advocate for a new bankruptcy law:

> In times like these, we find ourselves in the midst of a serious financial and industrial crisis. It just seems inconceivable that conditions can ever right themselves enough to have prosperous times in this country again. Trade and industry throughout the land are disorganized. Banks by the hundreds have failed. Securities have fallen to one half or even one quarter of their former values. The

problem of unemployment has become general, and in all large cities special committees have been organized to provide food and clothing of the poor and unemployed. Widespread want and distress have led to labor strikes. . . . Extensive competition, lowering prices, and unwise speculation have brought about a crisis.

Webster's sympathy for the financially disadvantaged may have been influenced by his own circumstances. His biographer, Robert Remini, describes him as a high-risk speculator who was likely hundreds of thousands of dollars in debt by 1837. Indeed, Webster viewed his situation as so serious that he considered giving up his illustrious Senate career to devote his attention to righting his financial affairs (Remini 1997, 452–53, 469).

The 1837 depression eventually motivated Congress to adopt a new bankruptcy law in 1841, again amid much controversy. Thirty-three thousand Americans sought relief under the new law, which unlike the 1800 statute permitted voluntary case filings. However, like its predecessor it proved highly unpopular. Not only was the law widely criticized for its high administrative costs and meager dividends for creditors, but constitutional challenges kept its legitimacy in doubt. The law was repealed in 1843 after being in effect for only fourteen months.

A postwar economic downturn led to the passage of yet another national bankruptcy law in 1867. Although the law was, like its predecessors, enacted over considerable congressional resistance (supporters achieved two-vote majorities in each chamber), it provided needed relief for many Americans. Over one hundred thousand cases were filed in the first four years following its enactment. Officers called registers (so named because debtors were registered as bankrupt once a district judge had adjudicated their petitions) performed the daily work of administering bankruptcy cases. However, unlike modern bankruptcy judges, registers had little judicial authority; federal district judges retained that power.

The law nonetheless included provisions that would have been familiar to modern bankruptcy practitioners. Both voluntary and involuntary petitions were permitted. Although aimed at merchants and other small businessmen, like the 1841 law, its provisions applied likewise to farmers and business corporations. Bankrupts' property was protected to the extent provided by their state laws.

A total of seven men served as registers in the Eastern District of Michigan during the eleven-year tenure of the 1867 bankruptcy law. The original appointees were B. J. Brown of East Saginaw, Hovey K. Clarke of Detroit, James E. Dalliba of Marquette (then in the Eastern District), and Charles Draper of Pontiac. They were joined by Eugene Pringle of Jackson in 1872 and Edwin Hadley of Adrian in 1874. Another register, Thomas M. James of East Saginaw, was appointed in 1873, possibly as B. J. Brown's replacement. The best known of the registers was Hovey Clarke, who was a prominent lawyer in Detroit. Clarke was born in 1812 and active in local politics and community affairs. His appointment as register extended over the entire duration of the 1867 act, and he continued to practice after its repeal until ill health forced his retirement. Clarke died in 1889.[1]

Although the law was amended several times, the changes were inadequate to satisfy the many objections raised to it. However, debtors and creditors were united in their criticism of the bankruptcy system's high administrative costs and low creditor dividends; over the course of the law's existence, creditors received, on average, less than ten cents on the dollar (Warren 1935, 1999, 113). The law was little mourned when Congress repealed it in 1878.

ENACTMENT OF THE BANKRUPTCY ACT OF 1898

By the time Congress repealed the despised 1867 bankruptcy law in 1878, the U.S. economy had rebounded from the financial panic earlier in the decade. A *New York Times* editorial at the end of 1880 described the country as "extremely prosperous."[2] Moreover, the nature of American business had changed. Where the economy before the Civil War had been mostly agrarian and local, the interstate sale of goods was the growth engine of the country's economy in the Gilded Age. Between 1870 and 1880, the length of railroad track in the United States increased from 52,922 to 93,262 miles (Gordon 2005 , 235). However, merchants' cross-country expansion of their customer base also posed new challenges. As they did with their local customers, vendors generally sold goods to their far-away customers on credit. Should those customers fall into financial difficulty, the long distances separating them from their interstate vendors gave their local creditors a distinct advantage. Given the limitations of communication in the nineteenth century, local creditors were likely to learn of their customers' financial difficulties earlier than their more distant counterparts would and thus take action more quickly. Moreover, jurisdictional rules required creditors to file collection suits in the local court in the customer's state. The overall result was that financially troubled debtors favored local creditors over those located farther away. Even local creditors were faced with a "race to the courthouse," sometimes bringing about a debtor's premature demise. Finally, proximity notwithstanding, the largest, best-financed creditors tended to prevail when competing with other smaller creditors for a debtor's limited assets.

Businessmen were troubled by another concern. The boom and bust cycle of America's nineteenth-century economy meant that some of their ranks were left with crushing debts when their businesses failed. The concept of voluntary debtor relief, which was part of the 1867 bankruptcy law, retained considerable salience among businessmen.

Motivated by these concerns, members of commercial trade organizations mobilized to put bankruptcy legislation back on the public agenda. They faced several serious obstacles that would combine to block enactment of a national bankruptcy law for nearly twenty years. First, the dissatisfaction that led to the repeal of the 1867 law remained strong. Opposition on this front took two forms. In practice, the cost of administering bankrupts' cases under the old act tended to exhaust any funds available for distribution to creditors. The generally held view was that case administration under the old act was at best inefficient and at worst corrupt: "So lasting was the impression made by the waste and frauds and defective machinery of the Bankruptcy Act of 1867 that, as late as 1893, it was stated that 'the prejudices created under the Act of 1867 make a fair discussion of any bankruptcy act difficult'" (Warren 1935, 1999, 127). Moreover, populist sentiments against a new bankruptcy law ran high. Southern and western farmers inherently distrusted any debt collection system proposed by commercial interests. They believed that the 1867 act had been little more than a tool used by northern and eastern merchants to wrongfully take away their property and their livelihoods. This attitude would persist through the eventual enactment of a new bankruptcy law in 1898, despite repeated concessions made by the legislation's sponsors to address populist concerns.

A second challenge faced by bankruptcy's proponents was that aside from commercial groups there was little interest in enacting a new national bankruptcy law. Recent economic growth had all but eliminated popular and congressional interest in a new law (Warren 1935, 1999, 128). However, the commercial groups' concerns were real and they had no alternative but to seek help from Congress. The existing state laws were well entrenched and inherently protected local interests. Moreover, Article I of the Constitution gave Congress exclusive authority to enact bankruptcy legislation. Finally, Congress was becoming increasingly interested in regulating the national economy, as evidenced by its adoption later in the decade of the Interstate Commerce Act (1887) and the Sherman Antitrust Act (1890).

With these factors in mind, the National Convention of the Representatives of the Commercial Bodies of the United States met in St. Louis in 1880 to draft and promote enactment of national bankruptcy legislation. These efforts would gain much attention, but they also garnered much opposition and no new legislation was passed. In fact, new comprehensive bankruptcy legislation would be promoted by the commercial groups and introduced in Congress in most biennial sessions for the next eighteen years until the Bankruptcy Act was finally approved in 1898.

Indeed, bankruptcy legislation might not have been enacted at any time in the 1890s had it not been for the depression of 1892–93. That depression is considered by many to be the worst the United States experienced until the Great Depression of 1929. While the 1892 depression was not in itself sufficient cause to enact bankruptcy legislation, complete opposition to any bankruptcy law was not a factor in subsequent legislative debates. Those debates instead focused on whether a new bankruptcy law should include provisions for involuntary bankruptcy, reflecting the concerns of populist forces in Congress at the peak of their political power. Even so, it would not be until 1898, in the wake of the Republicans' massive victories in the 1896 elections, that the legislation's supporters found a real chance of seeing it become law. The law's passage was nonetheless preceded by nearly two years of legislative maneuvering and resulted in two similar but different bills from each chamber.

The two bills were sent to conference committee, which issued its report with compromise legislation on June 15. The *Detroit Free Press*'s editorial writers joined those who supported the bill.[3] Opposition to the legislation remained strong in other quarters. Former Michigan congressman Levi Griffin gave an address at the Commercial Law League's annual convention in which he raised objections to the law that would be familiar to followers of legislative debates over later bankruptcy statutes. The proposed law, he said, would encourage debtors to take unreasonable financial risks and would promote fraudulent conduct. He urged that provisions for voluntary bankruptcy be stripped from the bill.[4] Like most opponents of the law, Griffin was a Democrat. Notwithstanding its 1896 electoral drubbing, the Democratic Party remained deep in the throes of the populist movement; its 1900 presidential candidate would again be William Jennings Bryan, who had been soundly defeated by McKinley in 1896. Democrats consistently opposed the proposed bankruptcy law. They linked bankruptcy laws to the reviled gold standard as a tool to be used by northern and eastern financiers to rob southern and western farmers and ranchers of their land and livelihoods. Ultimately, they preferred to take their chances with local judges in state court collection cases rather than distrusted federal ones appointed by the national government (Tabb 1999). Partisan identification with the legislation was strong; Michigan's congressional delegation consistently split along party lines in the many votes leading to the law's passage. However, the law gained the approval of both houses of Congress by the end of June, and President McKinley signed the bill into law on July 1, 1898.

THE 1898 BANKRUPTCY ACT

The 1898 act became the United States' first permanent bankruptcy law, remaining in force, with numerous and sometimes significant amendments, until it was replaced by the Bankruptcy Code in 1978. The act, like its predecessor, provided for both voluntary and involuntary bankruptcy, although farmers were excluded from the latter. It included the basis of the principle of the fresh start through its inclusion of state exemption laws. Moreover, it did away with the proverbial race to the courthouse by incorporating a principle of equitable treatment of all creditors. Therefore, the law included aggressive provisions that allowed for certain pre-filing payments to creditors known as preferences to be avoided, with the money coming back into the bankruptcy estate to be distributed to all creditors in accordance with the priorities established in the law. The act did not in its original form include provisions for anything like the modern Chapters 11 and 13, although some small businesses could seek to avoid liquidation through a proceeding known as an arrangement.

However, the most prominent feature of the new law was in the way it structured bankruptcy administration.

To a large extent, the creation of the position of referee reflected Progressive Era businessmen's faith in the ability of professional government managers to counter the waste and corruption of the Gilded Age. Just as urban reformers sought to replace political machine bosses with professional city managers, the proponents of new bankruptcy legislation sought to correct past abuses by creating the position of bankruptcy referee.

The referees were charged under the Bankruptcy Act with general case supervision. Their positions were somewhat analogous to those of today's bankruptcy judge but also included many of the duties performed by the United States Trustee and case trustees under the modern Bankruptcy Code. The referees' judicial responsibilities included the authority to grant or dismiss voluntary and involuntary bankruptcy petitions and conduct meetings of creditors, as well as to exercise such other additional duties that might be assigned them by the district judge. In addition to their judicial responsibilities, referees were also responsible for many administrative activities now performed by case trustees or the United States Trustee. In particular, referees themselves made all disbursements to creditors. By placing the lion's share of responsibility for case administration with a single official, moreover one whose compensation depended on successful outcomes, the drafters of the Bankruptcy Act believed they had resolved the accountability problems that had been the downfall of prior national insolvency laws. However, while the system worked well in the Eastern District of Michigan during Paul King's tenure, abuse continued and even thrived in some other jurisdictions. Moreover, abuses in the conduct of corporate reorganization cases, in which the referees played smaller roles, led to major investigations of the bankruptcy courts. King would give much of his attention over the remainder of his career to solving these systemic challenges.

While referees were properly considered judicial officials, they were unique in many important respects. Referees were not political branch appointees. In fact, no federal department or agency had the authority to supervise bankruptcy administration under the Bankruptcy Act. Instead, bankruptcy court supervision fell within the exclusive authority of the district judges in each federal judicial district. The judges appointed the referees for two-year terms, and appointments were generally renewed.

The appointments were originally conceived as part-time positions; almost all were lawyers who maintained a private practice (although they were barred from acting in other capacities in bankruptcy cases).

The bankruptcy courts were self-sustaining entities. Court operations were funded through a combination of filing fees and fees retained as a percentage of funds collected in asset cases. This extended to the referees, who were paid a small flat fee plus a percentage of the disbursements made in each case. In other words, most of a referee's compensation was in the nature of a contingency fee; the referee received no compensation beyond the flat fee unless assets could be liquidated and distributed to creditors. While intended to reduce gouging, the referee's fee-based system of compensation was frequently criticized, although it would not be replaced with a salary-based system until 1946.

Bankruptcy law in the United States is wholly a creation of Congress. The 1898 act established the fundamental template for U.S. bankruptcy laws that remains in place to this day. Even when those laws were overhauled, as they were in 1978, or substantially modified, as happened in 1938 and 2005, the new statutes are more an evolution than they are a replacement of the original act. Therefore, the 1898 act is necessarily the starting point for any account of the bankruptcy courts. However, how that law affected and was affected by a single place, the Eastern District of Michigan, is the story told in this book.

2

THE EARLY DAYS OF THE BANKRUPTCY ACT, 1898–1919

Although President William McKinley signed the Bankruptcy Act into law in early July 1898, it did not become effective until the Supreme Court approved court rules for its implementation, which did not happen until November of that year. Nonetheless, district judges around the country scrambled to appoint referees to oversee the new cases. Unlike the seven registers the Eastern District had under the 1867 law, it would initially have only a single referee. Chief District Judge Henry Swan appointed fifty-year-old Harlow P. Davock to be the Eastern District of Michigan's first bankruptcy referee in August 1898.

HARLOW P. DAVOCK (1898–1910): THE EASTERN DISTRICT'S FIRST REFEREE

The 1898 act did not establish a central supervising authority for the new bankruptcy courts. Instead, each new referee answered to the chief judge of his district. Given the lack of central authority, each of the new referees essentially had to create a new court from scratch, with the untested Bankruptcy Act and memories of the much-maligned 1867 law as their only guides. In that respect, Swan might have seen Davock's technical background as beneficial. Born in Buffalo, New York, in 1848, Davock was a latecomer to the practice of law. He graduated from the University of Michigan in 1870 with two degrees, a Bachelor of Arts from the university's Literary Department and a civil engineering degree. He worked as an engineer in Ohio, Indiana, Illinois, and Michigan's Upper Peninsula from graduation until at least 1877, during which time he helped with construction of the Soo Locks. Davock was admitted to the Michigan Bar in 1878 after reading law in the office of Maybury & Conely, a Detroit firm. However, he did not begin practicing law until 1882.

Although the automobile industry would not take root until the following decade, Detroit in the 1890s had moved away from its economic reliance on timber and mining, although those industries were still dominant in the remainder of the Eastern District. Instead, Detroit was a growing industrial town that was home to stove manufacturers, coach and railroad car builders, and cigar makers. The city's population expanded dramatically during this time, growing from about 205,000 residents in 1890 to 285,000 in 1900. The booming city provided many opportunities for Harlow Davock, in terms of both his legal career and his interest in public service. Davock was increasingly involved in public affairs throughout the 1890s. He served as a Republican member of the Michigan legislature for a single term in 1893–94 and was then appointed United States Supervisor of Elections in 1894. He was a member of the Detroit Board of Health from 1895 to 1900 and was an unsuccessful candidate for the Wayne County Circuit Court in 1905.

Case filings during Davock's tenure were few in number by contemporary standards, ranging from a low of 158 in 1903 to a high of 254 in 1909. However, the general nature of cases then was different than it is now. Provisions for business reorganization and wage-earner repayment plans were not added to the Bankruptcy Act until 1938. Moreover, wage earners borrowed little and so made up a smaller percentage of bankruptcy filers than they do today. Instead, in the first decade following the act's enactment, most bankrupts were small business owners, and their cases often included assets to be liquidated. The referees were more closely involved in the day-to-day administration of those cases than are modern judges. For instance, referees were responsible for presiding over first meetings of creditors, maintaining all accounts, and making disbursements from an estate.

In addition, the relative workload for Harlow Davock was greater than that for referees in other districts. As originally enacted, the Bankruptcy

Act authorized the appointment of a referee for each U.S. county. However, the sole authority for appointing referees rested with the chief judge in each federal district, and the act's referee per county requirement went mainly unheeded. Still, most major metropolitan areas had more than one referee-in-bankruptcy. Detroit had become the nation's ninth largest city by the 1910 and yet was served by a single referee. What was intended to be a part-time position dominated Davock's time, even with Lee Joslyn's appointment in 1904 as referee in the district's Northern Division. He maintained his office in the Albert Kahn–designed Trussed Concrete Building at West Lafayette Boulevard and Wayne Street (now Washington Boulevard) in Detroit.[1] That was also where he maintained his courtroom. In fact, the bankruptcy court would not be located in the same building as the district court in Detroit until the new federal building was completed in 1935.

Such arrangements were the norm in the early twentieth century. This was due in part to Congress's intention that bankruptcy administration be a part-time endeavor. However, it also reflected a general attitude, prevalent among federal judges in particular, that the bankruptcy courts should not benefit from the prestige of the federal courts.

Davock proved himself an able advocate for the new Bankruptcy Act in an interview with the *Detroit Free Press* on the first anniversary of his appointment. Expressing sentiments common among early supporters of the law, he said, "Every civilized nation has its bankruptcy law—some legal method of procedure for extricating from hopeless financial predicament those unfortunate businessmen that would otherwise be unable again to become independent in the battle of life."[2]

The contentiousness that accompanied passage of the Bankruptcy Act did not disappear with its enactment in 1898. The American Bankers Association, which had stayed on the sidelines during the eighteen years of debate that preceded the bill's passage, led efforts to repeal the legislation once it was enacted. Bills to repeal the Bankruptcy Act were regular fixtures on the congressional agenda in the years following its enactment (an editorial appearing in the *New York Times* on January 13, 1906, referred to "the biennial movement to secure the repeal of the bankruptcy law"). Seeking to protect their new system, several of the new bankruptcy referees, including Harlow Davock, organized quickly. They met in Chicago in late July 1899, just a year after the law's passage. Forming the first national referees' association, the assembled officials sought to head off opponents of the new bankruptcy law by proposing amendments dealing with its most problematic and controversial provisions. These mostly concerned objections to the discharge of debts and the recovery of certain payments made by bankrupts on the eve of filing their bankruptcy cases. The first bill to repeal the act was introduced in the House in January 1900. Its supporters were unable to gain sufficient votes for its immediate passage.

The referees' proposed changes were incorporated into different legislation introduced by Congressman George Ray on February 13, 1901. Predictably, supporters of repeal blocked passage of the Ray bill. The referees met again in Buffalo in August 1901 with the future of the Bankruptcy Act in question. Davock attended that meeting and was elected the group's second vice president. That conference resulted in a substantial effort to mobilize broader public support for retention of the act. Fourteen thousand letters were sent to businesses and business associations throughout the United States. The referees presented a report to Congress in December 1901 that summarized the responses. A great majority of the more than 1,000 responses indicated support in principle for a national bankruptcy law. However, most of the respondents also indicated that some change was needed: 794 indicated support for the Ray bill, while only 120 favored the act's repeal.

The referees' lobbying effort was a success; efforts to repeal the act failed. Congress instead passed the referee-supported legislation sponsored by Congressman Ray in February 1903. The referees' association was disbanded shortly after the Ray bill's passage. The referees did not again organize when another significant repeal bill was filed in 1906. That challenge was in any event unsuccessful, as was another in 1910.

As already noted, the act as passed in 1898 contained no provision for business reorganizations. Those kinds of matters were handled in state or federal courts through equity receiverships or similar proceedings. Most of the bankruptcy court's docket was filled with the cases of failed small businesses and their owners. Aside from the daily work of case administration, the routine business of the court included the consideration of involuntary petitions,[3] objections to discharge, and actions to set aside so-called preferential transfers and fraudulent conveyances. These cases rarely gained broad public attention. However, from time to time the bankruptcy court would hear cases of particular notoriety. The most prominent of these during Davock's tenure was that of the stock brokerage of Cameron Currie & Co. and its partners, Cameron Currie and Louis Case.[4]

Cameron Currie & Co. was Detroit's largest and most prestigious stock brokerage. Founded in 1892, it handled the accounts of many of Detroit's most prominent families. Louis Case started with the firm as a cashier in 1899 and quickly advanced in the organization; he was made a partner in 1902. By 1908, he was the brokerage house's managing partner.

Hayden, Stone & Co. was Currie & Co.'s eastern correspondent. Because of the logistics of conducting business cross-country in the 1900s, Hayden, Stone routinely advanced payment for Currie's stock purchases. It held the margined stocks and copper from Currie equal to 120 percent of Currie's indebtedness to secure payment. Stocks purchased by Hayden, Stone on behalf of Currie & Co. were held until payment was received, except when they could be delivered without diminishing Hayden, Stone's equity cushion.

Although it would later be proved that Currie & Co. was insolvent by the summer of 1907, the firm appears to have been unaware of its condition until a financial crisis struck the nation late in the year. Unlike the widespread effect of other panics, this one was mainly limited to the financial sector. Stock values fell by 50 percent, but the crisis quickly ended by November after eastern bankers led by J. P. Morgan worked cooperatively to stabilize banks (the incident led to the formation of the Federal Reserve in 1914).

However, the brief downturn was sufficient to bring Currie & Co.'s problems to the fore. Evidence later produced in the Wayne County Circuit Court established that it was at about this time that the firm "resorted to irregular and dishonest practices" to disguise its true financial situation and leave its customers and the general public unaware of its condition.[5]

Justice Joseph Steere, writing for the Michigan Supreme Court, later described the events leading to Currie & Co.'s collapse as "an instructive chapter in frenzied finance." Currie & Co. "kited" over $2.25 million in accommodation drafts from Hayden, Stone, usually rushing to cover them only at the last possible opportunity. Currie & Co. also developed a kind of Ponzi scheme, withholding delivery of stocks paid for by its customers and instead returning them to Hayden, Stone as collateral to secure delivery of stocks purchased for other customers. Currie & Co.'s customers were largely unaware of these activities and their complaints were relatively few.

Prior to June 1908, Currie & Co. conducted business with a few corresponding firms on the East Coast besides Hayden, Stone. However, reacting to considerable pressure from the company, Currie & Co. moved all of its eastern business to Hayden, Stone on June 22, 1908. At the same time, Hayden, Stone sent agents to Detroit, claiming a need to establish a new margin system and to evaluate the proportion of low-priced stock carried by Currie's customers.[6]

The timing of the request and Currie & Co.'s ready assent to Hayden, Stone's demands for both consolidation and an audit suggest that both firms' managers knew that the jig was up. However, Currie would testify that he was unaware of the firm's condition, stating that he had devoted all of his attention to overseeing the partnership's interests in Upper Peninsula copper mines and had left management of the firm to Louis Case. However, his testimony on this point was less than credulous. Currie later disclosed that he was aware of problems with some of the brokerage's accounts in the spring of 1908, which led him to pursue negotiations with Hayden, Stone and resulted in an infusion of $60,000 into the firm upon the deal's conclusion. Currie would later state that he and his wife turned over more than $1 million in stocks and securities to the firm in an effort to stem its slide.

When Hayden, Stone's examination was completed on July 13, 1908, it demanded that Currie & Co. be placed in receivership. Cameron Currie himself filed the application with the Wayne County Circuit Court on July 13, 1908. The court appointed Fred Austin of Detroit as receiver on July 18. In the meantime, Hayden, Stone took over the Currie & Co. offices and was running the brokerage house under its own name. The receiver obtained an injunction preventing Hayden, Stone from liquidating any stocks, including those held as collateral for Currie & Co.'s debt.

On August 10, 1908, Cameron Currie and Louis Case filed bankruptcy in their personal capacities and for their co-partnership. Referee Davock appointed Fred Austin as trustee in the three bankrupts' single case (it was common at the time for partners' estates to be administered in a single case; Davock even denied an investor's motion to appoint a separate trustee for Currie). Ironically, the effects of J. P. Morgan's efforts to stabilize banks were beginning to have a positive impact the financial markets. Stock prices began to rise quickly in the late summer, and Hayden, Stone and the trustee agreed that Currie & Co.'s stock collateral should be liquidated. The sale was successful enough to satisfy Hayden, Stone's claim of $1.34 million and still net $325,000 for the bankruptcy estate.

Despite its success, the stock liquidation did not end the disputes between Hayden, Stone and the bankruptcy estate. Various actions between the two continued in both state and bankruptcy courts until at least 1916. On the other hand, Davock moved quickly against Cameron Currie and Louis Case. On March 10, 1910, he entered an order denying their discharges. The trial revealed other efforts the firm had employed to disguise its condition, including the creation of fictitious accounts and a bookkeeping system Davock called "unintelligible."[7] Newspaper reports at the time noted that their defense was not helped by Case's testimony that he viewed the firm as free to do what it wanted with its customers' stock certificates and other property.[8]

The Currie case highlights some of the important differences between practices in bankruptcy courts under the early act and later. Conflicts of interest, which are of preeminent concern today, were given far less consideration then. The estates of Currie and Case were administered together with that of their co-partnership. An investor's motion to appoint a separate trustee for Cameron Currie was denied as unwarranted. The proceedings to block Currie and Case's discharges were even tried together. Moreover, legal and jurisdiction limits hemmed in the referee's authority. Davock officially presided over the discharge case not in his capacity as referee-in-bankruptcy but rather as a special master appointed by the district judge, to whom the act gave primary authority over such actions. Limited grants of jurisdiction to the bankruptcy courts also meant that more matters that would now be considered "core proceedings" were then litigated in state courts. Actions for turnover, like the Hayden, Stone case, as well as proceedings to avoid preferential or fraudulent transfers, were typically filed in the state courts.

Davock would not live much beyond his decision to block Currie and Case's discharges. He died suddenly on August 30, 1910, at age sixty-two, apparently of a stroke, while vacationing with his family in New Hampshire. A convert to the practice of law, he considered it central to a fair and just society. He summed up his beliefs in a lecture at the University of Michigan in 1907 when he said, "In these days of commercialism and Alladin-like [*sic*] fortunes, of trusts and combinations, let us not forget that it is upon those who prepare laws, who enact laws, who execute the law, who decide the law, that the weal or woe of the nation depends" (Davock 1907).

LEE E. JOSLYN (1905–19): THE COURT MATURES AND FACES ITS FIRST CRISIS

Harlow Davock's sudden death surprised everyone. He had been reappointed only a few weeks before leaving on vacation, and just the day before he died he wired his office with his upcoming itinerary so that his staff could stay in contact with him about ongoing court business.

Davock's desire to remain in contact with his office while on vacation reflected the Eastern District's growing caseload. With 254 new cases filed, 1909 had been the busiest year in the court's short history. Practically speaking, the increasing pace of the new filings meant that Davock needed to be replaced quickly. Therefore, it is no surprise that Judge Swan asked Lee Joslyn to move from Bay City to become Detroit's new referee-in-bankruptcy.

Judge Swan had appointed Joslyn referee in 1905 to relieve Davock's growing caseload and give the Northern Division its own bankruptcy court. Evidently pleased with his work, Swan saw him as the natural, and most expeditious, choice to take over the much busier Detroit court. Joslyn had been born in New York State in 1864 but was raised in Dryden and Lapeer, Michigan. Although he would later teach at the Detroit College of Law and even wrote a bankruptcy textbook, Joslyn attended neither college nor law school, but instead, as was still typical at the time, he "read for the law" under the supervision of two state circuit court judges and likely performed routine clerical duties.[9] During that time he also served as principal of the local high school, since like most clerks reading for the law, he was not paid. Despite the strenuous workload, Joslyn was admitted to the bar in 1886 when he was only twenty-one years old. A Democrat at a time when Michigan was a predominantly Republican state, he nonetheless served in a number of public offices in Bay County before moving to Detroit, including prosecuting attorney, county school commissioner, and circuit court commissioner.[10] He was later a member of the Detroit Charter Commission. Joslyn also had a bit of the political bug in him: he unsuccessfully sought elective office on three occasions: for Congress in 1898; for the Wayne County Circuit Court in 1923; and for the state legislature in 1926.

Public service notwithstanding, Joslyn had a busy practice in Bay City by the 1890s. In the later part of the decade, he represented a young African American man named Oscar W. Baker in a case against the Pere Marquette Railroad Company to recover damages for Baker's loss of a limb in a railroad crossing accident. Baker, who would later be active in Michigan's early civil rights movement, won the case and used the award to pay his way through the University of Michigan Law School. Joslyn hired Baker after his graduation in 1902, reportedly making him Bay City's first black attorney.[11]

Bankruptcy case filings in the Eastern District increased during Joslyn's tenure in Detroit, from 254 in 1909 to a high of 429 in 1918. Total assets in cases administered in the district rose to $856,616 by 1913; they dropped to $530,689 the following year and then tripled to $1,770,891 in 1915. By 1918, assets administered in the district totaled $2,705,381 but then dropped again to $1,136,392 in 1919.[12] Since referees' commissions were based on assets actually liquidated and distributed, their compensation to some extent fluctuated with the number of case filings. Total commissions paid to the district's two referees dropped from a high of $26,023 in 1918 to $10,128 the following year; they were $11,389 in 1920 and $9,907 in 1921.[13]

The district's Southern Division was by far the busier, at least in terms of case filings. In 1915, for example, 317 new cases were filed in the Southern Division, while the Bay City court saw 57 new filers. On the other hand, total assets administered in Detroit that year totaled approximately $600,000, while those in Bay City exceeded $1.1 million. These differences may seem contradictory on the surface but are explained by the court's relatively small caseloads. One or two large cases filed in any given year could affect the court's workload for years to come.

After resigning his appointment as referee, Joslyn practiced law with his two sons, specializing in bankruptcy matters. He was on the faculty of the Detroit College of Law and lectured at the University of Michigan. Joslyn's classroom lectures on bankruptcy were collected in 1925 in a textbook titled *Student's Manual of Bankruptcy Law and Practice*, the purpose of which he described as to provide "a model for conducting the ordinary Bankruptcy case, *voluntary or involuntary*, through the Court."[14] He died in 1936, two years after suffering a stroke while arguing a motion in a bankruptcy matter before Judge Ernest O'Brien of the United States District Court in Detroit.

Along with the growth of the bankruptcy court's workload came criticism of its administration of cases. Closely echoing the complaints that brought down the 1867 act, critics charged that the courts were controlled by tight groups of lawyers, referees, appraisers, and auctioneers, known as "bankruptcy rings," who monopolized bankruptcy work in their communities and drained cases of most of their value, leaving little if anything for creditors. The bankruptcy court in Detroit was not immune from such criticism, and it ultimately led to Lee Joslyn's resignation in 1919.

Criticism of the court became public in June 1916 at the monthly dinner meeting of the Detroit branch of the National Association of Credit Men. The topic of the meeting was "Should the National Bankruptcy Law Be Repealed?" Relying on national statistics for the previous year, Frank Hamburger, the association's secretary, argued that the law profited receivers, trustees, attorneys, and other professionals while trade creditors were left with nothing by the end of a case:

> An estate is scarcely ever closed in less than a year and usually in three years.... Who are the beneficiaries under the present law? They are the attorneys, the receivers, the trustees, the auctioneers, the referees, the bankrupts and a few others that have fastened themselves upon the estate. Finally comes the unsecured creditor and to him is given the "hank and bone." ... The national bankruptcy law is a farce to the unsecured creditor.[15]

To his credit, Lee Joslyn stepped into the lion's den, defending both the law and his own administration of it. "The law does not attempt to punish the debtor, but to see that there is an equal distribution among creditors," he said. "[Fees] to settle the Lozier [Motor Company] case involved only 3 per cent of the total amount involved."[16]

Joslyn's defense of the court did little to pacify its critics, some of whom apparently saw the referee as part of the problem. Creditors, particularly the Detroit Credit Men's Association, continued to express dissatisfaction with bankruptcy administration in Detroit, and by 1918 they were taking their complaints directly to District Judge Arthur Tuttle. Tuttle was appointed to the bench in 1912 as the district's only judge. Unlike his predecessors, he took an active interest in the bankruptcy court and involved himself deeply in its operations. He was noted throughout his long and distinguished public career as a lawyer and jurist of conscience and dignity, which extended to his treatment of the court and the law. Therefore, Tuttle paid close attention when confronted with charges of cronyism, conflicts of interest, and self-dealing in Joslyn's administration of bankruptcy cases in Detroit.

It is not clear whether Joslyn knew about the complaints that were made to Judge Tuttle. However, relations between him and the creditor community were tense enough by early 1918 that he took it upon himself to write to Judge Tuttle, referring to the aforementioned *Detroit Free Press*'s account of the 1916 Detroit Credit Men's Association meeting. Utilizing the same national data the association's members had proffered against him at the meeting, he showed that fees and distributions in Detroit were consistent with those in other districts.[17] Joslyn's defense missed the point, to some extent; to many of the Credit Men, the problem was that the Eastern District's bankruptcy court was too much like other courts around the country.

Whether or not Joslyn knew of the complaints, he probably did not expect Tuttle's next action. The judge cut Joslyn's request for fees in the *Lozier* case, a major case at the time and the one that Joslyn had cited at the credit managers' meeting as an example of his court's efficiency. Many creditors in the case did not receive their final distribution checks, which had supposedly been mailed in June 1917 by the Detroit Trust Company, the trustee in the case. Tuttle held Joslyn responsible for the lapse, denying his petition for fees in the *Lozier* case in an amount equal to that of the undelivered distribution checks.

Nevertheless, Judge Tuttle renewed Joslyn's appointment in the autumn of 1918. However, by January 1919 the judge had apparently concluded that some changes were in order in the bankruptcy court. Sending a letter to Joslyn by messenger, he demanded both an accounting of the retainers Joslyn had received from private clients and that his use of auctioneers to conduct sales be immediately suspended:

Dear sir:

Rumors have come to me of so many misfortunes, disadvantages and dissatisfactions in connection with the employment of auctioneers for making sales of bankruptcy estates, that it is my desire that in the future and until I change these instructions no sales be conducted by any one other than the trustee except on order made by the Court, and that no fees be paid to auctioneers except upon such order of this Court.

I would like to have accurate information as to all retainers which you now hold from any corporation, partnership, or individual. Please give me the name and address of such clients and the period for which such retainer has existed in the past, and the period for which you have agreed to serve in the future. I would also like to have an itemized statement of all fees which you have received since January 1, 1919, either for retainer, counsel or services of any kind.

I am sending this to you by messenger and would be glad to have your reply before the opening of court at nine o'clock tomorrow.[18]

Given the suddenness of Tuttle's letter and his insistence on an immediate reply, it is reasonable to surmise that he had received new information about Joslyn. This likely related to charges of conflict of interest that arose out of Joslyn's private law practice, specifically his representation of the National Cash Register Company. At the time, National Cash Register built and sold nearly all of the cash registers in the United States and would have been a major client for any attorney. Many of the company's machines were sold on conditional installment sales contracts under which the company claimed ownership of the machines until it was fully paid. Since virtually every commercial enterprise owned one of the company's registers, National Cash Register was a frequent plaintiff in both state and federal courts, as well as a creditor in many bankruptcy cases.

According to the Justice Department's subsequent investigation, Joslyn represented the National Cash Register Company in both bankruptcy and non-bankruptcy cases throughout the time he was on the bench. He eventually referred many of the company's cases to a colleague through a fee-sharing arrangement. The Justice Department's investigator later described the situation as "unethical, but not criminal."[19] It should be noted that such arrangements were not unique among the bankruptcy bench. The position of referee-in-bankruptcy was intended to be a part-time job. Conflicts were inevitable, particularly in a one-judge court. Nevertheless, the important point is that Judge Tuttle, who had sole authority to appoint referees in the Eastern District, believed it to be improper.

The other charge in Tuttle's letter relates to Joslyn's use of auctioneers. More accurately, the charge was about Joslyn's exclusive use of a single auctioneer, Charles Todd. In the report issued following its investigation, a Justice Department official described Todd as Joslyn's "official auctioneer and confidential friend."[20] In the matter of interest to Judge Tuttle, Joslyn endorsed a note that enabled Todd to acquire the stock of the Detroit Textile Fabric Company.[21] Joslyn later received $150 from Todd and, according to the Justice Department's later report, received 20 percent of the company's stock, which he held as trustee for his minor children.[22] In another case, Joslyn appointed Todd to liquidate the Savage Motor Car Co. Todd himself purchased several pieces of expensive mahogany furniture from the estate, which he resold to Joslyn after the case was closed for $175 (about $2,500 today).[23]

The other matter of concern to Judge Tuttle, which is not explicitly disclosed in his letter to Joslyn, was the charge that Joslyn had taken a large roll of wallpaper from an estate (approximate value $1,400, nearly $20,000 today) and appropriated it for his own use. Joslyn would later readily admit taking possession of the paper and storing it in properties that he owned. However, Joslyn claimed that the wallpaper had suffered water damage from a burst pipe at the debtor's place of business and that he stored it himself to minimize costs pending disposition of the paper, which he said had been rendered unusable by a second burst pipe while in storage. Though Joslyn would later claim that the paper was unsalable, he used portions of it to decorate two rental houses he owned.[24]

Tuttle sent a letter to Attorney General Thomas Gregory on February 5, 1919, asking that his office undertake an investigation of the affair. He described the charges against Joslyn as "unverified rumors" and went on to write:

> Ordinarily I would investigate this matter myself, without bothering your Department, but I am so overburdened with official duties that I can not possibly give it the necessary time.

The rumors do not concern any juggling of accounts in his office or any of those things which could be investigated by an examination of his office. The most serious allegations are to the effect that he has either directly or indirectly been the purchaser of property sold on bankrupt sale in his court. . . . I feel that in fairness to the reputation of the Federal Court in this District, this matter ought to be so thoroughly investigated that if the rumors are true I can promptly remove Mr. Joslyn from office, and if they are untrue, I can do Mr. Joslyn full justice by so stating."[25]

Assistant Attorney General LaRue Brown notified Tuttle by way of a letter dated February 15, 1919, that Agent Herbert Cole of the Bureau of Investigation's Detroit office would look into the matter.[26] Tuttle, however, did not await the bureau's report, suggesting that he considered the allegations against Joslyn to be more than the "rumors" he described them to be in his correspondence to the attorney general. Writing to Joslyn on March 16, 1919, Tuttle directed the referee not to represent any private clients or take any fees for any other matters, including notary fees, and suggested that Joslyn resign if he could not comply with Tuttle's instructions.[27]

Taking his time to respond, Joslyn sent Tuttle a letter on April 1, 1919, resigning from the court effective in three months, stating that he could not comply with the conditions the judge placed on his private law practice, and indicating that he wanted to set up practice with his son, who was soon graduating from law school. He professed his belief that his work was negatively affecting his health and that he no longer enjoyed it.[28]

Tuttle replied the next day, informing Joslyn that his resignation was accepted but would take effect immediately. The following day, a *Detroit Free Press* article announcing Joslyn's retirement quoted him as saying "that he needed a long rest and intended to take one before devoting his time in the future to private law practice in this city."[29] Although Tuttle would never publicly contradict Joslyn's account of his resignation, he nevertheless harbored deep suspicions about him. On the same day that the *Free Press*'s report appeared, Tuttle wrote a letter to the new attorney general, Mitchell Palmer, asking the department to thoroughly audit and examine Joslyn's office.[30]

By June 1919, the Justice Department had completed its investigation. It confirmed all of the particulars of Judge Tuttle's charges against Joslyn but concluded that while the referee's conduct "borders on inethical [*sic*]," he was not "willfully and knowingly guilty of any official misconduct." Because Joslyn had resigned, and because of the lack of cooperation from key witnesses and conclusion that no official misconduct had occurred, the special agent recommended that no further action was needed.[31]

Despite the fact that he was relieved of Joslyn and that his plans for the bankruptcy court's restructuring were going well, Tuttle was unwilling to let the matter go easily. On September 29, 1919, he asked the Justice Department to pursue the matter further. The department declined to do so, leading Tuttle to write one final letter on the matter to Attorney General Palmer in February 1920. Describing Joslyn's explanations to investigators as "very weak and unsatisfactory," he went on to write:

Perhaps we all ought to be thankful and satisfied to think the court is relieved of Joslyn as an official. . . . I repeat that his explanations are not at all satisfactory to me. He is not the childish ignorant sort of an individual who is stumbling into these raps; he is a very shrewd, penny-grabbing individual who always makes money out of everything which comes near him. His explanation of [the wallpaper incident] is really very silly. The idea that this paper was valuable enough to him so that he had been moving it around from one place to another and finally has moved it into his attic, and yet, it is without value to any one else. During the past few years paper of all kinds has been of high value, and even old paper has had sufficient value to warrant a sale, I feel that I cannot let this matter stand on this statement with this paper in his attic, even on his statement that it is of no value, and in spite of his statement that it has been damaged with water even a second time. I have, therefore, directed the present Referees in Bankruptcy to see to it that Mr. Joslyn at once brings this paper to the offices of the present Referees in Bankruptcy, at Joslyn's own expense. If it were worth enough so that he was willing to bear the expense of moving it into his attic, I am going to compel him to bear the expense of moving it out of his attic and into the offices of the Referees.[32]

In any event, no further action would be taken against Joslyn, who seems to have been unaware of Judge Tuttle's opinion of him. In resigning from the court, he wrote, "My greatest regret is that you may feel that your confidences have been misplaced or abused. If so it will be because of the barking and snarling of certain persons for their own sinister reasons."[33] Later, Joslyn would dedicate his bankruptcy textbook to Judge Tuttle.

In fact, Joslyn does not appear to believe that he did anything wrong. He cooperated fully with the Justice Department's investigators and readily provided explanations for each charge. Despite Judge Tuttle's feelings about these matters, Joslyn maintained his innocence. In a letter to the Justice Department's J. W. Gardner dated January 16, 1920, he admitted using the wallpaper in his own rental homes but claimed that it could not be sold because of water damage. He likewise acknowledged receiving payment for endorsing a note for Charles Todd (although he wrote in his defense that he first tried to refuse it). He denied receiving any stock in the Detroit Textile Fabric Company.

Of course, conflict of interest rules in the 1910s were less developed than they are today. Moreover, the fact that most referees were considered part-time officials who maintained separate private practices could create situations ripe for conflicts. The likelihood of at least occasionally having a case in which a client was involved was strong. However, National Cash Register was not just another client. As the dominant manufacturer of cash registers in the United States, it was a creditor not only in many bankruptcy cases but in state court collection actions as well. Being the company's Detroit counsel must have been a lucrative relationship for Joslyn. It inevitably must also have provoked resentment whenever Joslyn ruled in favor of the company in a bankruptcy case. To his credit, by the time of Tuttle's inquiry, Joslyn was recusing himself from many of the actual controversies involving his client.

The circumstances surrounding Joslyn's endorsement of a note for Charles Todd remain murky. However, his furniture purchase from Todd and his appropriation of wallpaper are considerably less so. Even without Judge Tuttle's commentary, Joslyn's explanations concerning the wallpaper make little sense. Was it a simple lapse of judgment or part of a systemic process of profiteering and deceit? Joslyn himself denied the latter but did not assert the former argument either.

On the other hand, Judge Tuttle appears to have considered nothing but the latter but never made his feelings public. Instead, his swift action, borne out of his close interest and careful supervision of the bankruptcy court, saved the court from the kind of controversy that would engulf it in the 1980s.

Moreover, Tuttle's discretion probably preserved Joslyn's reputation. Joslyn would go on to practice law with his two sons, specializing in bankruptcy matters. He returned to teaching, joining the faculty of the Detroit College of Law and lecturing at the University of Michigan, and published his classroom lectures on bankruptcy in 1925. He suffered a stroke in 1934 while arguing a motion in a bankruptcy case in the district court before Judge Ernest O'Brien. Although he recovered sufficiently to return to his practice, he died two years later, a well-regarded member of Detroit's legal community.

3

THE BANKRUPTCY COURT
AND THE DEVELOPMENT OF
THE AMERICAN AUTOMOBILE
INDUSTRY, 1900–1925

Automobile manufacturing was America's most dynamic business at the beginning of the twentieth century, and nowhere else in the United States did more hopeful new car makers try to start a business than in Detroit. A total of 239 new manufacturers entered Detroit's automobile industry between 1897 and 1933; 232 of those companies had disappeared by the end of that same period, leaving only seven producers. The failed manufacturers left the scene in different ways. Some of them were privately owned and financed; when these companies failed, most simply folded up shop (Davis 1988). Other nameplates disappeared through mergers and the like. Nevertheless, the bankruptcy courts and insolvency laws played a key role in shaping the auto industry in the early part of the century. This chapter explores the critical role that insolvency law and the courts played in the development of the automobile industry through examinations of proceedings concerning three companies: the Lozier Motor Company; the Chrysler Corporation; and the Lincoln division of the Ford Motor Company.

THE LOZIER MOTOR COMPANY

The Lozier Motor Company's story is typical of that of failed auto manufacturers of the time. Henry Lozier, a former bicycle maker from Indiana, started the Lozier Motor Company in Plattsburg, New York, in the 1890s. Although the company's first products were marine engines, it joined the growing ranks of American car manufacturers in 1900. Harry Lozier took over the company when his father died in 1903, and in 1910 he moved operations to a factory on Mack Avenue on Detroit's near East Side. The move was brought about by fifty Detroiters who collectively invested $1 million in the new company to bring it to the emerging center of the American automobile industry.

Lozier's products were well regarded but were priced outside of the reach of all but the wealthiest Americans. With its models in 1910 priced between $4,600 and $7,750, a Lozier cost more than ten times the annual income of a typical U.S. worker. By comparison, a Chevrolet cost $2,150 in 1912 and the new Model T sold for $850. As a result, Lozier never sold many vehicles. Although it produced 600 cars in 1912, total production during the company's entire existence was only a few thousand vehicles.

The company was not without its successes. In 1911, a Lozier was driven to second place in the inaugural Indianapolis 500. However, by 1913, many of the company's top employees had left to join other firms in the rapidly expanding automobile industry. Lozier's vehicles still enjoyed a good reputation, but the company struggled to sell its high-priced automobiles. In an effort to increase sales, Lozier produced a new, less expensive four-cylinder vehicle in 1914; however, that car struggled to compete with other, more established brands in that market segment.

These efforts were costly. Another investment of $2 million in 1913 did not stem the Lozier's flagging fortunes. By September 1914, the company's creditors forced it into bankruptcy. An involuntary petition filed by the Detroit Pressed Steel Company, the Welded Steel Barrel Company, and the Brightman Nut & Manufacturing Company asserted that the three firms were owed a total of $2,397.[1] Lozier contested the involuntary petition, claiming to be solvent. It asked that the petition be dismissed.[2] U.S. District Judge Arthur Tuttle appointed referee Lee Joslyn as custodian of the property pending a hearing on the petition. The company asserted at a hearing before Judge Tuttle a week after the filing that it was solvent but short of capital. He did not dismiss the petition, but he did express some sympathy toward the company. He urged Lozier to find new capital and encouraged it to reorganize. The judge indicated that he might be persuaded to dismiss the petition if Lozier's shareholders were to submit a satisfactory plan to reorganize the company.

In the meantime, Judge Tuttle appointed the Detroit Trust Company as Lozier's temporary receiver. The receiver was charged with making an inventory and appraisal of the bankrupt's assets but was given no authority to operate the business. In so doing, Tuttle indicated his general objection to operating receivers, stating: "I do not believe in the adequacy of receiverships to serve the best interests of both creditors and stockholders of such a corporation."[3] He maintained that those interests were best served by liquidation if Lozier could not be reorganized.

The Detroit Trust Company submitted its report to Judge Tuttle the following month. It valued the bankrupt's assets, less real property, at $1.8 million, while its liabilities were estimated to be $6.7 million. The adverse report did not dim the company's hopes, however. At a hearing before Judge Tuttle on November 23, 1914, Lozier's shareholders' attorney, Charles Warren,[4] continued to claim the company was solvent but admitted that its cash flow was insufficient to presently allow it to pay its debts.[5]

The Lozier case illustrates the prevalence and importance of involuntary bankruptcy proceedings in the operation of the bankruptcy courts in the early years of the act. In 1914, Lozier was one of 83 debtors in the Eastern District against whom involuntary proceedings were filed. Those petitions accounted for 27.6 percent of the 301 bankruptcy cases started in the district that year. The district was by no means unique in this regard. The 5,035 involuntary petitions filed nationally accounted for 21.9 percent of 22,959 bankruptcy cases filed in 1914. In modern bankruptcy practice, by comparison, the number of involuntary cases filed in a given year is so small that the Administrative Office of the United States Courts no longer keeps separate track of them.

The modern Bankruptcy Code provides only two general grounds for granting an involuntary bankruptcy petition. An order for relief can be entered in an involuntary case only if the court finds either that the debtor is not paying its debts as they come due or that a custodian took charge of substantially all of the debtor's property within 120 days of the petition filing.[6] The Bankruptcy Act included a longer and more detailed list of grounds to support an involuntary bankruptcy filing. These acts of bankruptcy, as they were known, allowed for an alleged bankrupt[7] to be adjudicated as such if the court concluded that any of the following events applied to the alleged bankrupt within four months of filing the involuntary petition:

- Conveyed, transferred, concealed, or removed, or permitted to be concealed or removed, any part of his property with intent to hinder, delay, or defraud his creditors, or any of them; or
- Transferred, while insolvent, any portion of his property to one or more of his creditors with intent to prefer such creditors over his other creditors; or
- Suffered or permitted, while insolvent, any creditor to obtain a preference through legal proceedings, and not having at least five days before a sale or final disposition of any property affected by such preference vacated or discharged such preference; or
- Made a general assignment for the benefit of his creditors; or
- Admitted in writing his inability to pay his debts and his willingness to be adjudged a bankrupt on that ground.[8]

The Bankruptcy Act's drafters had intended that a large proportion of cases filed under the law be involuntary ones. Most supplier-merchant relationships were local ones until the latter part of the nineteenth century. Then the expansion of interstate commerce via the railroads meant that local businesses increasingly obtained materials and inventory from far-flung suppliers. Nonetheless, geographic distance could still pose a serious impediment to collection, as local creditors would often have better, or at least fresher, information about their struggling customers and so would frequently prevail in a "race to the courthouse." The 1898 act was intended to offset such advantages by putting all trade creditors on equal footing in a federal bankruptcy court, where the law's distribution scheme would determine the amount of their recovery.

Notwithstanding Judge Tuttle's suggestion, neither Lozier's shareholders nor any new investors were willing to make further contributions to salvage the foundering company. That left the company without options, as the act as then constituted did not include provisions for business reorganizations. On December 9, 1914, its attorneys appeared before Judge Tuttle and consented to entry of an order adjudicating it to be bankrupt. Tuttle assigned the case to Joslyn. He convened the first meeting of creditors at his courtroom in the Trussed Concrete Building in Detroit on December 29, 1914. The Detroit Trust Company, the temporary receiver in the case, was elected to be the trustee of the bankrupt. Charles Simons (who would later be appointed a U.S. district judge in the Eastern District) was appointed to be the trustee's attorney.[9]

The Lozier case was unquestionably the district's biggest bankruptcy case up to that point.[10] Its assets were considerable and spread out across several states. The Detroit Trust Company appraised the bankrupt's personal and real property. The personal property included the usual machinery, equipment, and inventory but also the company's name and patents. The real property included a 250,000-square-foot factory in Detroit and Lozier's original 115,000-square-foot plant in Plattsburgh, New York. The property was appraised at approximately $4.9 million, with a liquidation value of $1.37 million. In addition to the items associated with the two plants, the bankrupt's assets also included dealerships in Chicago, Philadelphia, San Francisco, Long Island City, and Westchester, New York. The trustee's working assumption was that a significant part of the assets would be sold intact to a buyer seeking entry into the automobile business.[11]

The auction of Lozier's property took place in Joslyn's courtroom on February 4, 1915. The machinery, equipment, inventory, and other personal property were ultimately sold in two lots for $840,000, substantially less than the amount estimated by the trustee in its appraisal: $200,000 of the bids was associated with the Plattsburgh facility; the remainder was for the Detroit items and the dealerships. The reasons for the difference can be understood from the circumstances surrounding the sale. A new group of investors wanted to acquire sufficient assets to build new, less expensive automobiles with the Lozier nameplate. The name was, after all, associated with high-quality motor vehicles. However, the investors acted through agents, presumably to keep from running up the bid price by making their interest known. In addition, the assets of another, albeit smaller, car company, KRIT, were sold at the same time as those of Lozier, creating a surplus in the region's inventory of used automotive manufacturing equipment and related goods.

Joslyn was present at the sale and described the bid for the Detroit assets "problematical."[12] The purchasers were ultimately forced to raise their offer to $1 million in order to gain confirmation of the sale. The court quickly made distribution of a portion of the sale proceeds equal to about 5 percent of claims.[13] However, as described in the preceding chapter, delays in making the final distribution raised protests from several creditors. Judge Tuttle blamed the delays on Joslyn's administration of the case and reduced his fees. That dispute arguably was the start of the sequence of events leading to Joslyn's resignation in 1919.

Once confirmation was achieved, the new investors,[14] who formally identified themselves as the Associated Lozier Purchasers, soon went to work developing a new product line. By the end of October 1915, the new entity purchased Lozier's Mack Avenue plant from the trustee for "considerably less" than the trustee's appraisal of $695,454 made a year earlier.[15] However, the new company's efforts proved to be no more successful than those of its predecessors. By September 1916, Associated Lozier sold the Mack Avenue plant and moved into a smaller facility. It developed a new car, the Lozier Six, but manufactured relatively few units before ceasing production in 1918, joining the ranks of defunct brands like Detroit Electric, King, Liberty, Regal, and Grinnell. In fact, the Detroit automobile industry was shedding companies by 1918. Between 1903 and 1916, the number of new companies annually entering the business in the city was commonly in the double digits, reaching highs of 31 in 1910 and 26 in 1914.[16] After 1916, however, the numbers of new entrants dwindled to a handful while the number of failed companies grew (Davis 1988, 86). One company that successfully overcame this trend was the Chrysler Corporation.

CHALMERS, MAXWELL, AND THE BIRTH OF THE CHRYSLER CORPORATION

Each of the three major U.S. automakers in some measure owes its modern form to insolvency and restructuring proceedings, but none more so than the Chrysler brand. In recent decades, the company has been saved from joining the ranks of failed car manufacturers, first by a government bailout in 1980 and then a government-managed and financed Chapter 11 case in 2009. Therefore, it is in a way appropriate that the brand itself was created from another bankruptcy manufacturer, the Maxwell Motor Corporation, through a receivership in the Eastern District in the 1920s.

The roots of the present-day Chrysler automotive manufacturing company[17] can be traced to the Maxwell Motor Corporation and its predecessor, the Maxwell-Briscoe Motor Corporation. Maxwell-Briscoe produced its first cars in 1904. Like Lozier, the company originally produced vehicles in New York State, in this case Tarrytown. The company was successful, annually producing more than 8,000 cars by 1908. By 1910 it operated plants in Tarrytown, Pawtucket, Rhode Island, New Castle, Indiana, and Highland Park, Michigan. Sales of Maxwell automobiles more than doubled by 1914 to 17,000, and then to 75,000 by 1917 (Hyde 2003, 21).

Despite the popularity of Maxwell's cars, a combination of factors combined in 1919 to virtually shut down the company's vehicle production. A postwar recession affected automobile sales in general.[18] In addition, labor unrest increased as manufacturers fought off efforts by workers to increase wages that had been frozen during the war. This problem was more acute among the auto manufacturers' unionized steel and coal suppliers. The resulting limited supplies of essential fuel and raw materials slowed vehicle production. For similar reasons, some of Maxwell's mechanics demanded higher wages, leading to work slowdowns when their demands were not met (Yanik 2009, 126–27).

Labor issues and the poor state of the economy were not the only serious problems contributing to Maxwell's difficulties. The Federal Reserve Board issued rules increasing the down payment for new vehicles from 25 percent to approximately 50 percent (Yanik 2009, 126–27). More specifically, Maxwell vehicles had earned a poor reputation in terms of their reliability, mostly because of axles that were prone to breaking when driven on rough roads (Hyde 2003, 22). The cumulative effect of these problems on Maxwell's success was dramatic; sales of its vehicles declined to 50,000 in 1919 and just over 34,000 in 1920. By mid-1920, Maxwell was $26 million in debt.[19]

By the same time, Maxwell's board had begun negotiations to merge the company with another Detroit automaker, the Chalmers Motor Corporation. Maxwell already leased some of Chalmers's facilities. The negotiations stalled owing to Maxwell's worsening finances. As Maxwell's troubles seemed to be coming to a head, its bankers stepped in. Those bankers already had at least one other automaker in financial difficulty on their hands, the Willys-Overland Company of Toledo, Ohio. They had hired Walter P. Chrysler, a well-regarded manager from General Motors, to oversee the reorganization of the company. Pleased with Chrysler's progress at Willys-Overland, the bankers asked him to undertake similar duties at Maxwell. Chrysler agreed so long as the bankers would extend $15 million in new financing for the reorganization, a condition with which they readily concurred. The bankers established a management committee for Maxwell, with Chrysler at its head. The members of the committee were mostly bankers and creditors, and included George Davison, president of the Central Union Trust Company of Detroit; E. R. Tinker from Chase National Bank; Ralph Van Vechten of Chicago's Continental and Commercial National Bank; Leo Butzel from the First and Old Detroit National Bank (and lead attorney in the Detroit law firm known today as Butzel Long); James C. Brady, representing Maxwell's existing investors; B. F. Everett, a businessman long associated with the Detroit auto industry, representing other creditors of the company; and Hugh Chalmers of Chalmers motor company.[20]

The banks agreed to advance $3 million to Maxwell for operating expenses pending reorganization.[21] One of Walter Chrysler's first actions was to recall approximately 26,000 vehicles from dealers to correct the various defects, most notably the fragile axles (perhaps the first major automotive recall). He then lowered prices on the repaired vehicles, reducing Maxwell's inventory by some $11 million (Hyde 2003, 22).

Chrysler's efforts were well received by Maxwell's bankers, creditors, suppliers, and shareholders. In little over a month, the management group reached agreement with suppliers and shareholders groups to reorganize the company. Under the terms of the agreement, the merger between Maxwell and Chalmers would be completed. Walter Chrysler would manage the new company, which would receive as working capital the remainder of the $15 million agreed to by the bankers.[22]

The agreement also stipulated that the company would reorganize through a friendly receivership action filed in federal court. A receivership was necessary because the Bankruptcy Act at the time made no provision for either voluntary corporate bankruptcy filings or reorganization (a form of reorganization, called a composition, was allowed for small unincorporated businessmen under §12 of the act). However, the use of receiverships to reorganize corporations predates the 1898 act. The method was developed in the mid-1800s to provide an orderly means of restructuring the newly created railroad companies, the first large American corporations (Skeel 2001, 56–60).

The receiverships, commonly known as equity receiverships, combined two existing forms of remedy, specifically the authority of a court acting in equity to appoint a receiver to preserve the property of a debtor and the right of a mortgage holder to foreclose on its collateral. Because they were almost necessarily cooperative projects, the equity receiverships broadly resembled today's prepackaged Chapter 11 cases or a secured lender's Article 9 surrender and sale. The cases were started by the filing of a pleading known as a creditors' petition or creditors' bill, in which creditors requested that the debtor's assets be placed in the care of a receiver. A second petition asked for authorization of a sale according to the prearranged terms, although sales were usually subject to bids. The sales were subject to court approval before becoming final.

A creditors' petition requesting appointment of a receiver for Maxwell was filed on April 10, 1921, in the United States District Court for the Eastern District of Michigan. Two similar petitions were simultaneously filed in the federal district courts in Dayton, Ohio, and Indianapolis, Indiana. The three separate petitions were necessitated by jurisdictional restrictions and the geographic spread of Maxwell's operations. The filing in the Eastern District of Michigan was the lead filing. In an official statement made upon filing the creditors' petitions, the Maxwell company announced that "the reorganization of the Maxwell motor company today entered upon the final stages leading toward successful completion."[23]

Judge Arthur Tuttle acted immediately, granting the creditors' petition. He appointed W. Ledyard Mitchell, Maxwell's president, as receiver in all three cases. He also ordered that the company's assets be sold with a minimum bid price of $10,915,000, at such time "when such a step would appear to be advantageous."[24] In addition, Judge Tuttle appointed a special master, William S. Sayres Jr., to actually conduct the sale.

Although all of the most involved parties had agreed to the receivership and terms of reorganization, not all of the affected parties were on board. Maxwell, like virtually all major corporations at the time, raised most of its capital from the sale of shares to investors rather than through loans. Maxwell had a complicated investment structure with several levels of shareholders. A preferred Maxwell shareholder, Holmes Jones of Wilmington, Delaware, filed a motion to block the sale, claiming that he and other first preferred shareholders were being inadequately compensated for their existing interests relative to other, more junior interests. Among other complaints, the intervenors claimed that second preferred shareholders were receiving more than three times what was to be given to the first preferred group. Judge Tuttle held a special Saturday session of the court to address this issue. After hearing the arguments of the parties, he did not rule on the objection, but he also did not block the sale.

The special master's sale of Maxwell's assets took place on May 12, 1921, on the front steps of Maxwell's offices on Oakland Avenue in Highland Park. Unsurprisingly, Walter Chrysler and Harry Bonner made the winning bid of $10,915,000, the minimum amount set by the court, on behalf of the new Maxwell Motor Corporation (Yanik 2009, 134). Judge Tuttle confirmed the sale at a session of the court held in Bay City on May 17, 1921. However, again taking up the objections filed by Holmes Jones, Tuttle did so only after members of Maxwell's management committee agreed that they would be individually liable to the objecting shareholders should the judge later find their claims to be meritorious.[25]

Once it was freed from Maxwell's old debts and obligations, the new company was able to complete the merger with Chalmers, effectively terminating that latter company's existence. Walter P. Chrysler became chairman of the new corporation, as planned. The company was soon producing an all-new vehicle that did not bear its name but was instead called the Chrysler Six. The company's sales revived, and by 1924 it ranked sixth among all U.S. automakers. Such was Walter Chrysler's success that by 1926 he was able to consolidate his control of the company and reorganize it again, this time as the Chrysler Corporation.

The Maxwell case demonstrates the importance of non-bankruptcy remedies before the act was overhauled in 1938 to include comprehensive provisions for corporate restructurings. The equitable nature of the proceedings gave them an ad hoc character. However, they in fact relied on overwhelming consent. A well-grounded objection could scuttle an otherwise agreed-upon plan. Hence, Maxwell's management committee was willing to effectively guaranty repayment to the dissenting preferred shareholders in order to resolve their serious objections. All in all, however, the Maxwell case represented a fairly straightforward example of an equity receivership. A less formal, more unusual case was the one that led to Ford Motor Company's acquisition of Lincoln.

FORD MOTOR COMPANY ACQUIRES LINCOLN

Lincoln Motor Company of Delaware was formed in January 1920 by Wilfred and Henry Leland, father and son, respectively. The Lelands were well-known in Detroit business and social circles. They had previously run the Cadillac Motor Car Company, first on their own and then for General Motors after the latter company bought it in 1909. They left Cadillac in 1917, forming the Lincoln Motor Company of Michigan. That company produced Liberty airplane engines during World War I.

The new company shipped its first car in August 1920 and sold 752 vehicles through the end of the year. Much like Lozier, Lincoln concentrated on high-quality, high-priced vehicles. At the time, new Lincolns sold for $5,400 and $6,000 (Nevins and Hill 1957, 183). The company was hobbled by high start-up expenses. Moreover, the Lelands refused to effectuate any significant cost-cutting measures.

The company was in deep financial trouble by the end of 1921. The Lelands unsuccessfully sought a loan from New York investors and alternatively tried to solicit a buyer for Lincoln that would retain them as the company's managers. However, Lincoln's finances were in such poor shape that its board of directors voted to place it in receivership, without the prospect of a buyer or a formal plan to restructure the company. The receivership was filed on November 8, 1921. Judge Tuttle appointed the Detroit Trust Company receiver of the company.

Once the receivership was started, a buyer appeared in the person of Henry Ford. Ford and the Lelands knew each other well but not always in a positive way. When Henry Ford's partners forced him out of the Henry Ford Company in 1902, Henry Leland convinced the partners to allow him to take over management of the company, renaming it the Cadillac Automobile Company (Davis 1988, 62). Given Henry Ford's noted prickliness, it is not hard to imagine a degree of tension between him and the Lelands. Nonetheless, their negotiations, although not secret, were almost entirely informal.

By the end of 1921, the popular consensus was that Ford would acquire Lincoln. Henry Ford himself was not so certain. He rejected the Lelands' proposals on multiple occasions and had no interest in adding a luxury car line to Ford's existing offering, the Model T. Ford was induced to step in only when it appeared that Lincoln had run out of options for survival. Popular sentiment was with Lincoln and the Lelands. The

Lelands were well liked in Detroit, and Henry's son, Edsel, portrayed the purchase as an act of personal and public charity, claiming that Ford had no use for the concern (Davis 1988, 123–24). Ford himself claimed that his wife, Clara, changed his mind. In fact, newspaper accounts at the time indicated that Clara Ford convinced Edsel that Lincoln should be saved, and he in turn convinced his father that the acquisition would be a good one for their company.[26]

The parties agreed that Judge Tuttle should set a date for the sale of the Lincoln assets. A meeting was held at Henry Leland's house at 1052 Seminole Street in Detroit's Indian Village neighborhood early in January 1922 to finalize the terms. It is at this point that the matter became unorthodox, at least by contemporary standards. First, Judge Tuttle not only attended the meeting, he took an active role in the negotiations. In addition, both Ford and the Lelands were represented by the same attorney, Harold Emmons.[27]

According to Nevins and Hill, Henry Ford offered to pay $5 million for Lincoln, stating that the amount would pay all of Lincoln's creditors. Judge Tuttle responded to Ford, stating, "If all creditors were to be paid, the minimum bid should be $8,000,000" (Nevins and Hill, 181). Ford then assented to the higher price. Judge Tuttle subsequently entered an order authorizing the terms of sale and setting a minimum bid price of $8 million. The terms of the order also required bidders to make a $250,000 cash deposit prior to the sale. Recognizing the unusual circumstances leading to the agreement, Judge Tuttle stated, "When it comes to protecting the creditors I feel the duty rests with the judge to do it by form of decree rather than relying on statements made to him privately" (Nevins and Hill, 181).

The terms of sale were nonetheless subject to some confusion. Some newspapers reported that Ford would pay up to $11 million to acquire Lincoln.[28] The Lelands would later join with some Lincoln creditors who continued to assert their unpaid claims notwithstanding the judicially ordered sale. Ford would eventually pay an additional $4 million to those claimants, although it steadfastly maintained that it was under no obligation to do so. Given Ford's initial reluctance to purchase Lincoln at all, and the events recounted by Judge Tuttle, Ford seems to have been on solid ground. However, it is possible that the Lelands were relying on statements Henry Ford might have made in the course of their informal discussions.

In any event, the sale was set for February 4, 1922. Ford, appearing through attorney Harold Emmons, was the only bidder at the public sale and offered the requisite $8 million. Judge Tuttle promptly confirmed the sale, and Lincoln's plant on West Warren Avenue in Detroit reopened on February 6, 1922.

One of the unformalized agreements Henry Ford apparently made to the Lelands was that they would continue to manage Lincoln after the purchase. In fact, Lincoln issued an immediate press release emphasizing that the company would continue to be managed by the Lelands. However, as is often the case when new owners retain the former managers of their new acquisition, the Lelands' expectations appear to have been different from those of Henry Ford, whose own statement to the press made no mention of the Lelands, or even Lincoln. Instead Ford's only comment was that "there is not much to say about the sale, other than that I am extremely happy that I was able to purchase the plant."[29] The Lelands had resisted putting the company into receivership and did so only when forced to by Lincoln's board of directors.[30] They predictably bristled under Ford's control and even offered to buy back the company. In any event, they were gone by June 1922.

The Lelands resented Ford for what they saw as his takeover of their company. Henry Leland would pursue Ford for the remainder of his life. By 1927, Leland had convinced a group of 1,800 former Lincoln shareholders to sue Ford in the Oakland County Circuit Court to recover the value of their original investments, notwithstanding the receivership and sale. That case was ultimately dismissed in 1931 (after two separate appeals to the Michigan Supreme Court), and Leland died the next year. Lincoln itself would, of course, become an integral part of the Ford line of vehicles.

Automakers would continue to go out of business during the Great Depression. Some of them would utilize the bankruptcy courts to wind up their affairs. However, the courts would not again play so integral a role in the restructuring of such companies until 2009, when both Chrysler and General Motors filed cases in the bankruptcy court in Manhattan. The Eastern District of Michigan's judges found other outlets to exercise their business acumen. The judges were known for the degree to which they would involve themselves in running bankrupt businesses. A report appearing in the *New York Times* in 1936 noted that the judges were managing a distillery, a pickle factory, a university, a large manufacturing concern, several hotels and apartments, and two hot dog stands.[31] While the judges reportedly enjoyed handling these cases, their activities were short-lived, as a major overhaul of the Bankruptcy Act enacted in 1938 would, among other things, provide bankruptcy companies with other avenues for reorganization. The person most responsible for that legislation would be the Eastern District judges' own referee-in-bankruptcy, Paul H. King.

4

PAUL KING AND THE MAKING
OF THE MODERN AMERICAN
BANKRUPTCY COURTS

As originally conceived, bankruptcy law was practiced before part-time officials in private offices often located far from the federal courthouse. In the early twentieth century, especially, bankruptcy courts were commonly criticized for lax administration, cronyism, and corruption. Paul King saw greater potential in the courts. No one in the first half of the twentieth century had a greater impact on improving the quality and reputation of the bankruptcy courts in the United States than King, who served as referee-in-bankruptcy in the Eastern District of Michigan from 1919 until his death in 1942.

Paul King's influence can be seen today across the broad range of his endeavors. He began his career as a Michigan Republican Party official and played a key role in securing President William Howard Taft's renomination for president in 1912 against Theodore Roosevelt's insurgent bid to regain the office. However, his political endeavors very nearly cost him his career and freedom in one of the most notorious political trials in American history. Forsaking politics, he became a tireless leader of the local and national bankruptcy community and of many civic and charitable organizations. Though he is virtually forgotten today, his influence is still felt in each of these areas.

EARLY LIFE AND CAREER

Paul King's family moved often.[1] His father was a surgeon but desired greater fortune than that profession provided at the time. Dr. John King's belief that financial success would be found in farming led the family to Arapahoe County, Nebraska, where Paul was born in a sod house in 1879. However, Dr. King's expectations of wealth were not satisfied in Nebraska and the family moved again, first to Chicago and then to Iowa before settling in Minnesota. Dr. King died in 1891, when Paul King was twelve. Young Paul needed to work to supplement his mother's small schoolteacher's income. At fourteen, he found work as a page in the Minnesota House of Representatives.

In 1897, King's mother moved the family to Dowagiac, Michigan, to be near her relatives. King again found work as a legislative page, this time in the Michigan Senate. In a pattern that would repeat itself throughout his life, he quickly achieved success through his skillful behind-the-scenes work on behalf of legislative leaders. He advanced to the position of assistant secretary of the Senate in 1901. When the Senate was not in session he served as the secretary of state's private secretary.

King was nineteen when he graduated from Dowagiac High School, perhaps delayed by his family's recent move and his need to work to support his family. He did not attend college. Instead he continued working in the legislature and studied privately for the bar, a practice that remained common even at the turn of the twentieth century. He was admitted to practice in 1904, scoring highest of twenty-three applicants taking Michigan's bar examination that year. Thereafter he practiced law in Lansing and later Detroit. In 1910, King married Sarah Bidwell in Lapeer, Michigan. Together they would have four daughters.

Not unlike his father, Paul King divided his attention between his chosen profession and other endeavors. Though he practiced law, his interests were increasingly drawn to politics and business. He moved from assistant secretary of the Senate to assistant chief clerk of the Michigan House of Representatives, before advancing to chief clerk in 1909. In 1907 and 1908 King was the secretary of the Michigan constitutional convention. He chaired Charles Townsend's campaign for the United States Senate in 1910 and afterward became secretary of the Republican State Central Committee. His time with the Central Committee was particularly eventful. In 1912, the Republican Party was divided between supporters of the incumbent president, William Howard Taft, and an insurgent campaign to return his immediate predecessor, Theodore Roosevelt, to office. The party's state convention devolved into fisticuffs when one of Taft's supporters physically attacked a speaker advocating Roosevelt's candidacy. While the state police were called to maintain order on the convention floor, they could do nothing to maintain order in the party. Michigan's Republicans sent two slates of delegates to the national convention in Chicago.

Despite the Roosevelt forces' insurgent successes, Taft and his people controlled the national convention. King and most of Michigan's Republican establishment supported Taft. King worked behind the scenes with the president's campaign to seat Michigan's Taft delegates, helping ensure the incumbent's renomination.

By 1912, Paul King had turned his professional attention to the world of business, particularly railroads. While not abandoning his law practice, he became secretary to the president and general manager of the Grand Rapids Railway Company. In 1914 he joined the Grand Rapids, Holland & Chicago Railroad as its assistant secretary-treasurer. By that same year King had gained the attention of Federal District Judge Arthur Tuttle of the Eastern District of Michigan, who appointed him to be the operating receiver of the Pere Marquette Railroad, a position he held for three years.

CRISIS: THE 1918 UNITED STATES SENATE ELECTION

In 1918, the Michigan Republican Party's establishment called on King again, this time to chair Truman Newberry's campaign for election to the U.S. Senate.[2] It became one of the most notorious political contests in the state's history and nearly destroyed King's career. Newberry was heir to one of Detroit's great fortunes, an early investor in the Packard Motor Company, and a former secretary of the navy for Theodore Roosevelt. Two former governors and auto pioneer Henry Ford opposed Newberry in the Republican primary. Ford wished to appear non-partisan and so also ran in the Democratic primary. Newberry won the Republican nomination, Ford the Democratic one.

King's diligence as Newberry's manager resulted in the great crisis of his adult life. Newberry's election campaign was dogged by rumors of massive spending. At the time, federal law prevented Senate candidates from spending more than $10,000 on their election. The Newberry campaign indisputably exceeded that threshold. Estimates indicate that the campaign spent nearly $200,000, almost twenty times the legal limit. The amounts spent by the campaign were an open secret, and many Republicans voted for Ford. However, Ford's refusal to actively campaign on his own behalf gave Newberry a narrow victory in the general election.

Frustrated by his loss, Henry Ford used his considerable resources to conduct an investigation of the Newberry campaign and ultimately turned over much of the information obtained to the federal government. The claims against the campaign had implications that extended beyond Michigan. Newberry's election gave the Republican Party a two-vote advantage in the U.S. Senate. The change of a single seat would evenly divide the chamber, giving control to the Democrats through Woodrow Wilson's vice president's tie-breaking vote. On November 29, 1919, a federal grand jury in Grand Rapids charged Newberry, King, and 124 others with four counts of violating the Federal Corrupt Practices Act in connection with the primary election and violating federal bribery and mail fraud statutes in the primary and general election.

The *New York Times* described the trial as "one of the greatest legal battles ever waged in Michigan."[3] Newberry himself never testified; King was the defendants' primary witness. Responding to charges of heavy-handed political tactics and rampant fund-raising, King testified for several days. At the conclusion of his direct examination, he collapsed and was hospitalized; the *New York Times* described it in an article dated March 10, 1920, as a nervous breakdown. Whatever the cause, the prosecution never cross-examined him.[4]

The jury (ten of twelve of whom professed at voir dire to be Republicans) deliberated for less than two days before returning verdicts against King, Newberry, and seventeen others on the first count of the indictment. King was sentenced to two years in Leavenworth Penitentiary,

Kansas, and fined $10,000. He made a statement protesting the verdict the next day:

> No jury and no court can make a criminal out of me nor out of my splendid associates. . . . There is, thank God, another day and another court, in which justice will ultimately be done, and this monstrous thing made right. . . . There was not a single act of corruption in the Senatorial campaign, and the final result will demonstrate that this was the cleanest campaign ever conducted, and not a criminal conspiracy.[5]

King's statement betrays an internal dissonance between the fact of the conviction and his self-image as a person of great integrity. It may have created in King a blind spot to his culpability in the scandal. However politicized the trial might have been, and however often the campaign spending limits might have been exceeded in other elections, it is clear that the Newberry campaign spent more than the law allowed. However, the prosecution's case was weak and its presentation of the facts ambiguous. One of the jurors told a reporter at the conclusion of the trial that "without Paul King's testimony that he told Senator Newberry that the campaign would cost $50,000, the Government had a weak case, and without the King-Newberry letters [voluminous correspondence between the two about the conduct of the campaign that was introduced by the defense] no case at all" (Ervin 1935, 57). It is entirely conceivable that for all of King's political and legal acumen, his belief that he was being unfairly prosecuted and his desire to clear his reputation may have blinded him to the pitfalls of testifying until it was too late.

The Newberry defendants' choice of counsel for their appeal to the Supreme Court was a savvier and certainly more prestigious one: the former and future Supreme Court Justice Charles Evans Hughes. Hughes obtained a reversal of his clients' convictions but not on a clear-cut finding of innocence. Instead, on May 2, 1921, the Court unanimously reversed the convictions on the grounds that the Federal Corrupt Practices Act did not regulate primary elections.[6]

Truman Newberry's name became synonymous with electoral corruption. He went on to take his seat in the Senate but was ostracized by his new colleagues, who conducted their own investigation. Newberry was so reviled by his new colleagues that when Charles Evans Hughes was nominated to be the country's new Chief Justice in 1930, his representation of Newberry was raised as grounds for denying his confirmation (Pusey 1951, 659). Newberry's own efforts to retain his Senate seat did not improve his reputation. Despite the overwhelming evidence produced at trial of his role in the campaign, he claimed through his allies that King kept him in the dark about the campaign's spending. He resigned his seat before the end of his term and never again sought political office.

However, it turns out that Paul King's worries about the harm the prosecution would cause to his reputation were unfounded. The respect with which others held King overcame any possible taint from the trial. Even King's indictment seven months after his appointment to the bankruptcy bench did not shake Judge Tuttle's support. Shortly after the indictment, Tuttle wrote King concerning the administration of particular cases, stating, "Let me suggest that you do not bother with this matter at this time. . . . I am certain that Referee Marston will be glad to look after this and all other matters in order to relieve you of these details at the present time."[7]

Later in the year, a Justice Department official wrote to Tuttle to ask whether King's indictment required his removal from office. Tuttle categorically rejected the inquiry, replying in a letter dated July 9, 1920, "I have already given careful consideration to this question and reached the conclusion that it does not disqualify him and that it should not do so."[8] On the one hand, Tuttle was an ardent Republican and, like many others, may have seen the Newberry matter as a case of partisan political excess. On the other hand, Tuttle was famous for his sense of integrity. He would not tolerate even the appearance of misfeasance or impropriety. However reluctant he might have been to do so, had Tuttle believed the charges against King were legitimate he would have sought his resignation. That he did not reflected the high regard for King that he shared with many others. Some later accounts of King's life mentioned his role as Newberry's campaign manager, but none of them mentioned his prosecution or conviction.[9]

Paul King withdrew from partisan politics after the trial. However, freed of the threat of prosecution and imprisonment, he embarked on an illustrious public career that would bring him the universal respect and admiration of his contemporaries.

BANKRUPTCY IN THE EASTERN DISTRICT
OF MICHIGAN IN THE 1920s AND 1930s

Arthur Tuttle was the Eastern District of Michigan's only judge in 1919, and he took a particular interest in bankruptcy administration. This was partly attributable to the fact that until the enactment of the Volstead Act in 1920 (which flooded the federal courts with prosecutions against bootleggers and speakeasy operators), bankruptcy cases made up a significant portion of district judges' dockets. However, it was also in Judge Tuttle's nature to do so. A man of great personal and public dignity, his attitude toward the court and its staff was described as paternal, and he took an active interest in the court and its operations. By 1919, he was anxious to revamp the bankruptcy court's operations.[10] Bay City and Detroit had each had their own referee since 1907. Judge Tuttle devised a plan under which new cases filed anywhere in the district would be assigned jointly to both trustees, which would even out the workload between the two divisions (Detroit was increasingly the busier of the two) and would promote quicker administration and faster case closings.

Judge Tuttle was greatly impressed by Paul King's performance as the operating receiver of the Pere Marquette Railroad. He credited King's management with sufficiently improving the company's financial condition to make its reorganization possible. Tuttle believed that King's managerial skills and legal background would make him the ideal person to implement his plan. However, King was not seeking the job. It would also seem that Tuttle saw King as the ideal answer to the crisis provoked by Joslyn's removal. Therefore, Tuttle approached King and enlisted him for the position.[11] King readily accepted the appointment and began work almost immediately. Tuttle was pleased with his choice. The two formed a close relationship, and he frequently expressed to King his satisfaction with the new arrangement.

In both theory and practice, the duties traditionally associated with judging made up only a small part of the work of the early bankruptcy referees. Case administration occupied the larger part of the referees' attention. Although Paul King would play a significant role in shaping the Chandler Act, which made substantive changes to bankruptcy law in the late 1930s, his professional career primarily focused on improving bankruptcy administration both in his own court and nationally. This was partly by inclination; since he was a young man, King had been drawn to the organizational and managerial aspects of his endeavors, whether it was state legislatures, political campaigns, or law.

However, King's efforts to improve bankruptcy administration were also compelled by necessity. Despite the efforts of the act's drafters, some critics continued to assail the bankruptcy courts as being at best inefficient and at worst corrupt. In some jurisdictions this was undoubtedly true. The title of a 1923 exposé published in the *New York Times* by a noted bankruptcy authority was self-explanatory: "The Wolves of Bankruptcy and the Tactics They Employ."[12] Small cliques of attorneys and other professionals dominated the bankruptcy courts in many major cities; they prospered while leaving little of a bankrupt's assets for creditors. Conflicts of interest were common and widespread, with one attorney frequently representing trustees and creditors in the same cases. Contributing to the problem was bankruptcy's unseemly image. Prominent law firms avoided the practice in the same way that they left criminal and personal injury cases to smaller, unprestigious firms.

Such problems were of particular concern to King at the time of his appointment. His predecessor had resigned in the face of charges by Judge Tuttle of cronyism, conflicts of interest, and mishandling estate assets. King wished to elevate the reputation of bankruptcy administration in general and referees in particular. He frequently offered the opinion that better administration of cases would remove some of the stigma that attached to bankruptcy. Judge Tuttle, whose interests were more parochial, encouraged his efforts. Tuttle's concern was to run the cleanest court possible. In 1940, Tuttle reflected on his twenty-year association with King, stating, "For years I have been trying to hold the expenses of your office down to such a point that when criticism came it would not hit us and that we should have not only done justice but that we could prove that we had."[13] Their complementary efforts made the Eastern District of Michigan's bankruptcy court a model of both efficiency and propriety.

Therefore, King's initial efforts were aimed toward improving the workings of his new court. In 1919 and 1920 King and Tuttle focused on improving the bankruptcy court's financial reports. King implemented organizational and procedural changes to the court with the goal of improved efficiency. He believed that referees should strive to reduce case expenses, thereby enhancing the distribution to creditors. Therefore, he made enthusiastic use of the relatively new field of program evaluation, carefully studying data in search of further improvement. His penchant for statistical analysis was evident in a tribute to his colleague George Marston that he wrote in 1928. King emphasized the connection between the changes made in court operations and improved outcomes for creditors:

> All references of cases are made to us jointly and severally, so that either Referee may act in any matter, at any stage of the proceedings and in any part of the District. [Then as now, the Eastern District extended south from the Straits of Mackinac to the southern state line.] The work is evenly divided, one of us presiding in Detroit one month and the other "out-state" so to speak, the next month. Compensation is also equally divided.
>
> During the nine years of our administration 4753 cases have been closed at an average expense ratio of 14.81% of the proceeds realized, and in an average period of administration of 14.03 months per case. $25,506,394.33 in proceeds have been realized and the sum of $20,883,040.02 has been paid to creditors, the difference being in expenses of administration, exemptions and reclamations. There are now pending 823 cases with $1,552,331.76 on hand in cash.
>
> The great volume of business is handled systematically by a well-organized staff, and the plan by its flexibility has proved highly efficient. It is giving, we think, general satisfaction to litigants, attorneys and the public. Referee Marston and I . . . are constantly striving to make the offices of the Referees in this District a model of efficiency and service. (King 1928)

These efforts were successful. By 1926, the Eastern District of Michigan ranked as one of the nation's most efficient bankruptcy courts.[14] By that same year, King extended his efforts to the local bankruptcy bar. He organized regular meetings with himself, Judge Tuttle, Marston, and local attorneys. These meetings provided the officials with a forum to explain procedural reforms, but King valued the opportunity to enhance the overall camaraderie of the bankruptcy bar.

Bankruptcy scholars have noted the positive correlation between easy access to credit and bankruptcy filings. This was just as true in the 1920s as it was in the 1990s. Case filings in the Eastern District increased from 200 in 1920 to 962 in 1929. Moreover, the total debt in those cases likewise increased, from $4,378,751 in 1920 to $19,061,147. Banks and merchants commonly complained (as they do now) that their customers were using the bankruptcy laws to hoodwink them. By 1926, King was publicly contradicting this argument, offering his opinion that most businessmen went bankrupt because they were unqualified to run a business and not because they were dishonest or corrupt (King 1926b, 6–7). King would refine and expand this theme throughout his career. By 1939, after overseeing a decade of Depression-era bankruptcy cases, he was quoted in the *New York Times* as describing bankruptcy as "a social agency as well as a necessary economic device." He added, "We may look at its possibilities from the point of view of the rehabilitation of business units as commercial agencies which mean progress, instead of merely as a means of clearing away wreckage."[15]

NATIONAL BANKRUPTCY REFORM

King believed that bankruptcy courts should be thought of as more than government-run collection agencies. However, after seven years on the bench, he was convinced that his vision of the courts would not be achieved unless the quality of bankruptcy administration throughout the United States was improved. However, its diffuse structure and lack of a central authority stood in the way of effective reform. Therefore, King decided to focus his considerable organizational skills on his own profession.

In 1926, King and his fellow Eastern District referee, George Marston, hosted a conference at Detroit's Book Cadillac Hotel to establish the National Association of Referees in Bankruptcy. King organized the conference and was elected the association's first president. The themes discussed at the conference reflected King's concerns. Despite the resistance voiced by some of his colleagues, many of whom enjoyed the autonomy the bankruptcy system provided them, he pushed for the adoption of at least some uniform practices. He also urged the conferees to adopt the administrative practices of their most efficient colleagues. Finally, he suggested that the public's perception of bankruptcy would be improved if the first two goals were successfully achieved (King 1926b).

In the course of the following year, King identified the most and least efficient referees through a comparative study of administrative fees and creditor distributions for all eighty-four federal districts, which he apparently compiled himself (King 1926b). His other major project during his term as the organization's president was the preparation of a uniform Code of Ethics for referees. The code was adopted at the association's second annual meeting in Buffalo in 1927.

King had great faith in voluntary organizations and strongly believed that the referees could and should regulate themselves. However, his efforts met with varying degrees of success. Despite his vigorous attempts through the association to promote the adoption of uniform practices among the referees, such rules were not taken up until after bankruptcy administration was brought within the Administrative Office of the United States Courts in 1946. Until then, bankruptcy administration varied widely between districts. Lax administration by referees in some districts fueled public perceptions of corruption. By the late 1920s, a major investigation of bankruptcy practices throughout the country led to calls for bankruptcy reform. King, as a recognized leader in the national bankruptcy community through his role in forming the National Association of Referees in Bankruptcy, was well placed to participate in the reform effort. His formidable organizational skills would make him the bankruptcy community's most important leader.

The National Bankruptcy Conference began as an informal group formed to draft and advocate changes in the 1898 act. Its members were representatives from the major bankruptcy-related organizations and influential professionals and academics. While the original idea for the group was not King's, he was active in its formation and was its chairman from its inception in 1932 until his death in 1942. The conference played a primary role in drafting the Chandler Act (named after its main congressional sponsor), a major overhaul of the 1898 act adopted by Congress in 1938. However, the organization did not exist at the start of 1932.

King took a keen interest in the proposed revisions to the Bankruptcy Act even before a bill was introduced, meeting with Solicitor General Thomas Thacher, who was responsible for the national investigation and the first drafts of the legislation (Honsberger 1985, 4). After the bill's introduction in early 1932, King (who thought many of its provisions were unworkable) undertook to prepare and disseminate, at his own expense, a detailed analysis of the legislation and corresponded with other professionals around the country (Honsberger 1985, 7). King had cultivated a network of like-minded bankruptcy specialists ready to insert itself into the policymaking process by the time congressional hearings on the proposed legislation had begun.

Congress in fact essentially delegated bill-writing authority to King's group by June 1932. When that group met in Boston in mid-June it designated King as its chair; his wife, Sarah, who accompanied him to Boston, served as the group's unofficial "house mother," tending to their meals, snacks, and refreshments (Honsberger 1985, 15). However, while the group's initial efforts were very intense, the pace of reform was slow. It would be six years before President Roosevelt finally signed the legislation into law. The National Bankruptcy Conference (NBC) met several times during this period, revising and adding to its proposals and reaching consensus with the various parties that showed interest in the legislation from time to time. Some of these parties raised challenges that threatened the NBC's efforts. The most significant of these arose in 1936, when the Securities and Exchange Commission (SEC), under the leadership of William O. Douglas (a noted bankruptcy expert himself), threatened to overturn much of the NBC's proposed reforms in favor of legislation more narrowly crafted to suit the commission's interests. King and his colleagues met repeatedly with the SEC and eventually found a way to accommodate most of its desired changes in the existing reform framework.

Nonetheless, the SEC's interjecting itself into the bankruptcy reform process probably delayed passage of the new law for at least a year. King held his core group together throughout, despite the fact that neither he nor they were compensated for their efforts and even paid their own travel and lodging expenses (Honsberger 1985, 22, 45). King organized the meetings and sent out weekly reports to the conference members on their colleagues' progress; reports note that he mediated the sometimes heated differences between the group's members (Honsberger 1985, 27; Hunt 1937b). In 1937, one of his colleagues in the conference resorted to sports metaphors to describe King's role in the group: "They remind me of a football team, [prominent Philadelphia lawyer Jacob] Weinstein is center, he passes the ball back to [Pittsburgh referee Watson] Adair, who passes the ball to Paul King, and Paul King always runs to a touchdown. He has held the Conference together for five years, and the suave way in which he keeps them good tempered is marvelous" (Hunt 1937b, 21). By the time the Chandler Act became law in 1938, the *New York Times* reported that "the conference has grown into a definite, recognized reference body on bankruptcy and corporate reorganization and, though unofficial, enjoys the confidence of members of Congress."[16]

King's substantive influence can be seen in the Chandler Act's treatment of referees. Despite the major revisions to the act, their authority was not only left untouched, but its scope was extended in corporate insolvencies and by the creation of personal reorganization cases. However, enactment of the Chandler Act, which incorporated these changes, also led to the appointment of a commission to investigate the disparity in administration between districts and the desirability of putting the referees on salary.

Despite the intentions of the original act's drafters, in practice the fee-based system for compensating referees was a common source of criticism of the bankruptcy courts. Opponents argued that it created an inherent conflict of interest by providing referees with an incentive to rule in favor of arguments that increased the distributable assets in the estate, notwithstanding the merits of doing so in a particular case. For all of his efforts to improve the standards of judicial administration in bankruptcy cases, King gave short shrift to such criticism. Responding to Judge Tuttle, who closely monitored referee compensation in his district and seemed in support of proposals to put the officials on salary, King stated that he was not aware of any instances of abuse by referees. He suggested that the real problem was that the referees frequently earned more than the district judges who supervised them.[17] However, by 1940 the NBC had come to support the concept of placing bankruptcy administration under a single national authority. Ever the consummate organizational leader, and perhaps frustrated by his own inability to encourage the referees to adopt their own uniform procedures, King provided his personal and organizational support to the Attorney General's Committee on Bankruptcy Administration.[18]

The referees were not made salaried employees under the central authority of the Administrative Office of the United States Courts until 1946. It was not until the early 1970s that Congress accorded them the title of bankruptcy judges. However, until those events, it is fair to say that no single individual did more to elevate the status or quality of the bankruptcy courts than Paul H. King.

PUBLIC AND CHARITABLE ACTIVITIES

Despite Paul King's long tenure on the bench and his prominence in the national bankruptcy community, he was better known to the general public for his charitable activities. He focused his considerable organizational skills on these endeavors with great success. King was the Michigan director of the Red Cross's first World War I war fund campaign, which raised more than $4 million for the organization's relief work. Following Theodore Roosevelt's death in 1919, Michigan's King-led effort to raise funds for a memorial to the former president raised more than $100,000 in small contributions, more than that raised in all states but Roosevelt's own New York. (King's involvement in this particular effort was somewhat ironic, given his efforts to defeat Roosevelt's bid to regain the presidency in 1912.)

King was deeply involved in the Rotary Club, serving in leadership roles at the local, state, and national levels. While having no formal connections, the Rotary Club was closely connected with programs that assisted disabled children. In typical fashion, King came to lead the state, national, and international branches of the Society for Crippled Children. Similar to his effort to organize bankruptcy referees, much of his attention was directed toward improving patient care by promoting discourse and cooperation between individuals and groups specializing in the problems of the disabled. He organized world congresses for people working with physically disabled children in Ostend, Belgium, in 1927, Geneva in 1929, The Hague in 1931, Budapest in 1936, and London in 1939. The international organization broadened its scope to include disabled adults during King's tenure as its leader.

By 1933, the Depression had dramatically restricted the national society's fund-raising. At its national convention that year, Paul King advocated the sale of stamps, or seals, as a way to raise money for the organization. He proposed that the Easter season would be an ideal time to conduct such sales. Thus the society's Easter Seals campaigns were born. The first Easter Seals were sold in 1934 and became so well known that the organization eventually renamed itself after the seasonal stamps. The stamps themselves continue to be one of the group's primary fund-raising tools.[19]

King was also an active member of the North Woodward Congregational Church, serving as president of its board of trustees for many years. This, along with his other civic activities, led to his election as the first lay president of the Detroit Council of Churches in 1930. Again he used his role to seek innovative ways to address the problems brought on by the Great Depression. Under King's direction, the council's board attempted in the spring of 1930 to alleviate Detroit's growing unemployment by encouraging church ministers to hire workers for odd jobs in and around their churches. Unfortunately the council's efforts did not find much success, as the city's profound economic downturn overwhelmed private efforts to provide relief (Pratt 2004, 40).

KING'S LAST YEARS

This high level of activity took its toll on King. By the late 1930s, he experienced health problems, particularly heart disease. His wife and close friends tried to convince him to slow down and take better care of himself. Although King made some concessions, he maintained his usual frenetic pace. Judge Tuttle, King's boss, mentor, and friend, sent him a poignant letter in June 1939 urging him to take better care of himself:

> You told me some time ago that you were planning to go to London for the Fourth World Congress of Workers for the Crippled. I am not only glad to have you make the trip but I am delighted to know that Sarah and Pauline [King's youngest daughter] are to accompany you. My only request is that you do not load yourself down with work. Your activities in connection with the crippled

children will be enough. Please do not take any work from the office or from this side of the Atlantic with you. You need a rest and I want you to get some real relaxation and recreation out of the trip. You owe it to yourself, you owe it to Sarah and you owe it to Pauline . . . I also note that immediately on your return you are going to Los Angeles for the annual meeting of the Referees in Bankruptcy. I think of that as so intimately connected with your work as referee in bankruptcy that I add my approval to that trip. I urge you, however, for many reasons, not to take on additional duties in connection with the crippled children or in connection with the conference of referees. You over-tax your energies by adding on so many outside activities and you do that extra work without any money compensation. It is your position as referee in bankruptcy that gives you your income. You not only owe it to the office to give your time, energy and effort to that office, but having done that you haven't enough time or energy left to give to these other things without over-taxing yourself. It just means that you are either going to overwork or else neglect the job which gives you the income. Neither one of those things is right. Please help Sarah and me figure it out in such a way that your working time and energy is given to your position as referee in bankruptcy and the balance of your time is given to real recreation.[20]

As it turned out, King did not go to the referees' meeting in Los Angeles. He explained to Judge Tuttle in a letter dated August 14, 1939, that he could not justify the cost of the trip ($200), given the decline in case filings (resulting from the region's slowly improving recovery) and his daughter's school expenses.[21] However, it was the first referees' conference that he had missed since he formed the association in 1926. Given Judge Tuttle's concerns, one wonders whether King felt physically up to making a second long trip.

King suffered a heart attack on May 14, 1942, and was taken to Highland Park General Hospital, where he died three days later. Such was his devotion to public and private service that his colleagues were moved to profess their affection for him in the most profound terms. Judge Tuttle wrote, "I do not know when I have been so shocked and grieved by the death of anyone outside of my own family circle as in this loss of Paul. . . . I wonder if he knew how much we all loved him and how much we needed him. As I think about it, I imagine he did. He was such a modest and unassuming little chap, and yet I think he must have known that he had a great ability or he would not have taken a laboring oar and done all the work in connection with all these things with which he was associated."[22] The NBC eulogized him as "a man of large vision, deep insight, good judgment, and splendid open mindedness which made him a wise counselor and a foresighted, patient and tactful presiding officer at all meetings of the Conference. He was an uncompromising foe of anything which, openly or by implication, destroys honor and integrity, in public or private affairs. He was a jealous guardian for the oppressed and unfortunate, a fighter for the right, as God gave him to see the right. . . . This was the man, and yet we cannot write of Paul King without emotion, we are all moved by a sense of deep loss. As men love men, we all loved him, and mourn him."[23]

Few of Paul King's personal papers exist today, and his life must be pieced together from the recollections of his contemporaries. Those accounts, almost without exception, express acclaim for King's character, his generosity, and his commitment to service to others. His leadership of the bankruptcy community raised the status of bankruptcy courts throughout the country and influenced the reforms enacted by Congress in the late 1930s and 1940s. His work for the Society of Crippled Children resulted in the creation of one of charitable fund-raising's most famous tools and established a model for sustaining other public charities. King may be all but forgotten today, but the effects of his efforts, in court and in the community, were long felt.

5

THE BANKRUPTCY COURT
IN THE 1940s AND 1950s

Paul King's death in 1942 marked the end of a period of innovation and expansion of bankruptcy law and administration. The 1940s and 1950s were a relatively quiet time for the bankruptcy courts, both in the Eastern District of Michigan and nationally. The years of World War II saw the full engagement of America's economic capacity. The number of bankruptcy filings not only fell during the war but reached their lowest levels since the Bankruptcy Act was first adopted in 1898. The postwar period was notable for administrative changes made in the bankruptcy courts, such as the adoption of the Referees Salary Act, but was otherwise unremarkable for its bankruptcy cases or legal decisions. However, this interregnum would set the stage for the next, more eventful period in the history of the court.

GEORGE MARSTON

Paul King's unexpected death in May 1942 left George Marston as the Eastern District's only referee, a circumstance he had not experienced in his three decades on the court. Indeed, although the district's two referee positions were formally of equal rank, Marston had always been the junior member of its bankruptcy bench. However, with King's passing,

Marston would be the Eastern District's only referee-in-bankruptcy until Judge Tuttle appointed Walter McKenzie to replace King in March 1943.

The delay in McKenzie's appointment was not for lack of applicants. In fact, several people applied for the position, including court clerk Archie Katcher. Another applicant was Florence Clement, an attorney in the Michigan attorney general's office. She was recommended to Judge Tuttle by Michigan's solicitor general, Edmund Shepherd,[1] and would have been one of the United States' first female referees in bankruptcy.

However, Judge Tuttle was in no hurry to appoint King's successor. Responding to Shepherd's letter of recommendation, Tuttle wrote that "our bankruptcy work became very slack and we simply have gone along with referee Marston as the only referee on the job."[2] Bankruptcy filings in the Eastern District declined precipitously during World War II as Southeast Michigan mobilized to become the "Arsenal of Democracy." The state's industrialized economy, stymied through the 1930s by the Great Depression, was a prime beneficiary of the nation's military buildup. Michigan had 4 percent of the nation's population but received more than 10 percent ($21,754,000,000) of the war supply and facilities contracts awarded by the U.S. government between June 1940 and September 1945. Wartime employment in metro Detroit increased from 396,000 at the end of 1940 to 867,000 in November 1943. One in five Michigan residents was employed in some war-related business by the end of 1944. The per capita income of Michigan workers rose dramatically during this period as well, increasing from $591 in 1939 to $1,273 in 1945 (Clive 1979, 34, 36). Moreover, Depression-weary Michiganders were careful with their money, avoiding new debt and using their newfound wealth to retire old obligations (Clive 1979, 51).

As a result, the wartime workload of the bankruptcy court was light. Even though Marston was sixty-nine years old in 1942 and had been a referee for more than thirty years, his ability to keep up with the caseload was satisfactory in Judge Tuttle's estimation. However, by 1944, Walter McKenzie had assumed Paul King's former spot on the bench, and Marston's age and physical impairments may have limited his ability to carry out his everyday duties. Marston took a leave of absence from the court and moved to Arcadia, California, an affluent community north of Los Angeles.

In California, Marston, a longtime bachelor who had lived at the Detroit Athletic Club during much of his time on the bench, got married.

He also grew increasingly blind. He returned to Detroit in the summer of 1946 but only to visit. Even though the district judges appointed him to another term during his visit, it seems clear that Marston had no intention of resuming his duties as referee. Longtime court employee Archie Katcher was appointed temporary referee while Walter McKenzie served in Japan with the international war crimes tribunal. On July 3, 1946, Katcher wrote to McKenzie, then in San Francisco, "Mr. Marston is back and I believe in very good health except for his eyes. We haven't seen too much of him down here. He was reappointed for another term, with all four Judges signing his order."[3] Another letter to McKenzie from George Read, clerk of the district court, dated July 25, 1946, indicates that Marston "was in the office a couple of times and looked very well, though he said his eyes were giving him considerable trouble, and that he had trouble recognizing people even though he knew them very well. I understood that he planned to return to California soon, although I have not learned whether he had done so."[4]

Marston in fact returned to Arcadia and retired in 1947.[5] His reappointment can be explained by the passage of the Referees Salary Act of 1946. From the inception of the Bankruptcy Act in 1898, all costs associated with the operation of the bankruptcy courts were paid exclusively from statutorily determined commissions based on the distributions made to creditors in cases administered in each court.[6] Efforts to put the referees on the federal payroll had been around for years. However, case filings, distributions, and referees' commissions reached record levels in the 1930s, and the referees unsurprisingly opposed any effort to put them on salary. The move to put the referees on salary gained momentum when it was included in the recommendations of a special commission formed by the attorney general to consider further improvements in bankruptcy administration in the wake of passage of the 1938 Chandler Act. This time, many referees supported the proposal. The decline in bankruptcy filings in the 1940s affected courts not only in Detroit but across the nation. Filings in 1946 barely topped 10,000, the lowest number since the act was adopted in 1898. Some referees lacked the funds needed to keep their offices open. Other courts, including the Eastern District of Michigan, considered employee layoffs.[7] As a result, the referees' traditional opposition to federal employment gave way to economic reality, and Congress passed the Referees Salary Act in 1946.

Passage of the act came at an opportune time for George Marston. In addition to placing referees on salary, the new law also provided active referees with benefits under the Civil Service Retirement Act and gave them full credit for all of their years of service.[8] Passage of the Referees Salary Act was anticipated for some time prior to its actual enactment. Marston's reappointment allowed him to delay his retirement until after the law's passage and enabled him to collect what would have been, with his thirty-plus years of service, a significant retirement benefit. The complicity of the district court bench in this ruse must be attributed in significant part to the respect Marston earned during his long term of service.

In any event, there is no record that Marston returned to the court after his visit in 1946. He remained in Arcadia, where he died on October 31, 1953.

WALTER INGLES MCKENZIE

Walter McKenzie's appointment as Paul King's successor in March 1943 was the first change in the officiating personnel of the Eastern District's bankruptcy court since King's own appointment in 1919. By the end of 1944, all of the officials who had run the court over the previous two decades would be gone. George Marston's leave of absence began in 1944, and Arthur Tuttle, who was just as much a part of the court as its two referees, died in December of the same year. Their departures marked the beginning of sixteen years of relative quiet in the bankruptcy court in the Eastern District of Michigan. That period, not coincidentally, coincided with the tenure of Walter McKenzie as referee-in-bankruptcy in the district.

Walter Ingles McKenzie was born in Muskegon, Michigan, on February 9, 1888. McKenzie was seven years old when his father died, and McKenzie spent his childhood and teen years working to help support his family, in his family's orchard, on other farms, delivering papers, and later in a sawmill. He also attended public schools in Muskegon and later Shelby (Oceana County), Michigan.

McKenzie continued to work following graduation from high school and was employed first in a general store and then as a shipping clerk for a clothing company. However, a financial panic swept the nation in 1907, and McKenzie found himself out of a job. He eventually made his way to the Literary and Law Departments of the University of Michigan, where he graduated with a Bachelor of Laws degree in 1915. He excelled at law school despite his hardscrabble upbringing and was a member of Woolsack and the Law Review. He practiced law in Lansing following graduation until he joined the federal Bureau of Internal Revenue in 1917.

Like many young men at that time, McKenzie tried to enlist in the military at the onset of World War I, first in the army and then the Marines. He was rejected both times because of poor eyesight but managed to find his way into the infantry by the end of the war. However, the war quickly ended after McKenzie's enlistment, and instead of joining the expeditionary force in Europe he was assigned to the 339th U.S. Infantry Squadron of the Polar Bear Expedition and was posted to Archangel, Russia.

The Polar Bear Expedition remains one of the most unusual and little understood events in American military history. U.S. soldiers, mainly from Michigan and Wisconsin, and British troops were sent to the northeast corner of Russia, ostensibly to reopen to the Eastern Front in the waning days of the war. However, they did not do that. Some Polar Bear squadrons saw limited action against Bolshevik troops, although it is unclear if this was part of a larger strategic action. Instead, most Polar Bear soldiers simply camped in the bitter and miserable conditions of northern Russia, unaware themselves of their military purpose. Reports spread of a mutiny in McKenzie's company. However, in a diary entry dated March 29, 1919, McKenzie wrote in large letters "I Co's reputed mutiny all bunk."[9] In any event, the soldiers were called home from Russia by the summer of 1919 without understanding the purpose of their mission.[10] McKenzie was assigned following his return to the Judge Advocate General reserves.

Instead of rejoining the Bureau of Internal Revenue, McKenzie became an assistant U.S. attorney in the Detroit office, a position he held until 1922, when he left to reenter private practice. His departure coincided with and perhaps was motivated by his increased role in the Michigan Democratic Party. McKenzie was the party's unsuccessful candidate for lieutenant governor in 1922. He was a delegate to the Democratic National Convention in both 1924 and 1932, and in 1934 he served as chairman of the Michigan Democratic Party's State Central Committee. He was an unsuccessful candidate for Congress in 1930. McKenzie's last attempt at elective office was in 1937, when he narrowly lost a bid to become a justice on the state supreme court.

McKenzie's efforts to gain elective office within the legal community were more successful than his attempts at public office. He was at different times president and treasurer of the Wayne County Bar Association, as well as a commissioner and treasurer of the State Bar of Michigan. However, McKenzie was best known for his participation in the Detroit Old Newsboys Goodfellows Fund. That organization, which was formed in 1914 and still exists today, was formed for a single purpose: to ensure that there would be "No Kiddie without a Christmas." The group collects money throughout the year (most famously through its sale of newspapers in early December), which it uses to buy and distribute gift packages to underprivileged children in metropolitan Detroit at Christmastime. McKenzie joined the Goodfellows in 1922 and eventually served as its president. Moreover, he was chairman of the group's Purchasing Committee until he retired from the bankruptcy court in 1960, in which capacity he was responsible for purchasing and distributing Christmas presents to sixty thousand Detroit-area children.[11]

Judge Tuttle appointed McKenzie to be the Eastern District's new referee on March 1, 1943. McKenzie had actively sought the position, writing a letter to Tuttle asking for the appointment on May 21, 1942, just four days after King died. From an economic standpoint, it is not clear why McKenzie was anxious to receive the appointment. Case filings at the court continued to drop. Within a year of his appointment, the court's declining revenue was forcing McKenzie to consider laying off some of the court's ten employees.[12]

For McKenzie, at least, the problem of declining caseloads was short-lived. He was granted a leave of absence from the bench commencing on March 1, 1946 (the third anniversary of his appointment as referee-in-bankruptcy), to serve as an assistant counsel for the United States in the International Military Tribunal for the Far East. There, he would serve as part of the team prosecuting Japanese military and civilian leaders for war crimes. McKenzie served on the tribunal for a year (the trials themselves ended in January 1946). His participation mostly involved prosecutions connected with the Japanese invasion and occupation of Manchuria from 1937 to 1945. McKenzie himself only appeared before the tribunal once. Most of his attention was directed toward assembling the prosecution's case.[13]

With both referees on leaves of absence, the bankruptcy court in the Eastern District was left without a judicial official. The problem was quickly resolved when the district judges appointed Archie Katcher, King and Marston's former clerk, as temporary referee. Katcher served in that capacity until McKenzie returned from Japan, and then returned a year later with a regular appointment.

The court to which McKenzie returned was much different than the one he had left. George Marston had finally formally retired, though he had effectively left the court in 1944. Of greater importance was the enactment of the Referees Salary Act. Instead of receiving compensation based on a continuously declining caseload, McKenzie would be paid an annual salary of $10,000 (the equivalent of approximately $97,000 today). For a referee like McKenzie who had not experienced the boom times of the 1930s, this must have come as a welcome relief.

Being a referee at this time was still primarily an administrative rather than a judicial position. Referees were responsible for conducting first meetings of creditors, supervising the liquidation of assets, and making disbursements to creditors. Moreover, the Eastern District's referees covered the entire district. Venue rules at the time required the court to hear cases in the county of the bankrupt's residence. In McKenzie's case, this meant holding court in multiple locations during the 1940s. Besides presiding over cases in the federal courthouse in Detroit, McKenzie held hearings in the federal buildings in Bay City and Saginaw, in a courtroom in the Genesee County Probate Court, in the Port Huron City Council chambers, and in a private law office in the Peoples State Bank Building in Pontiac. Traveling to and from these various locations would have been a significant burden at any time, but must have been particularly challenging in the days before the I-75 and I-94 freeways were built.

In addition to his formal duties, Walter McKenzie followed in the footsteps of his illustrious predecessor, Paul King, by participating in the activities of the National Association of Referees in Bankruptcy. He was elected to the group's board of directors in 1944 and served as its president in 1953. He periodically spoke at its national conferences and contributed a few articles to its journal.[14]

One of the highlights of McKenzie's tenure was his receipt on May 1, 1957, of the L. E. Phelan Award from the Detroit Association of Credit Men. The award is notable because it highlights the different standards that governed referees then and because it demonstrates the degree of informality between the referees and the parties that regularly appeared before them, which would contribute to the problems of the court in the early 1980s. The award was given to McKenzie for "outstanding service to credit men."[15] The Detroit Association of Credit Men (later changed to "Credit Managers") was a branch of the National Association of Credit Men, the principal representative body representing unsecured creditors. Both the group and its members were regular and significant players in bankruptcy cases at the time. The acceptance of such an award for "outstanding service to credit men" by a bankruptcy judge today is unthinkable. It would create, at the very least, an appearance of a conflict of interest (if not an actual one) prohibited by the canons of the federal Code of Judicial Conduct.

However, in 1957, the receipt of such an award was not discouraged. In fact, it brought McKenzie wider commendation. The award was presented to McKenzie by the Eastern District's chief judge, Arthur Lederle. Moreover, few days after the award ceremony, McKenzie received a letter congratulating him on his award from Earl Warren, the Chief Justice of the United States.[16] These events indicate that the standards of judging judicial conflict in the 1950s were considerably different than they are today. As will be seen in the next chapters, such relationships, however proper they might have seemed at the time, led to an atmosphere that fostered even closer connections that would lead to corruption and calamity in the future.

McKenzie retired from the court on March 31, 1960. He initially lived in East Jordan, Michigan, but moved to Tucson, Arizona, because of his poor health. He died there six weeks after his move, on May 11, 1962.

ARCHIE KATCHER

Case filings began to pick up in the late 1940s. That fact, coupled with the broad area for which the Eastern District referees were responsible, necessitated the appointment of a replacement for George Marston. As a result, the district judges brought Archie Katcher back to the court in 1948.

Archie Katcher (pronounced with a long "a") was born in North Dakota on November 21, 1914. His family moved to Detroit when he was young and he graduated from Western High School in 1932. He attended both the Lawrence Institute of Technology and the Detroit Institute of Technology until 1935, receiving training (but no degree or certificate) as a printer.[17]

It was as a printer that Katcher first came to the bankruptcy court, in 1934. At the time, the court was responsible for preparing and distributing its own numerous notices and reports. It maintained an in-house print facility for this purpose, and it was as a printer that King and Marston originally hired Katcher. However, the position apparently spurred in Katcher aspirations for bigger things, and he enrolled in the Detroit College of Law, where he attended night classes until graduating cum laude in 1940. He continued to work at the court while in law school, and his duties expanded to include legal research and briefing for the referees.[18]

He continued to work at the court following his admission to the bar until 1943, when he left to join the law firm of Miller, Des Roches & Stern. He left that firm after a few years for solo practice but was soon appointed temporary (and only) referee-in-bankruptcy in the Eastern District while Walter McKenzie served as prosecutor for the war crimes tribunal. When he returned to private practice, it was with another Detroit firm, Freud, Markus, Gilbert & Lubbers. Shortly thereafter, in 1948, the Eastern District judges decided to replace George Marston, and Katcher fulfilled his longtime goal.[19]

As already noted, the position of referee-in-bankruptcy in the 1940s and 1950s was mostly considered an administrative rather than legal one, even though almost all of the referees were lawyers. Most contested matters, and certainly the most legally complex ones, were heard not by bankruptcy referees but were instead heard by district judges. Being a referee was not for the most part a scholarly endeavor. That changed in the 1960s as newer, younger referees sought to enhance both the authority and prestige of the bankruptcy courts (Mund 2007). Although Katcher preceded this group by a generation, he shared their goals. He published at least four separate articles in legal journals and was highly respected for his studious approach to bankruptcy issues. Moreover, like his old boss Paul King, he was keenly interested in improving the image and standard of practice of the bankruptcy courts. A decade after he retired, the National Association of Referees in Bankruptcy held its annual meeting in Detroit in honor of the fortieth anniversary of the group's founding there in 1926. The organizers of the event invited Katcher to speak; the title of his talk was "The Image of the Bankruptcy Court." His speech provided insight into his own experiences as referee and a more general meditation on the state of the profession in the 1950s.

Katcher remarked on the enhanced prestige of the bankruptcy bench that had occurred during his tenure, which he attributed to the fixing of the location of bankruptcy hearings to a few places with regular court-rooms, the wearing of judicial robes by the referees, and increases in the referees' salaries. He urged that further improvements be made, many of which would not be seen until the adoption of the Bankruptcy Code in 1978. These changes included granting referees greater authority to review fee applications and broader summary jurisdiction over matters before the court. Other changes proposed by Katcher were less formal. He urged the referees to abandon the practice, apparently common at the time, of attend-ing hearings on the appeals of their orders. More important, he suggested that it was time for referees to end the practice of informal hearings, espe-cially the unofficial and unrecorded meetings that did not include all of the concerned parties (Katcher 1966). This recommendation would be mostly ignored in the Eastern District of Michigan. As described in a later chap-ter, these ex parte meetings were commonplace in the court.

The adequacy of judicial salaries has been a constant source of con-cern within the federal system. Federal judges, including those in the bankruptcy court, have historically been compensated in amounts con-siderably less than those earned by attorneys of similar experience. Some judges, especially those with families to support, have resigned their posi-tions to take higher-paying ones in the private sector.

The annual compensation for the Eastern District's bankruptcy judg-es was $12,000 at the beginning of 1956 and would increase to $15,000 (approximately $120,000 today) by year's end.[20] Although Archie Katcher loved his work, he found himself unable to support his family on a ref-eree's salary. Therefore, he resigned his position effective April 30, 1956.[21] Katcher cited the low compensation of the job as the sole factor influenc-ing his decision to resign:

My leaving is with extreme reluctance and is purely a matter of economics. I had hoped to make this my life's work, but it requires too much sacrifice of the well-being of my family. Con-sidering the duties and responsibilities of the position, the salary provided by Congress has been most inadequate. And the Salary Increase Bill now pending in Congress, is still far short of rea-sonable compensation for the work.[22]

Katcher reentered private practice in Detroit, where he had a prominent and well-regarded career, serving in the leadership of numerous professional, civic, and religious organizations, including the Wayne County Bar Association, the Detroit College of Law Alumni Association, the NAACP, the Union of American Hebrew Congregations, the Anti-Defamation League of B'nai B'rith, and New Detroit, Inc. Archie Katcher died in Royal Oak, Michigan, on November 28, 1974.

JOSEPH C. MURPHY

Although Archie Katcher found his referee's salary inadequate, the pay was sufficient to attract sixteen applicants to replace him.[23] Joseph C. Murphy, a former acting U.S. attorney in the Eastern District, was selected by the district's judges to be Katcher's replacement. Unlike Katcher, Murphy had no prior bankruptcy court experience. Like McKenzie, he had an active background in Democratic Party politics.[24]

Joseph C. Murphy was born in Milwaukee, Wisconsin, on August 3, 1907, and moved with his family to Grosse Pointe Park as a child. He attended both college and law school at the University of Detroit, graduating from the latter in 1930. Murphy practiced law following graduation, but his real interest was in politics. He was a member of the local Young Democrats Club. Murphy was elected to the Michigan House of Representatives in 1932, rising to the rank of Democratic House Majority Leader in 1939. Upon his first election, he was quoted as saying, "In my legislative service, I shall attempt to carry out the principles of the Democratic State platform. I shall work for the economy in the administration of State affairs and devote myself to aiding [newly elected Democratic] Gov.-Elect Comstock in such programs as he may present."[25] One of the more attention-grabbing pieces of legislation that Murphy authored during his time in the legislature would have authorized police to mark with a large "X" the automobile of any driver found guilty of causing a motor vehicle accident while driving drunk or in which a person was injured or killed.[26] Needless to say, the proposed legislation was not adopted.

Despite having achieved the top position in the Michigan House, Murphy resigned in 1939 to join the U.S. attorney's office in Detroit. He rose to be a top trial and appellate lawyer in the office, becoming chief assistant in 1947 (with a two-year leave of absence in 1944–45 for service in the U.S. Navy). Murphy twice served as interim head of the office, once in 1949 and a second time in 1951. He left the U.S. attorney's office in 1953 to enter private practice but then successfully sought to replace Archie Katcher in 1956. Murphy resigned his appointment in 1964 to return to private practice, publicly giving no reason for leaving the post. He joined the Wayne County Prosecutor's office in 1966 and remained there for five years. Murphy died on January 26, 1987.

Murphy's eight-year tenure as referee was the shortest of any referee up to that time and one of the shortest ever in the Eastern District. It also straddled a period of significant change in the court. The volume of new cases filed increased dramatically, setting records each year. However, Murphy's own tenure was unremarkable, and he left no lasting impression on the court. Unlike his predecessor, Archie Katcher, but like his colleague, Walter McKenzie, his main emphasis appears to have been administrative rather than legal. As will be seen in the next chapter, the position of referee would fundamentally change in the 1960s as newer referees, including Eastern District referee George Brody, focused more on the legal side of the position.

HARRY G. HACKETT

By 1957, the number of cases filed in the Eastern District of Michigan had grown sufficiently to warrant the creation of a new seat on the bankruptcy court, the first since Lee Joslyn's appointment in 1905. This time, the district judges did not look beyond the courthouse for a new referee and appointed to the position Frank Picard's law clerk, thirty-four-year-old Harry G. Hackett. Hackett's appointment was a bold and pioneering one, as he became the United States' first African American bankruptcy referee.

Hackett was born in Cedar Bluff, Arkansas, and later moved to Birmingham, Alabama.[27] Hackett worked as a coal miner and in Birmingham's steel mills following his high school graduation before moving to Detroit in 1943. He entered the army soon thereafter. Hackett served in the Philippines and rose to the rank of second lieutenant before his discharge in 1946.

Hackett enrolled in Wayne University[28] after he left the army, eventually graduating from its law school in 1952. He supported himself while in school by driving buses and doing janitorial work for the DSR, Detroit's public transportation service. Hackett did sufficiently well in law school that District Judge Frank Picard hired him to a $6,300 per year job as clerk after his graduation.

The spot to which Hackett was appointed was created after the Judicial Conference of the United States recommended that the Eastern District of Michigan needed to increase its bench to include seven district judges and three full-time bankruptcy referees. Hackett was one of six applicants for the referee position. He benefited from the support of his boss, Frank Picard. Upon Hackett's appointment, Judge Picard told reporters, "I hate to lose Harry, but I don't want to stand in his way. He's the best law clerk of all the good ones I've had."

However, support for Hackett's appointment was not unanimous. Arthur Lederle, the district's chief judge, opposed appointing Hackett or any other nominee to the position. He in fact advocated for the complete abolition of the bankruptcy bench: "The National Judicial Conference has recommended seven judges and three fulltime salaried referees for our district. It is my opinion that we could greatly improve our judicial administration if we had 10 judges and no referees instead of the proposed seven and three."

Lederle's statement reflected the broader disdain with which many members of the federal judiciary viewed the referees-in-bankruptcy. Judge Arthur Tuttle's deep interest and involvement in the operation of the bankruptcy court was unusual among district judges, and the referees of the Eastern District of Michigan had benefited from it. For example, the referees of the district were among the first in the nation to have regular courtroom facilities in the federal courthouse, which in itself contributed greatly to the respect they were accorded not only by judges but also by lawyers and the general public (Katcher 1966).

However, many federal judges had little interest in bankruptcy administration and less regard for the referees who oversaw those cases. These attitudes came to a head in the lead-up to the passage of the Bankruptcy Act in 1978, when Chief Justice Warren Burger and the Judicial Conference of the United States vigorously opposed congressional efforts to grant bankruptcy judges the same authority and status as they themselves enjoyed under Article III of the Constitution. The Chief Justice told a congressional staffer that "a magistrate is three times more important than a bankruptcy referee" and that "elevating the referees to judicial stature is like elevating clerks of courts" (Mund 2007, 184–86). Judicial attitudes toward the referees took on petty dimensions in other jurisdictions; referees were denied reserved parking spaces at some courthouses, and others were forbidden to wear judicial robes (a practice that was begun in the 1960s). In some courthouses, the referees were even barred from the judges' dining rooms.

Fortunately Lederle was the only Eastern District judge who advocated eliminating the referees, and Hackett received the votes of the other judges. Hackett was sworn in on May 28, 1957, and was originally assigned to preside over cases in Flint and Bay City. He would shortly move to Detroit and serve there until the early 1980s, when scandal would overwhelm his accomplishments.[29]

6

THE 1960s AND 1970s

George Brody and the End
of the Administrative Era

The bankruptcy court that Walter McKenzie left when he retired in 1960 was in important ways a significantly different place than the one he joined in 1943. For one thing, it was a much busier court. New case filings in the Eastern District in 1960 totaled 2,915 (and would increase to 3,720 in 1961), more than five times the 562 cases filed in 1943.[1] The growing caseload meant more referees were needed; Harry Hackett's appointment in 1957 had increased the number of referees in the district to three. Still, there was no question of letting the other referees take up for a time the void left by McKenzie's retirement, as George Marston did following Paul King's death in 1942. Instead, the district judges quickly selected Chief Judge Theodore Levin's law clerk, George Brody, as the new referee.

George Brody was born in the Williamsburg section of Brooklyn, New York, in 1913.[2] His parents were poor Russian immigrants. Brody's father was a garment worker; he didn't earn much and was frequently unemployed (Brody 1996, 5). He died in 1937. Although Brody's mother had no formal education and was illiterate, she was, according to Brody, the "dominant force in the family" (Brody 1996, 2). Her sons' education was of paramount importance to her. She would go to the newspaper stand in the mornings to buy the *New York Times* for young George to read before he went to school.

Brody recalled Williamsburg as being a tightly knit community whose residents looked after each other: "I remember very vividly the owner of the corner grocery store extending credit—a running charge account—to my mother when my father was out of work, knowing that he would be paid when my father returned to work" (Brody 1996, 2). However, he also remembered his father selling apples on street corners during the Depression. Brody would later specifically invoke his memories of Williamsburg when he noted with satisfaction his presiding over cases involving the successful reorganizations of a synagogue and a nursing home.

Locked in poverty, Brody enrolled in the City College of New York after his high school graduation, which provided free tuition to qualifying students like Brody. Attending the college also allowed him to live at home while he took night classes. He worked at a variety of day jobs while in school: as a clerk, as a cashier, as a Works Progress Administration athletic director, and for the New York Board of Health. Brody graduated from City College of New York with a degree in social sciences in 1942.

The United States had entered World War II by then, and most men Brody's age either volunteered or were drafted for military service. Brody avoided conscription and military service during World War II. Upon graduation from college, he found a job at the federal minimum-security prison in Lewisburg, Pennsylvania. Brody apparently took the job anticipating that he would be the athletic director at the facility. Instead he spent six months there as a prison guard before quitting.

According to Brody, his former supervisor at the New York City Health Department then arranged for him to take a job as a management trainee with the Chrysler Corporation, apparently leading to his first contact with Detroit. He claimed to have no interest in or aptitude for the work, although he worked in various departments at the company's Dodge Main plant. Wholly dissatisfied, he left Chrysler after about a year and set his sights on law school.

George Brody enrolled at the University of Michigan Law School in 1944. His interest in law was apparently inspired by the success of his younger brother, David. George was two and a half years older than David, and although according to George they were not particularly close (Brody 1996), by the middle of the 1940s David Brody was well on his way to what would be a successful career, a path that must have looked very attractive to an older brother casting about to find his place in the world.

Like George, David attended the City College of New York, followed immediately by Columbia University Law School, from which he graduated in 1940. After Columbia, he moved to Washington, D.C., where he worked in the Department of Agriculture from 1940 until 1943 and again from 1946 to 1949, with a stint in between in the Department of the Navy's legal office.

David Brody left the Department of Agriculture in 1949 to work for the Anti-Defamation League of B'nai B'rith in 1949. He remained there for forty years; he became the group's chief Washington lobbyist in 1965, a position he held until his retirement in 1989. David Brody was well-known and highly respected throughout the nation's capital. He was frequently referred to as the "101st Senator," a moniker bestowed on him with respect and affection by the one hundred actual senators. His home was often the site of popular D.C. off-the-record dinner parties.[3] The German ambassador once stated (jokingly) that he had seen more senators in David Brody's home than on the Senate floor.[4]

While George Brody had little of the social skills of his younger brother, he did possess a formidable intellect. A career in the law, with its multiplicity of options to fit every personality type, proved to be an inspired choice. Brody entered the University of Michigan Law School in 1944 and graduated three years later, in 1947. He excelled in the endeavor; he finished third in his class, served on the law review, and was awarded the prestigious Order of the Coif. While he professed to enjoy himself socially, he lived by himself in a room in the Law Quadrangle and reported that he experienced anti-Semitism for the first time while at the University of Michigan, both socially and within the law school (Brody 1996, 14).

Given his academic success, Brody was able to secure an appointment as an assistant professor at the University of Toledo Law School, where he taught courses in equity, domestic relations, and torts.[5] However, Brody claimed to be uncomfortable with teaching because, at least in his mind, he lacked the "practical background to teach effectively." Instead he seemed to be most gratified by his time as coach of the University of Toledo's freshman basketball team, which he described as an "enjoyable and rewarding experience" (Brody 1996, 15). In 1948, Brody coached the team to the championship of the Ohio Amateur Basketball Federation tournament, defeating the University of Kentucky's freshman team in the process. Brody proudly related that his players referred to him as "Doc," in recognition of his Juris Doctor degree, which at the time was a kind of special law school honors degree (Brody 1996, 16).

However, Brody left the University of Toledo in 1950 to join the federal Office of Price Stabilization in Washington, D.C. The new agency was headed by Mike DiSalle, the former mayor of Toledo, whom Brody knew through coaching basketball (Brody 1996, 15–16). Congress established the Office of Price Stabilization at President Truman's request in response to fears of price gouging and runaway inflation provoked by the start of the Korean War. Brody joined the agency's legal counsel's office in Washington. He described his duties in the following way: "I handled all the legal aspects of the price control program for the industry unit to which I was assigned. I drafted price regulations, I held conferences with industry representatives relating to adoption and modification of ceiling prices, and I also spoke extensively to many industry groups on the policy of the price control program and its operation" (Brody 1996, 19).

The price stabilization program ended in early 1953 after Dwight Eisenhower became president. Brody sought to obtain another federal job in the Justice Department but was unsuccessful. For reasons unexplained, he moved to California, where he passed the bar and briefly joined a law firm.[6] He soon left that job for a position with the State of California.

However, as he had been in his other post-college efforts, Brody was unhappy in California. When his mother, who still lived in New York, became ill, he decided to move back in with her while he studied at New York University (NYU) Law School to obtain a Master of Laws in Taxation. He supported himself with a teaching fellowship at the law school. Near the end of his time at NYU, the school held a conference for judges and litigators. One of the attendees was Eastern District of Michigan Judge Theodore Levin. Brody knew the judge through his son (and future Michigan Supreme Court justice) Charles Levin. The elder Judge Levin and Brody met for breakfast during the conference, at which time Levin asked Brody to replace his law clerk, who had just been drafted. Having no better plan other than to return to California to seek work, Brody decided to move back to Detroit.

At this point, Brody was in his early forties. Over the course of his adult life, he had become somewhat of a personal and professional drifter, never staying at a place for more than a few years and never forming the kinds of relationships that might have provided stability to his life. Judge Levin's offer changed that and afforded him a professional and personal anchor at 231 W. Lafayette Boulevard that would last for the next three decades.

Brody himself described the job offer as "a kind of miracle" (Brody 1996, 20). Of Judge Levin he would say, "He was a great human being. He was compassionate, and understanding. Well, there aren't enough laudatory adjectives for me to describe him" (Brody 1996, 21). Indeed, the Levins became the family that Brody possibly felt he never had. In response to a question from Philip Mason, his oral biographer, as to whether his family was close, Brody answered, "Well, I don't know. We were together, but I don't remember any significant interchanges about anything. My brother and I went our different ways" (Brody 1996, 3). On his relationship with the Levin family, however, Brody said, "I wouldn't have traded that for anything. I was a member of the judge's family. He used to invite me to his home for dinner, and I kept in touch with him and his wife, Rhoda.... I considered Judge Levin my surrogate father" (Brody 1996, 26).

Brody's professional relationship with Judge Levin as his law clerk was similarly rewarding. Brody did legal research and wrote memoranda and draft opinions for the judge. Levin adopted many of those opinions without changes. Brody also sat in on Levin's trials, which he found to be a valuable learning experience when he became a referee. More important for Brody, Levin was a mentor. As Brody said, "If I had a problem and wanted to discuss it with him, he always found time to accommodate me" (Brody 1996, 24).

The respect was apparently mutual.[7] When Walter McKenzie retired, Levin asked Brody to replace him and lobbied the district's other federal judges for his appointment. With Levin's support, Brody handily won appointment to the bankruptcy bench.

Although the bankruptcy courts were much busier places in 1960 than they had been in earlier years, being a referee continued to be a mostly administrative job. Referees were rarely called on to decide complex legal issues. Many hearings were informal affairs conducted off the record in chambers. Although the court had limited its hearing sites to Detroit, Bay City, and Flint, the district continued the practice started by Judge Tuttle in 1919 in which the referees all shared duties for the three locations. The district's referees also shared cases—the referee presiding over a case could vary on any given day depending on where the judge was sitting. Therefore, Brody traveled every two weeks to Bay City and Flint to hear cases until Harold Bobier was appointed to hear cases in the court's Northern Division in late 1961 (Brody 1996, 33).

However, by the early 1960s a divide formed nationally within the ranks of the bankruptcy referees. This division was less a formal rift and more a difference of perspective. On one side were the mostly older referees satisfied with the largely administration-oriented status quo. On the other side of the divide were those referees, mostly younger and more recent appointees, who wanted to improve the status of the bankruptcy bench, in part through external changes and partly by improving the overall quality of their officiating. These referees tended to emphasize the legal decision-making functions of their positions.

These kinds of issues had been of longstanding interest to at least some of the referees in the Eastern District of Michigan. As seen in the preceding chapters, Paul King's desire to improve the quality of bankruptcy administration led to the creation of both the National Association of Referees in Bankruptcy and the National Bankruptcy Conference, as well as local bench-bar meetings. King's efforts led to the Detroit bankruptcy court's being one of the first to be located in a federal courthouse when the new courthouse opened in 1936, which King believed enhanced the overall authority and prestige of the bankruptcy court.

Not all federal judges, however, were as supportive of their bankruptcy courts as was Judge Tuttle. Many shared the sentiments of Judge Arthur Lederle, who instead of supporting Harry Hackett's appointment in 1957 opined that the entire bankruptcy bench should be abolished. Latching onto the administrative and often informal nature of bankruptcy practice at the time, these judges considered the bankruptcy courts little more than glorified collection agencies. So, for example, while some jurisdictions had followed the Eastern District's lead and relocated their bankruptcy court to the federal courthouse by this time, some referees in other courts were denied the perks accorded the judges, such as being barred from the judges' parking lot and dining room (Mund 2007, 184–85).

However, the referees bore some responsibility for this state of affairs. The Brookings Institution's study of bankruptcy administration made public what insiders had long known about the American bankruptcy system:

> Looking at the interrelations of all these people as a personnel system, we draw some unfavorable conclusions. Referees, selected by the judges on a personal-political patronage basis, try to bother the judges as little as possible with bankruptcy matters—which is the way the judges want it. Referees can grant favors to attorneys or withhold them. Attorneys, either as individuals or as the organized bar, can by their behavior and their comments affect the referees' reputation and future. Trustees, and their attorneys, must perform in a way that will at once remunerate them satisfactorily, keep creditors reasonably satisfied, and fit in the referees' policies and methods. Appraisers, auctioneers, accountants, and others employed to help liquidate estates must satisfy the trustee and referee. . . . In short a philosophy of "don't rock the boat" or "let's take care of one another" prevails. There are few incentives in the present situation for high standards of performance, and resources for supervision and inspection are too scanty to achieve significant change. (Stanley and Girth 1971, 164)

The efforts of the newer referees to change the conditions described in the study were not without precedent. Paul King's main purpose in creating the National Association of Referees in Bankruptcy in 1926 was to improve the quality of bankruptcy administration. However, membership in the organization was not mandatory, and its annual conferences were poorly attended (Brody 1996, 38). As a result, its efforts found limited success.

By 1964, however, the referees, led by Asa Herzog of the Southern District of New York, began working with the Bankruptcy Division of the Administrative Office of the United States Courts to hold annual conferences in Washington to train new referees. The sessions were expanded in 1965 to include refresher courses for veteran referees (Mund 2007, 4–5). Although he was a relatively new referee, George Brody was selected to serve as a panelist at the initial conference, a role that he repeated for the next three years (Brody 1996, 39). The conferences served two purposes.

First, they improved the overall quality of bankruptcy administration and in the process elevated the bankruptcy courts' level of respectability. Second, these conferences provided a venue for referees to discuss their various broader concerns, which would be one of the impetuses for the overhaul of bankruptcy law that would result in Congress's adoption of the Bankruptcy Code in 1978.

The content of the sessions at the Administrative Office conferences and the articles in the referees' own quarterly publication, the *Journal of the National Association of Referees in Bankruptcy*, reflected a deeper interest among the new referees in the legal, as opposed to administrative, aspects of bankruptcy cases. George Brody's own scholarly inclinations placed him comfortably within this new breed of referees, and he began to develop a national reputation for the quality of his written opinions.[8] By the 1970s, he was selected to join the National Bankruptcy Conference.[9] As a member of the NBC, Brody took an active (although not a lead) role in the adoption of the code.

However, Brody was best known, and had the greatest impact both nationally and locally, for his rulings that invariably limited or denied attorneys' fee requests. Concerns about excessive fees were not by any means limited to the Eastern District of Michigan. In fact, bankruptcy in the United States had long been dogged by complaints of excessive professional fees. The 1867 bankruptcy law was repealed in 1878 in large part because of the high cost of administration due to professional fees. Of the experience under that law, Professor Charles Warren wrote in his definitive chronicle of early bankruptcy laws: "So lasting was the impression made by the waste and frauds and defective machinery of the Bankruptcy Act of 1867 that, as late as 1893, it was stated in Congress that 'the prejudices created by the abuses under the Act of 1867 make a fair discussion of any bankrupt act difficult'" (Warren 1935, 1999, 127).

The Bankruptcy Act of 1898 generally provided for the review of attorneys' fees by the court, but at least in its original form it did not include any specific standards governing such awards. While the referees were intimately engaged in what are now called "asset cases" (i.e., cases in which non-exempt property of the debtor exists that can be liquidated, with the proceeds distributed to creditors), they commonly did not scrutinize attorneys' fee requests in the absence of an objection. The primary device for mitigating the review of attorney fees was the bankruptcy ring.

These "bankruptcy rings" ensured that objections were few. In point of fact, relatively few lawyers in any given locale practiced in the bankruptcy courts. Members of this small community were unwilling to object to each other's fees for fear of provoking retaliation against their own fee requests. Brody described bankruptcy rings thusly:

> The Bankruptcy Bar is a relatively closed society. The same attorneys generally appear in varying capacities in almost all substantial chapter II cases. Such continuing association fosters a club atmosphere which militates against effective client representation in matters relating to compensation. The court, thus, is faced with the difficult and delicate task of fixing fair and just compensation without the input of those who are in the best position to evaluate the fee request.[10]

In the absence of objections, few judges independently scrutinized fee requests. In their major study of bankruptcy practice conducted for the Brookings Institution, published in 1971, David Stanley and Marjorie Girth reported that 47 percent of attorneys indicated that their compensation requests were never reviewed by the bankruptcy court, while another 22 percent indicated that it rarely happened (Stanley and Girth 1971, 183).

These percentages held in the Eastern District of Michigan. Of the three referees in Detroit, Brody was the only one who routinely scrutinized fee applications. Brody said, "My colleagues were a whole lot more liberal [on granting attorneys' fee requests]. They in many cases, for one reason or another, gave the attorneys whatever they asked for. I took the time to review applications very carefully. In fact, I used to reserve Sunday mornings to come down to court and work on fee applications when I had undisturbed time to do so" (Brody 1996, 62–63).

Brody believed he was obligated to review fees, even in the absence of objections, and he was highly critical of judges who did otherwise: "Unfortunately, some judges, in the absence of objection, award whatever fees are requested. This is unfortunate and wrong and is responsible for the many documented sordid chapters in the history of fees in bankruptcy cases" (Brody 1996, 61–62). In other words, something more than an interest in effective bankruptcy administration was behind Brody's careful scrutiny of fee applications. A lifelong bachelor, he was himself a notoriously thrifty man. However, as played out in the courtroom, Brody's review of attorney fees took on the character of a moral crusade. In fact, he followed the foregoing statement with this comment: "Actually, the exorbitant fees reflect the breakdown of morality in society" (Brody 1996, 62). Moreover, Brody seemed to take great pride in his fee rulings. When interviewed by Philip Mason, Brody pointed out (presumably with favor, since the choice of including this passage in the oral history was his) his former colleague Stanley Bernstein's acknowledgment of Brody's efforts in a book he authored on bankruptcy compensation: "In commemoration of Judge Brody's terribly long and lonely 'winter war' to establish standards for reasonable compensation, I dedicate this work" (Brody 1996, 65).

George Brody justified his close scrutiny of fee requests with this simple statement: "An attorney is entitled to reasonable compensation for services rendered. He is entitled to nothing more."[11] Of course, what Brody considered a reasonable fee award for services an attorney rendered in a bankruptcy case was almost always less (and often substantially less) than the amount the attorney thought he or she should be paid. Although attorneys would not speak on the record about this issue, Brody was widely seen as a "pennypincher."[12] As already noted, Brody's Detroit colleagues, Harry Hackett and David Patton, granted significantly higher attorney fee awards than he did. The causes and consequences of these differences eventually became public in a series of newspaper articles and radio news broadcasts.[13]

By 1980, the courthouse controversy over Judge Brody's fee rulings garnered the attention of the Detroit media. Irving August was the district's busiest lawyer specializing in Chapter 11 reorganization cases under the then new Bankruptcy Code. He received a $5,500 retainer in July 1979 to represent Hamilton Hardware of Milan, Michigan, filing the case on July 21, 1979. August filed a plan of reorganization for the debtor on September 19, 1979, and successfully gained confirmation of the plan on October 24, 1979, a quick conclusion by any standard. August filed a request for an additional award of fees in the amount of $10,000. The requested sum was effectively a bonus for August's rapid success in the case. Neither the debtor nor any creditor objected to August's request, but Brody set the matter for hearing.

In his opinion, Judge Brody[14] quickly disposed of August's request for an additional award of fees, indicating that the then new Section 330 of the Bankruptcy Code had effectively overruled prior case law that allowed judges to award increased fees when cases were handled efficiently.[15] He then responded to arguments by August that the court should not independently review fees when no objections were filed, citing his judicial obligations as described above.[16] Ultimately, Brody concluded that the requested fees, when combined with the amount already awarded to August, would have given the attorney an effective billing rate of $300 per hour for the case (a modest amount today but a significant, if not unheard of, sum in 1981). He denied August's request for additional fees as excessive.

In Brody's mind, any criticism of him arose out of his rulings on fee awards. Brody was called to testify at Irving August's trial. When later asked under oath whether attorneys disliked practicing before him, he replied, "On the contrary, a number of lawyers have told me that they prefer trying cases in my court but would rather have someone else set their fees."[17] However, when interviewed upon his retirement, Brody admitted to a less than tolerant judicial demeanor: "Brody concedes that he becomes 'upset' in court and there have been instances where he should have 'registered my disturbance in a more controlled manner.' 'Each day, prior to going to the bench, I tell myself that nothing is going to happen that will upset me,' he says. 'But despite my resolve, I have no patience with lawyers who come to court unprepared. I never would have the courage to do that.'"[18] Indeed, Brody too often lost his temper and criticized attorneys in open court for major and minor infractions alike, provoking intense dislike from some attorneys who believed that he had demeaned them in front of their clients and other lawyers.

However, lawyers were also quick to acknowledge his intellect and the quality of his decisions. Besides the *Hamilton Hardware* decision, which courts around the country quickly adopted to define the bounds of proper fee requests, Brody also authored an important decision in the *Roman Cleanser* case,[19] which was one of the earliest cases holding that trademarks could be collateral subject to a secured lien on general intangibles under Article 9 of the Uniform Commercial Code. His other notable cases included those of Fred Sanders Co. (cited often for Brody's published opinions on administrative expenses and on the application of set off rules in bankruptcy cases), Bob Lo Company, and Adat Shalom synagogue.

Over the course of two decades, George Brody and other legally inclined judges gradually pushed bankruptcy law and practice in directions that led to a more professional handling of cases and ultimately to the overhaul of the nation's bankruptcy laws in 1978. In the Eastern District of Michigan, however, those changes would prove to be traumatic. Brody's decisions on fee requests and his zeal to take on what he saw as the corrupting influence of bankruptcy rings would be major factors in provoking the scandal that would engulf the Eastern District's bankruptcy court and dominate virtually every aspect of its operations for years to come.

7

THE 1978 CODE

Bankruptcy Comes of Age

By 1970, bankruptcy courts across the United States faced ever-growing caseloads, fueled by the postwar expansion of the American economy and the related rise of consumer credit. Nationally, annual personal bankruptcy filings, which had remained below 20,000 as late as 1949, increased to 131,402 by 1960 and 178,202 by 1970 (Skeel 2001, 137). Case filings in the Eastern District of Michigan followed a similar pattern, growing from 609 cases in 1949 to 2,915 in 1960 and 4,848 in 1970.[1] Most of these were individual, or consumer, filings. On the business side, case volumes were in themselves rarely burdensome. Rather, the increased complexity of commercial transactions and a shifting emphasis toward rehabilitating troubled companies rather than liquidating them spurred formation of a widespread consensus among bankruptcy specialists in favor of overhauling the Bankruptcy Act.[2]

Congressional action began in 1968 when a bankruptcy trustee told North Dakota's Democratic senator Quentin Burdick about the difficulties he faced administering his cases because of the referees' limited authority in business cases (Mund 2007, 6). Burdick had been a practicing attorney before entering politics, and his interest was piqued by the trustee's complaint. He sent a letter to each referee seeking comments on the existing system. The number of responses citing a need for reform was overwhelming and led Burdick to introduce legislation creating a bankruptcy review commission. Congress enacted Burdick's bill, establishing the Commission on the Bankruptcy Laws of the United States[3] in 1969. Once appointed, the commission selected the University of Michigan's Frank Kennedy to be its executive director.

Kennedy was one of America's leading bankruptcy scholars and was held in high esteem throughout the bankruptcy community. Born in southwest Missouri in 1914, he joined the faculty of the University of Iowa Law School after serving in the navy in World War II. He remained there until 1961, when he became the Thomas M. Cooley Professor of Law at the University of Michigan. A hugely popular teacher who mentored innumerable students and lawyers, Kennedy published many articles, and his writings were at the forefront of bankruptcy scholarship.[4] Of equal importance to his new role was his service as the reporter for the Advisory Committee on Bankruptcy Rules of the Judicial Conference of the United States from 1960 to 1976 (he would be the primary draftsman of the original 1973 Rules of Bankruptcy Procedure).

The commission began work in June 1971, conducting four public hearings and deliberating as a full committee for a total of forty-four days (Klee 1980, 277). Frank Kennedy and his colleagues, Philip Shuchman of the University of Connecticut and Walter Phillips of Texas Tech, naturally devoted more time and effort to the project than did the general committee members. They worked for two years in a small Washington, D.C., office north of the White House on Sixteenth Street, N.W. Gerald Smith, the commission's deputy director, described one of Kennedy's key roles this way: "With Frank in attendance, you really needed no other research tool. He brought his own library, primarily stored in his head, but amplified by meticulously accumulated notes and materials relevant to every conceivable matter having any impact on bankruptcy law, which of course includes the universe" (Brody 1983). The commission's chairman, Los Angeles attorney Harold Marsh, echoed remarks made repeatedly about Kennedy throughout his career when he referred to his "unlimited capacity for work" and "his incredible patience and unfailing courtesy in dealing with all of the persons who dealt with the commission" (ibid.).

The National Bankruptcy Review Commission submitted its final report, including a draft bill, to Congress on July 30, 1973. The commission's proposed legislation was introduced simultaneously in both the House and Senate later that year. The changes to the Bankruptcy Act contained in the bills were dramatic. On the commercial side, the old and cumbersome Chapters X and XI would be replaced with an all-new Chapter 11, which provided, among other things, for greater debtor control of reorganizing companies. The bill also included a new Chapter 13 bankruptcy that would allow consumer filers the opportunity to repay all or a portion of their obligations over time without losing their non-exempt property.

These provisions, although radical and far-reaching, were generally well received. A proposal to eliminate the incorporation of state exemptions in consumer cases in favor of uniform federal ones met with more resistance, mainly from legislators from states with generous homestead provisions like Texas and Florida, and would eventually lead to a compromise that granted states the authority to "opt out" of the federal scheme, that is, limit their residents' ability to use the federal exemptions in their personal bankruptcy cases. However, two other proposals, one that called for the creation of a national bankruptcy administrator and another that would have enhanced the authority of bankruptcy judges, brought into the open longstanding tensions between the bankruptcy bench and the district judges and threatened to scuttle any attempts at reform.

Under the commission's proposal, the appointments of all existing bankruptcy judges would be terminated on the effective date of the new law. An all-new independent bankruptcy court would take the place of the old one; judges would be appointed by the president and confirmed by the Senate and would serve fifteen-year terms. The district judges would retain important powers over the new bankruptcy court, with responsibility for setting the number of seats on the new courts, for appointing the bankruptcy clerks of court, and for hearing appeals from the new judges' decisions.

The bankruptcy judges (as they were identified after the adoption of the 1973 bankruptcy rules) had already been at work on their own proposal, which would have provided them with broad authority in bankruptcy cases. They had strong congressional support; as a result, their bill was introduced alongside the reintroduction of the commission bill in

1975.[5] The result was a kind of legislative standoff, and the prospects for any kind of reform dimmed until congressional sponsors insisted that the NBC/commission group and the judges resolve their differences. The product of their compromise was reflected in yet another bill, this one drafted by congressional staffers. It elevated the bankruptcy judges to full Article III status subject to presidential appointment and Senate confirmation.

This legislation might have quickly gained congressional approval but for the opposition of the federal judiciary, more specifically the Judicial Conference of the United States. The Judicial Conference remained opposed to any measures that would bring the bankruptcy judges closer to gaining the privileges and authority possessed by Article III judges.[6] The Chief Justice of the United States, Warren Burger, was one of the referees' most vocal opponents. As recounted by Judge Mund in her series of articles on the adoption of the Bankruptcy Code, "Burger had told a [House staffer] that 'a magistrate is three times more important than a bankruptcy referee' and that 'elevating the referees to judicial stature is like elevating clerks of courts'" (Mund 2007, 186). The members of the Judicial Conference barely veiled their official concerns in terms of policy and instead were explicit in their belief that giving referees full judicial status would diminish the prestige of their own Article III appointments (Mund 2007; Posner 1997; Skeel 2001). As a result, bankruptcy reform again stalled amid efforts to reconcile the positions of the bankruptcy and federal benches.

However, in the long history of bankruptcy law and Congress, major legislation, including the code, stalled and was reintroduced multiple times over several years before it was finally approved. Bankruptcy legislation (again in separate House and Senate bills with small but significant differences) was on the congressional agenda again when it came up for hearings before a Senate Judiciary subcommittee in November 1977. The Judicial Conference sent a full complement of judges to the hearing to express opposition to the bill, including Eastern District of Michigan Judge Robert DeMascio. This Ad Hoc Committee on Bankruptcy Legislation (as they identified themselves) had little interest in the substantive terms of the proposed bankruptcy law. Its concern was keeping the bankruptcy judges from achieving any kind of parity with the federal bench. However, their efforts may have been counterproductive to their goal. Many of the legislators and their staff had formed strong, mutually respectful relationships with the bankruptcy judges as they had worked together to formulate the new law. A particular problem was the federal judges' testimonial demeanor; some of them simply could not (or would not) conceal their disdain for the bankruptcy bench, which, according to Judge Mund, came across to the members of the subcommittee as petty and small-minded (Mund 2007, 184).

Judge Mund singles out Judge DeMascio for particular criticism on this score; she quotes the Senate Committee's deputy counsel, who describes DeMascio as "kind of nasty."[7] DeMascio was, without a doubt, "a self-described 'no nonsense' judge who could be intimidating and abrupt" on the bench (Chardavoyne 2012, 316). However, a review of his Senate testimony reveals nothing to support Judge Mund's harsh characterization of him. DeMascio spoke about the federal judges' proposal for the creation of a national bankruptcy administrator. He was careful to point out that the proposal should not be interpreted as a criticism of the bankruptcy bench. For instance, while explaining that the ad hoc committee's proposal to have the administrator select case trustees would insulate the bankruptcy judges from charges of cronyism, he was quick to indicate that he did not believe that bankruptcy judges in fact preferred one trustee over another.[8] On the whole, DeMascio's testimony was limited to a judicious discussion of the technical aspects of the proposal. If he shared his fellow ad hoc committee members' low regard for the bankruptcy bench, his testimony did not show it. So, while the public record might not convey Judge DeMascio's demeanor or any private comments he might have made outside of the hearing room, it nonetheless remains the only definitive record of his position, and it does not support Judge Mund's description of him.

Once the hearings were over, Congress's continued efforts to accommodate the federal bench's opposition to granting Article III status to the bankruptcy judges would delay passage of a new bankruptcy law for nearly another year. Superficially, the all-new Bankruptcy Code that was signed by President Carter on November 6, 1978, was a victory for the federal judges in that it did not grant Article III status to the bankruptcy bench. Instead, bankruptcy judges would be Article I judges, nominated by the president and confirmed by the Senate. They would serve fourteen-year, not lifetime, terms. However, despite the bankruptcy judges'

Article I status, they would have virtually all of the judicial authority of their Article III counterparts. By most measures of importance to the bankruptcy judges, the new code was a victory.

The 1978 code ushered in a sea change in American bankruptcy law. It streamlined reorganization provisions to give business debtors substantial discretion in shaping their own exits from bankruptcy as the debtor-in-possession, a legal status that allowed the debtor to manage its own business while reorganizing without the supervision of a court-appointed trustee. In fact, trustee appointments were eliminated in all Chapter 11 cases except in instances of debtor misconduct. Instead, the new code provided for the appointment of unsecured creditors' committees, which were given special standing to monitor the activities of debtors-in-possession, authority to hire their own attorneys and accountants (to be paid by the debtor), and generally act as a watchdog to protect the interests of debtors' trade creditors, who otherwise occupied the lowest rung on the distribution ladder. However, the new provisions encouraged courts to give great consideration to negotiated outcomes. Generally, the code promoted efforts to reorganize troubled businesses instead of immediately liquidating them.

The new statute's provision for wage-earner reorganizations, relabeled Chapter 13 under the new code, provided debtors broader discharges and relief from home foreclosure than was available under Chapter 7, in exchange for an agreement to make monthly payments to their creditors from their future income. Procedures for the appointment of Chapter 7 case trustees were dramatically modified. While cases would continue to be filed in the bankruptcy court, most consumer Chapter 7 cases were handled by the trustees without formal judicial intervention, particularly those where there were no assets to liquidate after allowance of the debtor's exemptions. In particular, judges would no longer conduct the first meetings of creditors or hold discharge hearings in every case. They would no longer appoint case trustees under the code. Instead, the trustees would be appointed and supervised by a new administrative agency within the Justice Department, the Office of the United States Trustee. The case trustees, not the judges, conducted the initial (and usually only) hearing in Chapter 7 cases, reviewed claims, and distributed proceeds from liquidated assets to creditors. While at first glance the U.S. Trustee bore some resemblance to the proposed administrative agency that had provoked the judges to draft their own bill in the early 1970s, it in fact was a very different entity and not the threat that the judges had feared. Moreover, ending the judges' authority to appoint trustees and other case professionals ended the rumors of "bankruptcy rings" once and for all. On the whole, the changes contributed to the elevated perception of the bankruptcy courts, which had been the judges' primary goal. Freed of routine ministerial duties, the new judges (most of whom were reappointed referees) could devote their efforts to judging instead of the administrative duties that had been their primary responsibilities under the former act.

The code granted bankruptcy judges expanded powers comparable to those of full-fledged Article III judges. Unlike the act, which gave the district judges authority over many significant matters, the code empowered bankruptcy judges to decide most of the matters arising in cases in their courts. Moreover, the new provisions for business reorganization meant longer cases with more judicial involvement. Those changes, with the possibility of significant legal fees, attracted established law firms to the bankruptcy courts for the first time. Overall, the effect was to improve the status of the bankruptcy courts almost instantly. Bankruptcy courts were perceived as courts of law instead of low-level collection agencies.[9]

Stuart Hertzberg, who was already one of Detroit's most prominent commercial bankruptcy lawyers by 1978, reflected in an interview on the positive effect the new code had on him and his colleagues.

> Well, there was more legal work under the code. Plenty of legal work. And, as a result, that brought in more lawyers to handle the legal work. And you had creditors' committees who were then appointed by the U.S. Trustee. They selected their counsel, and you had that position in the case, and you had an attorney for the debtor, and there were those who specialized as counsel for the debtor. . . . So you had a lot of people involved in the proceeding who became trained in the bankruptcy field, and enhanced the size of the Bar that was practicing over there. It was no longer a small, select set. (Hertzberg 2008, 36)

The new code took effect on October 1, 1979, and case filings increased dramatically: nationally, they leaped from 214,399[10] in 1977 to 331,264 in

1980, the first full year under the code. Consumers filed the overwhelming majority of these cases (87 percent) under the new, streamlined provisions for Chapter 7. The increases were even more striking in the Eastern District of Michigan, where overall case filings increased from 4,663 in 1978 to 5,819 in 1979, and then to 9,649 in 1980. Consumers filed 97 percent of the district's new bankruptcy cases.

Although Chapter 11 cases composed a small percentage of new filings, they occupied an increasing portion of the courts' time, in part because much of the work in routine consumer cases had been moved out of the courtroom, and in part because the reorganization cases were generally bigger and more complicated than their counterparts under the act. President Lyndon Johnson was quoted as saying that a town that can't support one lawyer can always support two. And so it was with practice under the new Bankruptcy Code. The Chapter 11 cases, with their increased complexity and multiple lawyers, brought increases in the fees paid to attorneys. In Stuart Hertzberg's view, "You got paid more postcode because there was so much more involved legally as a result of the formality of the type of proceedings" (Hertzberg 2008, 43).

Of course the increased fee requests were often accompanied by greater scrutiny. Some of this was again due to the nature of the new code. There were simply more parties with a formal role in the new cases who stood to gain if attorneys' fees, with their superior statutory priority of payment, were reduced. However, as described in the preceding chapter, some of the Eastern District's judges were less critical of attorneys' fee requests, regardless of the amount. These factors would prove to be the driving forces behind events that provoked a crisis that tore apart the court and affected bankruptcy practice throughout the Eastern District for years to come.

8

SCANDAL ENVELOPS
THE COURT

Aside from certain mega-cases in the Southern District of New York and the occasional celebrity filing, bankruptcy courts generally attract little media attention. However, on December 6, 1980, the *Detroit News* reported that the bankruptcy court in Detroit was under investigation by the FBI and that the way in which new cases were assigned to judges was the central focus of the investigators. In addition, the clerk of the court, William Harper, had been placed on administrative leave. Harper, Judge Harry Hackett, Chief District Court Judge John Feikens, and the bankruptcy court's acting clerk would not or could not provide further comment.[1]

Another *News* article at the end of January 1981 elaborated on the earlier report, stating that Harper was placed on leave because of complaints of sexual harassment made against him by court employees.[2] The same *News* article also indicated that District Court Judge James P. Churchill had for a second time reversed a fee award made to attorney Irving August by Judge Harry Hackett in the *Martin Place Hospital* case.[3] However, as startling as these reports may have been, they only hinted at the controversy that would soon rip apart the Detroit bankruptcy court.

On February 23, 1981, WJR, one of Detroit's premier radio stations, broadcast the first of what would eventually be twenty-three stories detailing multiple improprieties involving the bankruptcy court. In that first episode, WJR reporter Gene Fogel revealed that Western District of Michigan Judge Douglas Hillman had been appointed by the Sixth Circuit Court of Appeals to conduct administrative hearings on the complaints against clerk William Harper. Fogel also indicated that officials from the Administrative Office of the United States Courts had investigated complaints against Harper alleging "intoxication, abusive language, and solicitation of sexual favors," leading to the FBI investigation.[4]

The claims mentioned in the report had been brewing since the preceding fall. Several female court employees had formally complained to the Administrative Office, asserting claims of sexual abuse and other improprieties. One source told the *Detroit News* that the women contacted the Administrative Office only after being told by Harry Hackett that they would lose their jobs if they pursued their charges.[5]

The harassment charges were not limited to the clerk's office. The Administrative Office had received a similar complaint involving Judge Harry Hackett. Victoria Toensing, an assistant U.S. attorney, wrote that during a conversation at a bar near the courthouse, Hackett told her that "women should be kept 'barefoot, pregnant or in the kitchen' and left after saying he would know how to handle her if she ever appeared in this court."[6]

The Administrative Office quickly determined that the scope of potential wrongdoing in the Detroit court included more than the claims of sexual abuse and went well beyond its capabilities to investigate, let alone punish. It turned the investigation over to the FBI. In the meantime, WJR's investigative team was already covering much of the same ground. On the day following WJR's initial broadcast, the station's newscasts featured another story about the bankruptcy court by reporter Rod Hansen. Hansen revealed that he and his colleague had been investigating the court for six weeks. Referring to the allegations against William Harper, he said,

> It's no secret in the whole federal court establishment in Detroit that the sooner and more quietly the Harper case goes away, the better. The questions of federal judicial and FBI Investigators, and those of WJR reporters, have rubbed nerve ends raw. For it also is no secret that special relationships exist between two, and

quite possible all three bankruptcy judges, some court employees, some lawyers and some trustees. Even if there is no hard evidence of illegality, there are tough questions hanging in the fire about judicial ethics and propriety.[7]

Hansen went on to provide details, naming names along the way. He reported that attorney Irving August was dating one of the clerks in charge of assigning newly filed cases to the bankruptcy judges. That clerk and at least two others had received money, trips, and other gifts from attorneys. Moreover, Hansen indicated, the court's "blind draw" case assignment system was alleged to be rigged, possibly through an arrangement between attorneys and court employees, by the judges themselves, or by outright tampering.

Hansen added that two of the court's judges maintained close relationships with particular attorneys, allegedly traveling with them on business and vacation trips to locales such as Atlanta, Toronto, Hawaii, and Mexico. One of the attorneys was identified in the report as John Dougherty, who had been appointed by the three Detroit judges to be the standing Chapter 13 trustee in all Chapter 13 cases.[8]

The next day's report, again from Hansen, provided more details about the relationship between Irving August and Judge Harry Hackett, indicating that they had an out-of-court friendship that included golf outings and a 1980 trip to Toronto with two female court employees.[9] Other suspicious activity, according to Hansen's story, included Judge David Patton's transfer of the Allied Supermarkets case to Hackett shortly after it was filed in November 1978. Allied Supermarkets was the parent company of the Great Scott chain of stores and was one of the biggest companies in metro Detroit to seek bankruptcy relief up to that time. Its attorney was Irving August. Hansen also reported that Hackett sometimes signed orders in other August-filed cases assigned to Judge Patton even when those cases had not actually been transferred to him.[10]

The week ended with reports from both Fogel and Hansen alleging details of Hackett's trips to Toronto with Irving August and to Atlanta with Dougherty. The reports stated that female court employees accompanied the men on both trips. The reports also asserted that female employees identified as companions of Judge Hackett had received cash gifts from August or Dougherty.[11]

As alarming as these stories were, the next week brought further revelations about the court. On Monday, a WJR report highlighted the pervasiveness of the close relationships between judges and attorneys in the Eastern District, stating that even the notoriously tough George Brody had taken two trips with attorney John Dougherty. Although Judge Brody paid for the trips himself and was not accompanied by any female court employees, he admitted that the trips might have appeared to be inappropriate.[12]

However, the most damning story came the next day, Tuesday, March 3, 1981.[13] Rod Hansen identified the intake clerk who had handled all but possibly two of 44 Chapter 11 cases filed by August's firm in a twelve-month period as August's "girl friend." Hansen reported that the clerk had received gifts from August including an apartment, trips, and a new car. The clerk was responsible for processing new cases, which included assigning the cases to one of the court's three judges using a blind draw system. This system was constructed to impede judge shopping by attorneys. The three judges' names were printed on individual cards, which were collected in 100-card decks and shuffled. Judge Brody's and Judge Hackett's names would appear in each deck 37 times, Judge Patton's on 26. (Chapter 13 cases were not part of the draw and instead were automatically assigned to Patton; his relative draw for the other cases was adjusted to reflect his Chapter 13 caseload.) Cards were then drawn from the top of the deck until the deck was exhausted. Assuming that the deck was shuffled and drawn from at random, the likelihood of a case being assigned to Judge Brody and Judge Hackett was 37 percent each and Judge Patton 26 percent.

However, when WJR's reporters examined the 44 Chapter 11 cases filed by August's firm,[14] they found that 24 (55 percent) had been assigned to Judge Hackett, 19 (43 percent) had been assigned to Judge Patton, and only one (2 percent) had been assigned to the relatively stingy Judge Brody. Hansen cited a University of Michigan statistician to report that the odds of Brody's name being drawn in only one case was 1 in 1,000, creating a strong inference that August's cases were not, in fact, assigned to judges at random but that they were being steered away from Brody.

Given that Hansen's and Fogel's reporting was ultimately proven to be accurate, it is perhaps unsurprising that neither the court nor the various individuals in question had much of a public response. Hackett, Patton, August, and Dougherty all denied the accusations. Brody claimed to have asked the deputy court clerk to look into allegations that the blind draw was being tampered with but stated that there was no evidence of such behavior (Brody 1996). However, others, including the U.S. Attorney's office, the Eastern District's federal judges and those of the Sixth Circuit Court of Appeals, and even private litigants were giving the reports careful attention.

In the immediate wake of the WJR broadcasts, Blue Cross-Blue Shield of Michigan, a major creditor in the Martin Place Hospital bankruptcy case, filed a motion asking Judge Hackett to formally recuse himself from the case in light of his close relationship with Irving August, the hospital's attorney. Copies of WJR's broadcast transcripts were provided to the court with the motion. At the end of March, the Sixth Circuit appointed a blue ribbon merit-screening panel to review Judge Hackett's bid for reappointment when his term expired on July 30, 1981. While the appointment of such panels was routine under the provisions of the new code, the scrutiny could not have come at a less welcome time for Judge Hackett. The panel would spend the next two months receiving public comments and making its own investigation. However, that investigation, for all of its importance, would have to share court-watchers' attention with the rapidly developing prosecution of William Harper.

Harper was placed on administrative leave on November 26, 1980, but was reinstated on March 16, 1981, when Judge Hillman issued his finding that the evidence presented to him did not support sanctions against Harper for misconduct. However, Harper's relief would be short-lived. On April 23, 1981, a federal grand jury in Detroit handed down an indictment against Harper, charging him with violating the federal law forbidding court employees from purchasing property from bankruptcy sales. The indictment, however, did not involve the claims of misconduct and sexual harassment that had been made against Harper. Neither did it involve the blind draw manipulation described in the WJR reports. Instead, the indictment involved something astonishingly simple (and easier to prove). The grand jury charged that Harper had purchased a boat, motor, and trailer from a bankrupt's estate in 1976, using the name of his son-in-law, Carl Sturdevant, to conceal his identity. Then, as now, federal law forbade court officers from buying property from bankruptcy estates.[15] One reason for the statute was that the temptation and pressure to give favorable treatment to court officials in bankruptcy sales would be overwhelming. Such were the facts as presented in Harper's case; according to the indictment, he allegedly paid only $135 for the boat, motor, and trailer.

Faced with the criminal prosecution of their chief clerk, the Eastern District's bankruptcy judges met and decided not to suspend Harper again despite the gravity of the charges against him. Why they did this is not certain; the judges neither announced their meeting nor published their decision not to suspend Harper. It is possible that they felt deterred by Judge Hillman's recent refusal to uphold Harper's previous suspension. Regardless, the bankruptcy judges' inaction infuriated the Eastern District's federal district judges. Unable to take direct action against the bankruptcy court because of statutory restrictions, the district judges made a unanimous plea for action to the Sixth Circuit Court of Appeals.[16]

On May 6, 1981, the Judicial Council of the Sixth Circuit Court of Appeals exercised its supervisory authority over the Eastern District's bankruptcy court and placed the court in what it later described as a "virtual receivership."[17] The operative provision of the Judicial Council's order stated:

> The Council concludes that the effective and expeditious administration of the business of the courts within this circuit requires that the administration of the Bankruptcy Court for the Eastern District of Michigan be placed under the supervision of the United States District Court for the Eastern District of Michigan. Such supervision should include the oversight of the general operation of the Bankruptcy Court Clerk's Office, the appointment of an Acting Clerk of the Bankruptcy Court and the approval of all personnel actions affecting employees of the Bankruptcy Court.[18]

The Judicial Council also acted directly with respect to William Harper, ordering that he be immediately suspended with pay pending the outcome of his trial: "It is inconsistent with the maintenance of public confidence in the integrity of the federal judiciary for any person to continue to function in a position of public trust as an officer of the court while under formal charges alleging the conduct in the indictment."[19]

Twelve days later, on May 18, 1981, the judges of the U.S. District Court for the Eastern District of Michigan entered their own order directing

Chief Judge John Feikens to assume supervisory responsibility for the bankruptcy court in order to carry out the terms of the Judicial Council's order. Judge Feikens, however, took action soon after receiving the Sixth Circuit's order, naming David Sherwood, the deputy district court clerk, as acting clerk of the bankruptcy court on May 7, 1981. Within a week, Sherwood had issued a tough new set of rules governing the conduct of employees of the clerk's office.[20] He banned the longstanding practice that allowed court employees to accept gifts and favors from attorneys, appraisers, auctioneers, and others. The new rules also prohibited clerks from interfering with judicial case assignments: "A clerk should never influence the assignment of cases or perform any discretionary or ministerial function of the court in a manner which improperly favors any litigant or attorney."[21] Sherwood also terminated certain employees he viewed as being unproductive or disruptive influences within the office.[22]

While these actions of the Sixth Circuit Judicial Counsel, Chief Judge Feikens, and David Sherwood would ultimately go a long way toward resolving the crisis engulfing the court, they only brought limited relief from its immediate problems. William Harper's trial for illegally buying a boat, motor, and trailer began before Federal Judge Horace Gilmore in Detroit on June 11, 1981. Harper testified on his own behalf; he admitted buying the boat but claimed that it had been common for court employees to purchase items from bankruptcy estates and that in any event he was not a court "officer" within the meaning of the statute.[23] His assertion that his actions were legal left unexplained why he hid his identity in the transaction, making the purchase under the name of his son-in-law. David Patton, the judge who presided over the case, also testified, saying that he would not have approved the sale had he known that Harper was the true buyer. In reality, Harper had no defense, and the trial lasted barely two days. The jury quickly reached a verdict, deliberating only an hour before finding Harper guilty.[24] Harper was stripped of his $50,000 per year job, as required by the statute, when he was sentenced a few weeks later.

Just as Harper's conviction and removal from office were expected, it came as no surprise to court-watchers when Sixth Circuit Chief Judge George Edwards issued his report on June 24, 1981, denying Harry Hackett's reappointment to a new term. Edwards's report, which was based on the findings of the merit-selection panel, covered much of the same ground reported by WJR in February. He concluded that Hackett had shown favoritism in awarding fees to Irving August at a time when they were in "frequent social contact." Furthermore, Edwards wrote, "Judge Hackett permitted attorneys practicing before him to make gifts to female court employees with whom Hackett was maintaining a relationship." Moreover, he concluded, "There is strong evidence that gifts, entertainment, travel costs, and money have been tendered to and received by strategically placed bankruptcy court employees and by lawyers practicing before Judge Hackett, with his knowledge and apparent approval." And finally, in a charge that had not previously been described publicly, Edwards wrote that there was evidence that Hackett had been drunk while on the bench.

Acting court clerk David Sherwood conveyed Chief Judge Edwards's decision to Harry Hackett. Although the decision would not be effective until his term ended a few days later, Hackett, in an expression of anger, immediately resigned.[25] By the end of the day, he had cleaned out his office and was gone.

Thus within the space of two months, the long-festering problems within the courthouse were largely under control. Harry Hackett was gone. William Harper was gone, too, replaced by a new clerk who imposed tough new standards of conduct in the clerk's office. But the court was by no means clear of controversy. WJR had broadcast another series on the court, this one focusing on the activities of Chapter 13 trustee John Dougherty. A replacement for Hackett needed to be named, an appointment made all the more important by the fact that Judges Patton and Brody had themselves received their share of criticism in Judge Edwards's report. And last, but certainly not least, the federal government was preparing its prosecution of attorney Irving August. It would be a long time before the court would escape the media spotlight, and even longer before it would fully recover from the harsh effects of scandal.

9

FALLOUT FROM
THE SCANDAL

The August Trial

As noted earlier, the Bankruptcy Code's all-new Chapter 11 provisions were a boon for lawyers, providing not only more work but also new kinds of legal work and larger fees for bankruptcy specialists. This was true for no one more so than Irving August and his firm, August, Thompson, Sherr, Clarke & Schafer. Not only was the August firm among the Detroit court's most prominent Chapter 11 case filers,[1] but August also tended to receive consistently large fee awards in his cases. However, by 1981, the size of the fee awards sought and awarded to August had become a matter of broader interest and some controversy. In May, George Brody used August's petition seeking what was essentially a bonus as a platform for his precedent-setting decision in the Hamilton Hardware case. As a report in the *Detroit News* made clear, that case was only the most recent in a series of decisions by Brody in which he awarded lesser fees to August than what he requested. Moreover, creditors in some cases balked at August's fee requests, filing objections and, in the *Martin Place* case, appeals of fee awards.

As might be expected, August's manipulation of the court's case assignment system had become a source of tension among its staff well before the WJR reports made it known to the public. Brody's secretary, Helen Guercio, asked Brody if he was aware that he was assigned to very few of the Chapter 11 cases filed by Irving August's firm. Brody professed to have no knowledge of any discrepancies in the assignment of new cases but asked the deputy court clerk to investigate. According to Brody, the clerk reported back to him that he found nothing amiss, and Brody possibly gave the matter no more thought until the allegations about August became public in WJR's February 1981 reports.

The public attention, which was intensified by the story's sexual undertones, probably made Irving August's prosecution inevitable, and on March 19, 1981, a federal grand jury sitting in Detroit handed down indictments against the fifty-one-year-old August and his girlfriend, twenty-five-year-old court clerk Kathleen Bogoff. The seven-count indictment included charges that August and Bogoff conspired to manipulate the court's blind draw system for assigning new cases to judges to avoid assigning August's cases to George Brody, that August "corruptly endeavored to influence" Bogoff to manipulate the blind draw, that Bogoff accepted August's gifts and payments, and that August illegally sought to influence Judge Harry Hackett by loaning money to Hackett's friends, and by paying Hackett's expenses at golf outings. In addition, the indictment charged that August fraudulently concealed a $75,000 claim for unpaid pre-petition legal fees against one of his Chapter 11 clients, the House of Imports, instead cutting a side deal in which he would be paid in full while the debtor's other unsecured creditors would receive only 35 percent of their claims.

The charges against August arising out of the House of Imports case were less notorious than the ones alleging that he had rigged the blind draw, but they were illustrative of the extent to which, prosecutors claimed, August was willing to manipulate the rules for his own financial gain. The Bankruptcy Code bars the employment of an attorney by the debtor-in-possession if the attorney holds an interest adverse to the estate.[2] Any fees owed to the lawyer prior to the filing of a petition are a claim against the estate and constitute an adverse interest of the kind prohibited by the statute. Therefore, an attorney with unpaid fees who wishes to represent a debtor in a Chapter 11 case has two choices: he may retain his claim but forego representing the debtor in bankruptcy, or he can waive his claim to eliminate the adverse interest but in doing so give up any opportunity for repayment.

The indictment against Irving August charged that he had followed a third path; not only did he not waive his claim for pre-petition legal fees, but he instead kept it out of the bankruptcy case altogether and made a separate deal with the House of Imports to receive full payment outside of the Chapter 11 case. If all went according to plan, according to prosecutors, August would receive full payment of his $75,000 pre-filing bill while the debtor's other creditors could hope to receive no more than 35 percent of their claims.

August's defense was based on his assertion that he had never formally billed House of Imports for the unpaid fees. Instead, according to his lawyer, Miami attorney Albert Krieger,[3] August told the company president that once the House of Imports was out of bankruptcy, it could pay him "what I'm entitled to, or 35 cents to the dollar, or nothing at all, because [technically] you don't owe me anything."[4]

August's trial on the House of Imports charges was split off from the rest of the case and began before District Judge Ralph Freeman on October 18, 1982. August essentially admitted to the side deal with this client. His defense was that he had done nothing illegal, or even underhanded, in seeking payment of his fees. Attorney Albert Krieger pointed out in support of this defense that August had mentioned the fee deal in a letter he sent to House of Imports' president; a copy of that letter was also sent to the attorney for the debtor's creditors' committee. According to Krieger, "If [August] wanted to conceal the reviver agreement,[5] the last person in the world he would let know about it would be the vigorous attorney for the creditors."[6] One of those attorneys was Conrad Duberstein of New York. In the interim between the conclusion of the House of Imports case and the criminal trial, Duberstein had been appointed a bankruptcy judge in the United States Bankruptcy Court for the Eastern District of New York. He would go on to become one of the country's most prominent bankruptcy judges, just as he was one of its most respected practitioners before his appointment. Duberstein admitted under questioning by Albert Krieger that parts of the agreement were unclear to him. Krieger then led Duberstein through a parsing of the letter to suggest that it might be interpreted in multiple, less damning ways. The examination placed sufficient doubt in the minds of jurors; after deliberating for several days, they found August not guilty on the House of Imports charges.

Those charges were the lesser part of the case against Irving August, however. The trial against him and Kathleen Bogoff was delayed for several months but finally began before Judge Freeman on March 22, 1983. Assistant U.S. Attorney Martin Reisig told the jury in his opening statement that August had given Bogoff thousands of dollars in gifts and payments in return for which she had manipulated the court's blind draw to keep August's cases away from Judge Brody.[7]

The prosecution's case extended over the better part of the next month as it called several witnesses, including court employees, experts, and even Judge Brody, who testified that he was unaware of the disproportionately small number of August's cases that had been assigned to him until his secretary brought the discrepancy to his attention. The prosecution's witnesses portrayed August as brazenly determined to keep his cases away from Judge Brody. As recounted by the Sixth Circuit, "In 1978, August told Judge Brody that he could not afford to handle such cases if Judge Brody continued to reduce his fee awards so much. He asked Judge Brody to transfer all of the August firm cases to which Judge Brody had been assigned to Judge Hackett (a personal friend of August). Judge Brody refused to do so."[8]

However, the key parts of the prosecution's case were contained in the testimony of two witnesses. One of those witnesses was David Doane, a statistician from Oakland University. Doane examined the court's assignment of the August firm's cases before, during, and after Bogoff's tenure at the filing window. He found that while the filings before and after Bogoff's employ conformed to the expectations of a random distribution, Brody was assigned only 4 of 62 cases processed by Bogoff. Doane testified that had the assignment cards been distributed at random (i.e., without manipulating the order of the deck), the probability that Brody would have received only 4 were 5,121-to-1.[9]

The prosecution's other essential witness was Sharon Hughes, Harry Hackett's former court clerk. Hughes had been Judge Hackett's courtroom deputy and provided an insider's view of August's and Bogoff's activities. She described Bogoff as having been her best friend. Hughes testified that Bogoff had complained to her that August would drop off new cases to be filed at her home to be filed the next day. She also testified that she often saw lawyers from August's firm leave new cases on Bogoff's desk for filing. Of August himself, she testified that he used the court's offices as if they were his own. Hughes said that August "had the run of [Hackett's] office. . . . He made his own adjournments. . . . He put over to another time cases he didn't want heard at that time, or he would come in with added cases and put them on [the hearing docket]. He'd use the phones freely."[10]

Hughes was a classic insider-informant in that she was a direct source of important evidence necessary to the success of the prosecution's case but also because she had significant credibility problems. Hughes was Harry Hackett's girlfriend and the companion described in the WJR reports. She testified that she and Hackett often dined and socialized with August and Bogoff, sometimes during the court's normal working hours. However, Hughes's close relationship with Hackett put into issue questions of her own credibility. When examined by August's lawyer, she admitted that she had received numerous gifts and cash payments over the years from both Harry Hackett and Irving August. Hughes was also questioned her about unrelated charges that she had received more than $20,000 in welfare payments through fraudulent applications made while an employee of the court and that she had lied on her application to work at the court.

Finally, Hughes had been fired when the court was placed under Judge Feikens's receivership in 1981. According to court clerk David Sherwood, she was dismissed for "lack of productivity and disruptive behavior." Hughes, however, claimed that her termination was in retaliation for her cooperation with federal authorities, and she sued the court for wrongful discharge, a case that remained pending at the time of the August trial.

Even with these flaws, Hughes's testimony provided a critical link in the prosecution's case. The government's case was necessarily built on circumstantial evidence. As the Sixth Circuit stated on appeal, "In the instant case, there was no direct evidence of guilt. No one testified to having observed any tampering with the judge selection cards. No one confessed to having subverted the process. The government's case consisted of a showing of motive and opportunity, coupled with circumstantial evidence that a disproportionately small number of August's cases were being assigned to Judge Brody."[11]

Of the many witnesses called by the prosecution, Sharon Hughes was the only one that could be considered to have had inside information on the sordid relationship between August, Bogoff, and Hackett. These kinds of witnesses are often imperfect; the circumstances for their proximity may also be the grounds for their impeachment. Still, the direct evidence provided by these insiders makes them powerful witnesses, and Hughes's testimony provided the prosecution with an essential element needed to convict August and Bogoff.

Albert Krieger approached August's defense on several fronts. He attempted to minimize the gravity of the charges by repeatedly describing August's alleged actions as simple "judge shopping." In a pre-trial motion to dismiss, Krieger argued, "Judge shopping is a fact of life. If judge shopping is illegal, then I suggest there is not a lawyer, not a prosecutor who hasn't engaged in judge shopping."[12] Moreover, Krieger argued in his opening statement that not only was judge shopping not illegal, it was totally justified in the circumstances of the case. Krieger essentially placed responsibility for the entire matter on the shoulders of Judge George Brody, claiming that his treatment of lawyers justifiably provoked their efforts to avoid him.[13]

Another defense ploy was an argument that the blind draw could be manipulated without illegally involving the court clerk. According to Krieger, the blind draw decks were not perfectly random but instead were altered by the clerks after shuffling to ensure that no judge's name appeared twice in a row. Therefore, a filer seeking to avoid having his case assigned to Brody merely had to politely allow other filers to present their cases until the judge's name was drawn and then proceed to the clerk's counter to file the next case.

This defense might have raised some doubt in jurors' minds if only it were not easily refutable. The prosecution showed that only 18 of the 72 card decks (i.e., 2 out of 7) used while Bogoff worked as an intake clerk had been rearranged in the manner suggested by Krieger. Moreover, even if August and his colleagues had strategically filed their new cases, the odds of avoiding Brody in all but 4 of them were still an overwhelming 99-to-1.[14]

In general, the defendants seemed to find very little traction with their own case. Bogoff, testifying in her own defense, portrayed herself as the loving but honest victim of a statistical fluke. Under questioning by her attorney, Leonard Hyman, Bogoff said that she was in love with Irving August and planned to marry him, even though August was already married.[15] Because she loved him, she testified, she sought him out whenever he came to the clerk's office.[16]

However, Bogoff's expression of true love did nothing to counter the broader case of conspiracy developed by the prosecution. According to Bogoff, August took care of her "physically, emotionally [and] financially." Bogoff admitted that in 1980 alone August had given her more than $20,000, which according to the *Detroit Free Press* was more than twice her annual salary. He paid the rent on her Southfield apartment and for her sports car. Moreover, her desire to be with August whenever he came to the clerk's office did not explain why she was the go-to clerk for the other attorneys in August's firm. Despite all this, and without attempting to explain the discrepancies in the case draws, Bogoff nonetheless maintained that she handled August's cases no differently than those of any other attorney.[17]

Bogoff's testimony turned out to be the trial's climax. August chose not to testify, a fact that might have struck some members of the jury as something less than chivalrous given his girlfriend's appearance on the stand. Nonetheless, Albert Krieger had no problem playing the love card when it came time to make his closing argument. He began by telling the jury "love is a defense." Krieger argued that the relationship between August and Bogoff was an "affair of the heart" and the gifts August lavished on Bogoff were not "designed, motivated or used to influence her actions" but instead were expressions of love. He closed by telling the jury, "If your judgment comes from the adulterous relationship, then this past six weeks has been a travesty."[18]

The jury began its deliberations on Friday, April 29, and reached a verdict on the following Monday, May 2. August and Bogoff were each convicted of conspiring to defraud the United States of the due administration of justice and of impeding the due administration of justice. In addition, August was convicted of attempting to illegally influence Bogoff in the discharge of her official duties. Bogoff was acquitted of accepting illegal gifts from August, suggesting that her lovelorn testimony might have struck a chord with at least some of the jurors. The two were sentenced at the end of June; August received a prison term of two years, Bogoff one. In passing sentence, Judge Ralph Freeman stated, "The only motive for this offense would seemingly be greed."[19]

August and Bogoff's sentencing came as a coda to two and a half years of revelations and reforms that began with the WJR reports, or possibly even the complaints made to the Administrative Office about Harry Hackett's personal conduct. Other actions were taken between Hackett's resignation and August's conviction. As has already been described, acting (later permanent) clerk David Sherwood undertook immediate action to bring the clerk's office under control, adopting tough new rules of conduct and terminating several problematic employees. In August 1981, the Administrative Office of the U.S. Courts terminated all twenty-one of the court's Chapter 7 trustees, with the proviso that they could apply to be reappointed. According to David Sherwood, "Many of the trustees are hardworking, honorable persons. Only a few are problem members of the panel." Those "problem" trustees were described in the *Detroit News* as having been "closely associated" with Harry Hackett.[20]

The court's standing Chapter 13 trustee, John Dougherty, did not fare well either. Dougherty had figured prominently in the original WJR broadcasts. According to these reports, Dougherty had frequently given gifts to court employees and had accompanied Judge Hackett, and in one instance Judge Brody, on out-of-town trips. Another report indicated that he provided "gifts, favors and companionship" to Judge Patton's secretary.[21] Ultimately, nine of the twenty-three WJR broadcasts made some reference to Dougherty.[22] Moreover, by mid-1982, Dougherty was on his way out as a Chapter 13 trustee, as the clerk's office stopped assigning him new cases.

In October 1981, Dougherty sued WJR's owner, Capital Cities Communications, claiming defamation and related claims. Judge Gilmore dismissed the case on summary judgment in 1986. His decision reflected his weariness with the whole affair and perhaps specifically the protestations of innocence by various individuals implicated in the scandal while recognizing the institutional debt the court owed to the radio station and its reporters. In summarizing his reasons for finding against Dougherty, Gilmore wrote:

> It is impossible to discern any false information in the broadcasts. Each statement made had a factual basis, and where they were

not factual statements, as with the potential tactical advantage in knowing the judge's predisposition in a matter, they were statements of opinion that were not actionable as defamation. On this ground alone, this action could be dismissed. Furthermore, however, even if plaintiff could raise some question as to truthfulness based on innuendo and omission from these reports, the Court finds that summary judgment can be based on Michigan's qualified privilege to report on matters in the public interest.[23]

Certainly by 1986 the court had moved forward. George Woods was appointed to replace Harry Hackett shortly after the latter judge's resignation. Woods was a former federal prosecutor who had briefly served as interim U.S. attorney in 1961. Following his service in the prosecutor's office, he was in private practice for two decades, where he specialized in criminal defense work. Under the selection system in place at the time, Woods was picked by the Eastern District's federal judges over thirty-six other applicants to take Hackett's place. His selection was in effect a nomination subject to confirmation by a merit selection panel appointed by the Sixth Circuit Court of Appeals. George Woods had a reputation for toughness and integrity, and his appointment was widely viewed as an effort by the federal bench to clean up the bankruptcy court.

Although Woods's selection was generally well received, it did not come without controversy. Woods had been nominated in 1969 to be the U.S. attorney in Detroit. His nomination was withdrawn when local news outlets reported that he had represented reputed mobsters while in private practice. Upon learning of Woods's selection for the bankruptcy bench, Judge Brody's secretary, Helen Guercio, resurrected the old articles and sent them to the nominating committee, the Administrative Office of the U.S. Courts, the FBI, and various newspaper reporters.[24] Guercio was once described as a "professional busybody" whose demeanor rankled some people at the court.[25] Her efforts to stop Woods's nomination created a great deal of consternation within the court, and as a result she was fired. Guercio justifiably portrayed herself as one of the main whistleblowers during the court scandal, and she sued Judges Brody and Feikens, claiming that her firing was as much in retaliation for those efforts as it was for her attempt to block George Woods's appointment to the bankruptcy bench. Her case was dismissed on the grounds that the judges were immune from suit but only after much litigating and two rounds of appeals.[26]

Despite Guercio's reservations, George Woods served with great distinction during his brief tenure on the bench. Court veterans today point to him, along with David Sherwood, as the individuals most responsible for restoring the integrity of the court in the wake of the scandal. Woods was commonly described as a "no-nonsense" jurist who "did whatever he thought was right regardless of the criticism."[27] Woods also presided over some of the district's most significant cases of the time, including Allied Supermarkets (inherited from Judge Hackett), McLouth Steel, DeLorean Motor Company, and U.S. Truck Co. His decision in the latter case allowing the debtor to reject its collective bargaining agreement with its unionized employees was one of the most-cited opinions permitting such action under the code before the Supreme Court's decision in *Bildisco & Bildisco and Congress's adoption of 11 U.S.C. §1113* (effectively overturning those decisions) in 1984.[28] The success of Woods's efforts were implicitly recognized in November 1983, when he was nominated by President Reagan to fill the vacancy left on the district court bench when Patricia Boyle resigned to take a spot on the Michigan Supreme Court.

Another source of controversy over Woods's appointment to the bankruptcy court had come from Detroit's African American legal community, which advocated for a black jurist to replace Harry Hackett. Those concerns were assuaged shortly thereafter when thirty-five-year-old Ray Reynolds Graves, a former partner at the noted Detroit firm of Lewis, White, Clay & Graves and staff counsel at Detroit Edison, was nominated to replace retiring Judge David Patton in September 1981. While health was the announced reason for Patton's retirement, many court observers believed that the attention from the scandal had taken its toll on him as well, harming not only his health but also his reputation.

It would be wrong to pin blame for the scandal that rocked the court in the early 1980s on any single person, even Irving August. Bankruptcy courts have been accused of fostering self-dealing and the personal enrichment of officials and professionals for as long as they have existed; unfortunately those charges have sometimes been leveled with good reason. The WJR reports make it clear that a kind of petty corruption was endemic in the court and involved not only court officials and attorneys but trustees, auctioneers, and other professionals. Court veterans can still tell stories about such incidents that long preceded the news reports.

How did a court that had produced the likes of Paul King and Archie Katcher come to displace the interests of justice with banal and even tawdry scandal? Perhaps the best answer is Judge Freeman's, that in the end it was just greed—or perhaps more accurately, greed and stupidity. It remains hard to understand, even with the perspective of several decades, how a seemingly brilliant attorney like Irving August would have thought that he could get away with it forever.

However, in terms of the court history, the scandal has become a morality tale, a kind of warning of the perils of greed, and that it is something too easy to slip into. It serves as a marker from which court officials have ever after sought to distance and distinguish themselves. The scandal would cast a long and palpable shadow over bankruptcy practice and administration in the Eastern District for many years to come. New restrictions and strict norms limited the kinds of communications court employees could have with attorneys, leaving some in the latter group with the impression that they were perpetually and unjustly under suspicion. However, once the August trial concluded, the entire matter quickly disappeared from public attention. If the court garnered any press attention at all, it was for the cases being filed there, in particular the Chapter 11 cases being heard under the provisions of the still relatively new Bankruptcy Code. Therefore, the trial should properly be viewed as a needed if painful step in the court's effort to regain its institutional integrity.

10

CHAPTER 11 AND THE HEYDAY OF BUSINESS BANKRUPTCY IN THE EASTERN DISTRICT OF MICHIGAN

Of all the changes the 1978 code brought about in bankruptcy practice, none was more innovative or had a greater impact than those in Chapter 11,[1] the all-new provision for court-supervised business restructuring. The keystone of the new law was the creation of the "debtor-in-possession." The notion of the appointment of a trustee for all but the most egregious instances of misconduct was banished. Instead all operational, strategic, and decision-making authority remained with the debtor, or as formally designated, the debtor-in-possession. Moreover, the debtor-in-possession was given wide latitude under the code, having at least 120 days to propose a plan of reorganization, all the while operating under the protection of the automatic stay.[2] This period could be extended, and in practice often was, with leave of the court. Supervision of the debtor was in large measure delegated to committees of unsecured creditors that were given general standing to participate in most significant activities in a Chapter 11 case. The creation of these new bankruptcy-specific parties ensured that Chapter 11 cases would be thoroughly litigated, but it also encouraged flexible, negotiated outcomes.

Businesses in the recession-plagued early 1980s were quick to seek the benefits of the new law. Overall national business bankruptcy filings increased from fewer than 44,000 in 1980 to more than 69,000 in 1982. New petitions in the Eastern District of Michigan followed suit, with 602 businesses filing cases in 1980 and 1,018 two years later.[3] The rate at which new business bankruptcy cases were filed in the Eastern District dropped slightly from that number but remained fairly consistent throughout the remainder of the decade and into the early 1990s.

While Chapter 11 was a lifeline for many troubled businesses, the reasons they sought bankruptcy protection varied. Some of these companies were poorly, incompetently, and even criminally run. Others were simply not strong enough to make a long-term go of it. However, many vibrant, competently run companies find themselves the victims of events outside their control. Sometimes, such as during a recession, a business may need to resort to bankruptcy as a safe haven while it restructures its affairs. Other businesses are challenged by technological innovations and changing economic needs that render their products or processes unnecessary or obsolete.

In the last quarter of the twentieth century, the harmful effects of external economic forces profoundly affected Southeast Michigan. Because of the region's almost complete reliance on the automotive industry, it was especially buffeted by recessions, oil shortages, foreign competition, and technological change. Moreover, although the region's economic health once rose and fell with the fortunes of the automotive industry, the diffusion of the car business throughout the country and around the world left much of the region, not least the city of Detroit, in a state of long-term decline. In that sense, the case of McLouth Steel is a very representative one for the Eastern District of Michigan. Although McLouth was one of the nation's largest postwar steel producers, its business was mostly local, as its customers were mainly the Big Three automobile makers. However, domestic auto sales declined in the early 1980s in the face of a nationwide recession and increasing sales of foreign, mostly Japanese-made vehicles. As is typical for the industry, the decline hit many suppliers the hardest, leading some of them to seek protection in the bankruptcy courts. Unfortunately, as was true in the case of McLouth, bankruptcy too often provided only a temporary respite from these companies' troubles as the region was repeatedly challenged by economic change.

McLouth Steel began as a steel brokerage firm in Detroit in 1921 and by the 1940s had become a major steel producer. Specializing in rolled steel and with the American auto companies as its primary customers, McLouth rose to become the nation's eleventh largest steel company, no small feat for a firm located away from the industry centers of Pittsburgh, Pennsylvania, and Gary, Indiana. It was also one of the most modern American steel producers, with one of the few plants built after World War II. However, in the early 1980s, the Big Three's sales declined in ways they had not since the Great Depression. Overall, U.S. auto and light truck sales dropped from 14.98 million units in 1978 to 10.564 million in 1981. Moreover, the share of vehicles purchased from American manufacturers shrank as Americans increasingly turned to cheaper, more fuel-efficient Japanese cars. The foreign manufacturers' share of the U.S. auto market increased from 15 percent in 1976 to more than 27 percent in 1981.[4] Auto company sales accounted for 80 percent of McLouth's business.[5] As sales declined, suppliers like McLouth suffered in terms of overall sales and in the price concessions extracted from them by the auto companies. Though McLouth remained profitable at the end of 1979, it posted a loss of about $42 million in 1980, which increased nearly fivefold to $192 million in the first nine months of 1981.

McLouth responded to the changed market by paring down its operations, selling its stainless steel division of Jones & Laughlin for $23.5 million in June 1981 and laying off 2,000 of its 5,000 employees in October. Unfortunately for McLouth, the sale price reflected the parlous state of the steel industry; the same assets were valued at approximately $95 million according to the company's books at the end of the preceding fiscal year. Moreover, coupled with its declining revenue, the sale dropped McLouth's net worth to $103 million by October 1981, putting the company in breach of its loan conditions because of a requirement that the company was to maintain a value of at least $107.4 million. As a result, McLouth's secured lenders, led by Prudential Insurance and including other insurance companies, banks, and the United Steelworkers Union, declared a default under the loan agreements on December 7, 1981.

McLouth filed its Chapter 11 petition in the bankruptcy court in Detroit the next day. The case was assigned to Judge George Woods. It soon became clear that the company would not quickly exit Chapter 11. With the steel industry's continuing decline and the automotive industry's recovery still in the future, the case dragged on through the winter and spring without a feasible strategy for the company's reorganization. Supporters of the company and its employees began to consider other, less conventional approaches. The Michigan legislature passed a non-binding resolution urging the bankruptcy court to keep the company open. In late April 1982, scores of McLouth's employees and their families organized an overnight bus caravan to Washington, D.C., where they held protests at the Capitol and the White House demanding a federal bailout for the company.[6] Their pleas were flatly rejected.

In the meantime, McLouth tried to position itself as a more streamlined company. It received court approval to sell off its trucking subsidiary, its only non-steelmaking division. The company also sold its private jet, a luxury for which it had little need in its current state and was an irritant to both creditors and employees.

McLouth's options were dwindling by late summer when a savior for the company appeared in the form of Cyrus Tang, the owner of Chicago-based Tang Industries. Unlike other prospective suitors (including the notorious corporate raider Victor Posner), Tang had a real interest in maintaining McLouth Steel as an ongoing business. As a result, his offer quickly won the support of the company and its employees.[7] A formal agreement to sell the company's assets and inventory to Tang for approximately $75 million was reached at the end of September 1982.[8] With no other offers to save the 2,000-employee company, Judge George Woods confirmed the sale of McLouth Steel's assets and inventory to Cyrus Tang on October 20, 1982,[9] and the sale closed about one month later.[10]

As it turned out, the reorganization positioned McLouth[11] to take advantage of 1983's improved economic conditions, and by year's end it was able to show a modest profit.[12] However, the slimmed-down nature of the new company had its drawbacks as well. Once one of America's most modern steel producers, McLouth now had little ability to invest in new machinery and technologies to keep up with its competitors. In addition, some customers complained that the quality of the company's steel had declined.

Moreover, despite its early signs of possible success, the company continued to struggle. By 1987, the company was again in trouble and

Cyrus Tang was looking for a way out. This time, the State of Michigan facilitated an employee buyout of the company, with Tang retaining a 10 percent interest. The company continued to operate for several years but by 1995 had ceased making steel. Like its predecessor, the employee-owned company sought Chapter 11 protection on September 29, 1995. However, unlike in the earlier case, McLouth would not survive bankruptcy intact. A court-approved sale to Hamlin Holdings for $1.2 million in June 1996 disposed of the company's remaining assets. By 2005, developers were planning to turn the site of the company's once industry-leading plant in Trenton, Michigan, into a mixed-use development of condominiums, stores, and commercial space.

McLouth's story is a common one in the Eastern District of Michigan. As the automotive industry evolved over the decades following World War II, suppliers often found themselves bearing the brunt of the changes. However, the motor vehicle industry was not the only business faced with those challenges during that time. Almost from its inception, Chapter 11 has been the preferred stop for retailers facing financial trouble. The code's provisions for shedding or selling real estate leases and the latitude given debtors to restructure trade debt make it especially attractive to struggling retailers. This has been no less true in the Eastern District of Michigan. Some of the court's best-known cases in the 1980s and 1990s involved popular retailers that filed Chapter 11 to reorganize in the face of increased competition from both locally based stores and "big-box" national competitors. Southeast Michigan's supermarkets were early participants in this trend. In the early 1980s, Detroit consumers could shop at several well-established supermarket chains, including national retailers like A&P and Kroger and local brands like Farmer Jack, Great Scott (and its parent, Allied Supermarkets), and Chatham stores. A long-running price war between the companies would eventually contribute to pushing all of the local chains into bankruptcy or sales to the national companies. Great Scott and Allied Supermarkets were the first to face trouble, filing a petition for arrangement under Chapter XI of the Bankruptcy Act in Detroit on November 6, 1978.[13] Cases filed before the effective date of the Bankruptcy Code continued to be subject to the act, and so the court confirmed Allied/Great Scott's plan of arrangement under the old law on September 29, 1981. The case was notable for its use of bankruptcy to resolve its labor problems,[14] a practice that would be severely restricted by Congress's extensive 1984 revisions to the code.[15] Great Scott would nonetheless continue to struggle in the ever-competitive Detroit supermarket environment until national retailer Kroger acquired its remaining stores in 1990.

F&M Distributors was a one-time mom and pop pharmacy that grew into one of Southeast Michigan's major drugstore chains. Founded by Fred and Margaret Cohen in Ferndale in 1955, the store was popular for its deep discount prices. The Cohens sold the business in 1977, and by 1994 its owner had expanded the chain to more than 120 stores in metro Detroit, Chicago, and the Baltimore-Washington area. However, the burden of debt from its rapid expansion coupled with heightened competition from more generalized merchants like Target, Wal-Mart, Kmart, and Meijer led the company to seek Chapter 11 protection on December 5, 1994. Although it quickly shed more than half its stores, it was still unable to develop a confirmable plan of reorganization. The chain was liquidated and its stores were closed early in 1996.

Highland Appliance followed a similar path. Founded in a single store on Woodward Avenue in Highland Park, the electronics retailer expanded rapidly through the 1980s on the strength of the sales of new kinds of consumer products like the videocassette recorder and the portable cassette player. Highland's advertising was a staple of local television and radio stations and newspapers. However, declining sales of its core products coupled with competition from national retailers like Best Buy and Circuit City spelled its doom. It filed to reorganize under Chapter 11 in 1992 but instead was quickly liquidated.

Jacobson's Department Stores was different in kind from these discount retailers, but it suffered the same fate. Founded in Reed City, Michigan, in 1838, it moved its headquarters to Jackson in 1937. The high-end retailer of clothing and home goods traditionally avoided big mall locations commonly occupied by competitors like Hudson's (later Marshall Field's and, even later, Macy's) in favor of stand-alone stores in more affluent suburban communities like Birmingham, Grosse Pointe, and Rochester Hills. However, competition from retailers like Marshall Field's and Lord & Taylor and newer malls like the Somerset Collection in suburban Troy provided major challenges for the chain, and a multistate expansion strategy stretched its resources. It sought relief under Chapter 11 in 2002. Unable to find a buyer even after it shed its less

Bankruptcy Referee Paul H. King. (Historical Society for the Eastern District of Michigan)

First meeting of the National Association of Referees in Bankruptcy, Book-Cadillac Hotel, October 1926. (Historical Society for the Eastern District of Michigan)

(*Left to right*) C. D. Lincoln, clerk of the bankruptcy court, Assistant U.S. Attorney William G. Comb, Bankruptcy Referee George A. Marston, District Court Judge Arthur Tuttle, and Bankruptcy Referee Paul H. King, at the bankruptcy court in Detroit, June 1930. (Historical Society for the Eastern District of Michigan)

Bankruptcy Referee Walter McKenzie, arguing before the Far East War Crimes Tribunal. (Bentley Historical Library, University of Michigan)

Bankruptcy Referee Walter McKenzie. Historical Society for the Eastern District
of Michigan)

Future bankruptcy referee Archie Katcher (*right*) with his wife, Molly (*left*), and Judge Arthur Tuttle (*center*) in Bay City, 1939. (Courtesy Jonathan Katcher)

"KIRKWOOD LODGE"

Bankruptcy Referee Archie Katcher (*far right, with moustache*) at the National Association of Referees in Bankruptcy's 1950 conference. (Courtesy Jonathan Katcher)

Bankruptcy Judge George Woods. (Historical Society for the Eastern District of Michigan)

Bankruptcy Judge Ray Reynolds Graves. (Historical Society for the Eastern District of Michigan)

Bankruptcy Judge Stanley Bernstein. (Historical Society for the Eastern District of Michigan)

profitable stores, the company liquidated its remaining locations and by year's end Jacobson's no longer existed.

Not every debtor company sought protection in the bankruptcy court because of innocent misfortune. Some were led there by the misfeasance and even criminal conduct of their owners. The United States Bankruptcy Court for the Eastern District of Michigan has seen its share of these rogues. The DeLorean Motor Company sought bankruptcy protection in the court in October 1982 after its stainless steel gull-winged sports cars, later made famous in the *Back to the Future* movies, failed to capture much of a customer base. The company's CEO, former GM wunderkind John DeLorean, was at the same time arrested for drug trafficking in an FBI sting operation (for which he was ultimately acquitted on grounds of entrapment). The company failed and the case was converted to Chapter 7, but litigation in the matter continued for the better part of a decade. Another famous Detroiter, the Tigers' former pitching ace Denny McLain, was at the center of another notorious bankruptcy case, that of the Peet Packing Company. The company went bankrupt in 1996, two years after McLain and a business partner acquired it. McLain later served six years in prison after being convicted of embezzling $2.5 million from the company employees' pension fund. However, despite the fame of the central figures in these cases, perhaps no case in the history of the Eastern District was more notorious than that of Chatham Supermarkets and its CEO, Alex Dandy.

Chatham Supermarkets faced all of the same competitive pressures as Great Scott and would likely have filed bankruptcy for those reasons alone. However, while Chatham did wind up in bankruptcy, its story was a much different and more notorious one than that of its longtime competitor. Dandy controlled a Flint grocery store chain, Hamady Brothers Food Markets, through a family trust, beginning in 1981. Between 1981 and 1984, Dandy received well in excess of $1 million from Hamady's suppliers through direct and indirect kickbacks and through the diversion of other business funds to himself or relatives.[16]

In 1986, Dandy gained control of Nu-Trax, Inc., the owner of the struggling Chatham supermarket chain in metro Detroit. The Sixth Circuit Court of Appeals detailed how Dandy then gutted the company:

Using his control, defendant Dandy caused Chatham/Nu-Trax to greatly increase its purchases from certain suppliers whom defendant directed to inflate their prices in order to pay for such things as a sham salary to his son-in-law and kickbacks to defendant's solely owned corporations, ADI International and Michigan Milk Movers, Inc. The sham salary and kickbacks were for "consulting fees" even though these entities provided no services whatsoever for anyone. The suppliers involved in the schemes included M & B Distributors, McDonald Dairy, and London's Farm Dairy ("London's") and the schemes involved several hundred thousand dollars.

Defendant Dandy also diverted numerous Chatham/Nu-Trax assets to himself causing Chatham/Nu-Trax to sell tractors, trailers, and other equipment to its suppliers at very low prices. He then directed the suppliers to pay the remaining value of this equipment to his wholly-owned corporation, ADI International, as "consulting fees," even though ADI International provided no consulting services. He also directed Chatham/Nu-Trax to pay ADI International over $275,000 in bogus "consulting fees." By 1986, it was clear that bankruptcy was inevitable for Chatham/Nu-Trax. Defendant then sold his worthless option on Chatham/Nu-Trax's remaining stock back to Chatham/Nu-Trax, forcing it to pay him cash and transfer real estate worth over $7 million. However, he kept his proxy for exactly one year and one day in order to prevent Chatham/Nu-Trax from declaring bankruptcy during the one-year period within which his option sale could be rescinded as an avoidable transfer under bankruptcy law.[17]

On September 9, 1987, creditors filed an involuntary petition under Chapter 11 of the Bankruptcy Code against Nu-Trax in Detroit (Hamady had already gone into bankruptcy in Flint). The bankruptcy court entered an order of relief against Nu-Trax under Chapter 11 on October 1, 1987, at which point Chatham had only five stores and had been essentially sucked dry by Dandy during the preceding year (Henderson 1992). James McTevia was appointed trustee and recovered approximately $7 million of the money taken from Dandy. A handful of the remaining stores were sold to Kroger. The IRS and the Justice Department, building on McTevia's investigation, pursued Alex Dandy, who was eventually convicted of tax evasion, mail fraud, bankruptcy fraud, and obstruction of justice. He died in 2003.

The economic circumstances of retailers like Great Scott, F&M, Highland Appliance, and Jacobson's were by no means unique, even in Southeast Michigan. Fretter Appliance (filed Chapter 11 in 1996), Franks Nursery & Crafts (filed in 2001 and again in 2004), Borders Books (filed in 2011), and Kmart (filed in 2002) all sought to reorganize in bankruptcy; only Kmart managed to do so successfully. However, those cases differ from the ones discussed so far in this chapter in one very important respect. Even though each of these debtors both maintained their main offices and did a substantial part of their business in Southeast Michigan, they all filed their cases in jurisdictions other than the Eastern District of Michigan. Hence their cases are not part of the story of this court. However, like Sherlock Holmes's dog that didn't bark in the night, their absence is a key part of that story.

The exodus of big Chapter 11 cases from the Eastern District started rather inconspicuously; in fact, it was not an exodus at all. Instead, large law firms based in cities outside Michigan began to file major cases in the Eastern District. Highland Appliance (1992) was represented by Chicago-based Mayer, Brown & Platt. F&M (1994) was represented by Weil, Gotschal & Manges of New York. Dow Corning (1995) was represented by Sheinfeld, Maley & Kay of Dallas. The out-of-town firms generally had more bankruptcy lawyers than the smaller local firms, which at least on the surface augured in favor of their hiring. However, out-of-town firms likewise represented other key parties of interest in those cases, with the local bar mostly relegated to the largely nominal role of local counsel. This provoked no small amount of grumbling from the district's bankruptcy bar, but the whole issue quickly became moot as the national firms simply began filing major cases for Michigan companies in other jurisdictions, most notably the bankruptcy courts in the Southern District of New York (Manhattan) and Delaware.

This trend was by no means limited to the Eastern District of Michigan, as the Manhattan and Delaware bankruptcy courts became the locale of nearly every major Chapter 11 case filed in the United States. However, it seemed to especially impact the district. A brief survey of the Southeast Michigan companies that filed Chapter 11 outside Michigan in the first dozen years of the twenty-first century makes clear that, had their choice of venue been more traditionally limited, the Eastern District of

Michigan's bankruptcy court would have been one of the busiest and most essential courts in the country.

- *Franks Nursery & Crafts* (headquarters: Troy, Michigan). The garden supply and craft decorator famous for its wide selection of Christmas merchandise and post-holiday inventory reduction sales was founded in Detroit after World War II. Competition in the 1990s from larger retailers like Home Depot, Lowes, and Wal-Mart diminished the company's sales, forcing it into Chapter 11 in Maryland in 2001. Although it confirmed a plan in that case, it reentered Chapter 11 in 2004, this time in the Southern District of New York, and was liquidated.

- *Federal-Mogul Corporation* (headquarters: Southfield, Michigan). Automotive supplier Federal-Mogul filed for bankruptcy protection in Delaware in 2001, mostly because it had acquired two companies in the 1990s with massive asbestos liabilities. The company was plagued for years by reorganization issues both in the United States and Britain, but on December 27, 2008, it finally emerged from bankruptcy.

- *Kmart Corporation* (headquarters: Troy, Michigan). Detroit retailing pioneer Kmart filed for Chapter 11 on January 22, 2002, in the United States Bankruptcy Court for the Northern District of Illinois, based on the locale of a subsidiary. Despite speculation of its demise, it confirmed a plan of reorganization on May 7, 2003, based largely on financing from its primary shareholder, ESL Investments. The company later acquired another ESL holding, Sears, but remains the subject of persistent speculation over its ongoing viability.

- *Borders Group* (headquarters: Ann Arbor, Michigan). Borders was founded as a single bookstore in downtown Ann Arbor in 1971. Famous for its extensive inventory, it slowly expanded and then was sold to Kmart in 1992. Spun off by Kmart along with its Waldenbooks division in an initial public offering in 1995, the company embarked on a rapid national expansion strategy. Borders and its New York–based competitor, Barnes & Noble, dominated the national bookselling market and were responsible for the demise of many a local book-seller. However, inconsistent management in the face of new challenges from amazon.com, emerging e-reader technology, and persistent competition from the bigger Barnes & Noble chain and big discount retailers like Target, Wal-Mart, and Costco led the company to seek bankruptcy protection in the Southern District of New York in February 2011. With the prevailing wisdom being that there was no longer room in the bookselling business for two big brick-and-mortar retailers, neither buyers nor new financing emerged for the company. It was liquidated and all stores were closed by mid-2012.

Of course, the greatest challenge to the Southeast Michigan business community was the Great Recession of 2008, which pushed the American automobile industry, and with it the economy of Southeast Michigan, to the brink of collapse. The list of local automakers and suppliers seeking Chapter 11 relief in the second half of the century's first decade reads like a who's who of the region's top companies.

- *Lear Corporation* (headquarters: Southfield, Michigan). Lear filed a pre-packaged Chapter 11[18] on July 7, 2009, in the Southern District of New York, citing $3.6 billion in debt.[19] The Chapter 11 was quickly wrapped up and Lear confirmed its plan of reorganization on November 5, 2009.

- *Visteon* (headquarters: Dearborn, Michigan). The recession-related downturn in motor vehicle sales caused the major motor vehicle supplier Visteon to seek Chapter 11 protection in Delaware on May 28, 2009. Visteon completed its reorganization and emerged from Chapter 11 on October 1, 2010.

- *Delphi Corporation* (headquarters: Troy, Michigan). GM spin-off Delphi filed bankruptcy in 2005 in the Southern District of New York. Its problems were caused as much by mismanagement as by the economy. Mired in lawsuits and charges of management and investor irregularities, the company used its case to downsize, but it still had difficulty obtaining creditor support for a plan of reorganization. On October 6, 2006, the court approved the §363 sale of its main assets to a new entity owned by its lenders, which created a new Delphi Holdings.

And then there were the two biggest bankruptcies of all:

- *Chrysler Corporation* (headquarters: Auburn Hills, Michigan). On the verge of liquidation and out of cash, Chrysler Corporation filed for Chapter 11 relief in the Southern District of New York on April 30, 2009, as part of a unique, federal government–sponsored bailout. The court sidestepped many conventional Chapter 11 rules and procedures to permit the sale under 11 U.S.C. §363 of the company's assets to Chrysler Motors, a new entity co-owned by the U.S. and Canadian governments, the UAW, and the Italian automaker Fiat. The time from filing to conclusion of the sale was a mere forty-one days.
- *General Motors* (headquarters: Detroit, Michigan). Likewise out of cash, General Motors, perhaps the greatest industrial concern in the United States, followed Chrysler's lead by seeking Chapter 11 as part of a government-funded bailout on June 1, 2009, in the Southern District of New York.[20] A similar §363 sale to a new General Motors Company LLC was concluded on July 10, 2009.

This turn of events was by no means unique to the Eastern District of Michigan. By the beginning of the new millennium, the courts in Manhattan and Delaware, which already were the nation's busiest commercial bankruptcy courts, had effectively become courts of national venue as the great majority of major Chapter 11 cases (so-called mega-cases) were filed there regardless of the debtor's place of business. The reasons for this remain a source of some controversy. The venue statute provides that corporate bankruptcy cases may be filed in any district in which a corporation is domiciled, which includes its place of incorporation.[21] On the surface, this follows longstanding non-bankruptcy law, which subjects business entities to suit in their place of incorporation. Therefore, under existing law, it is entirely appropriate for a company incorporated in New York state or Delaware to file bankruptcy in those districts. However, the problem arises when attorneys for the debtors stretch or ignore those rules. Two recent filings by Michigan-based companies are a case in point. Chrysler Corporation had long been incorporated in Delaware and had its headquarters in Southeast Michigan (in Highland Park for many years, and then in Auburn Hills). However, it filed its Chapter 11 case in the Southern District of New York. It did so by first filing for Chrysler Realty Co. LLC, a subsidiary that was itself organized in Delaware and headquartered in Michigan but that owned the real estate of two New York dealerships; the aggregate value of these properties was less than 3 percent of the total value of Chrysler's assets.[22] Chrysler's lawyers then filed the petitions for Chrysler Corporation and its other subsidiaries, as permitted by the venue statute.[23]

The attorneys for Borders Group did not even try to make this weak connection to the Southern District of New York. Instead the company, which both was incorporated and had its headquarters in Michigan, filed its case in the district without even attempting to anchor it in the district. However, in the absence of any objection by creditors or the local United States Trustee (or the court's clerk, who has authority to transfer such cases to the appropriate court in the complete absence of venue), the case remained in Manhattan.

The question, then, is why large companies overwhelmingly elect to file their cases in New York or Delaware, foregoing the advantages traditionally associated with filing in their own backyards. Proponents of the New York and Delaware filings argue that those courts are more skilled in large matters than are ones located elsewhere in the country; hence they are able to handle these cases more efficiently and conclude them more successfully (Miller 2002). However, the reasoning behind that argument is circular: most cases are filed there because most cases are filed there. Moreover, critics of the practice counter that companies that file in these courts are, on the whole, no more successful at reorganizing than those that file elsewhere in the country, and they may in fact be less successful.[24]

These critics point to other explanations for the dominance of these districts as the venues of choice for most big Chapter 11 cases. One reason, they claim, is the willingness of these courts to side with debtors notwithstanding explicit restrictions in the statutes and court rules. For example, in Chrysler's bankruptcy case, Judge Gonzalez approved the sale of the company's assets to the new Chrysler Motors over the objections of secured creditors who argued that the sale deprived them of the collateral while effectively violating the absolute priority rule by effectively giving the UAW, an unsecured creditor that became one of the new company's owners, a much greater return on its claims than it otherwise would have under Chapter 11's requirements for plans of reorganization and distributions.[25]

Another example cited by the critics of the New York and Delaware courts' exercise of national venue is the development and application of the "critical vendor rule." In a series of cases in the 1990s, the Delaware court permitted debtors to pay the pre-petition claims of certain creditors at or near the beginning of the Chapter 11 case, notwithstanding the code's express prohibition on such payments. The court claimed general equitable authority under 11 U.S.C. §105(a) to avoid the statutory limitation.[26] The critical vendor rule was not widely adopted beyond Delaware, but some judges in other jurisdictions did follow suit. Lynn Lopucki argues that these courts were not motivated by legal considerations but instead that judges in those jurisdictions were seeking to attract large, high-profile Chapter 11 cases to their districts by easing statutory restrictions on the parties.[27] The rule's spread eventually stalled when the Seventh Circuit Court of Appeals reversed a bankruptcy court order in Kmart's Chapter 11 case[28] authorizing the company to pay up to $300 million in "critical vendor" claims, finding that such orders were prohibited by the Bankruptcy Code.[29]

The other reason most often cited by critics of national venue is the size of the fees awarded to attorneys in the major cases filed there. Certainly the perception that the Manhattan court approves the largest fee requests is founded in fact. The fees approved in the General Motors bankruptcy case topped $120 million; those awarded in the Lehman Brothers bankruptcy were ten times that amount. Lopucki again mounts a substantial argument that these large fee awards help explain the migration of cases to New York and Delaware (Lopucki 2005, 140–43). Moreover, since the most significant parties in these mega-cases retain local counsel, this argument calls to mind Judge George Brody's opinion in the *Hamilton Hardware* case advocating for the aggressive judicial scrutiny of attorneys' fee requests and raises the specter of the New York bankruptcy rings of the 1920s.[30]

However, like the arguments citing experience as the main justification for national venue, criticism based on the size of fees awarded in mega-cases is circular, too. It stands to reason that the greatest fees will be awarded in the biggest cases. It is simply speculation to assume that the fees would be lower had the cases been litigated in a different court.[31] However, what does appear inarguable is that, whatever the reasons, there is a persistent tendency within the American bankruptcy system that favors the filing of large cases in a few jurisdictions, and that is unlikely to change anytime soon.

This is not to say that no major cases were filed in the Eastern District of Michigan in the 2000s. Two companies, Key Plastics and Collins & Aikman, both major automotive suppliers, sought Chapter 11 protection in the Eastern District in 2000 and 2005, respectively. Key Plastics successfully reorganized,[32] but Collins & Aikman could not and closed via a liquidating plan in 2007.[33] Moreover, the controversy over national venue masks a much larger phenomenon affecting the bankruptcy court, not only in the Eastern District of Michigan but virtually everywhere else as well. Over time, the number of business cases (both Chapter 7 and 11) filed in the bankruptcy courts has dramatically declined. Annual Chapter 11 filings in the Eastern District reached their peak of 352 in 1991 and declined only slightly to 339 the next year. However, the rate at which new Chapter 11 cases were filed thereafter declined, reaching their historical low of 122 in 2000. With a few exceptions, the number of new cases filed in the Eastern District of Michigan has remained well below 200 filings per year. These trends are counter to those nationally, where filings dipped in the middle of the decade, rose briefly in 2009–10, and have since settled in at around 11,000 new cases per year. The difference between the local and national filing rates is not surprising, as Southeast Michigan generally did not experience the same mid-decade economic upsurge that occurred in much of the rest of the country. However, the explanations offered for the recent decline in national filings likely apply to the local decrease as well. The professional fees and other costs associated with Chapter 11 cases are always high, regardless of the jurisdiction, as is the uncertainty of outcome. Although assessments of the failure rate in Chapter 11 cases vary, even the most optimistic of them peg it at about 66 percent (Warren and Westbrook 2009). Factors of more recent development include lending arrangements and security devices that shift more authority to lenders and give troubled debtors less flexibility to work out their financial problems. Similarly, a more conservative lending environment in the wake of the 2008 financial collapse likely contributed to the reduced Chapter 11 filing rates as well, as lenders scrutinized potential customers more carefully before extending them credit. Moreover, in consideration of all of these factors, debtors and creditors might have been more willing to explore out-of-court workouts before resorting to Chapter 11.

All of this is not to say that the bankruptcy court for the Eastern District of Michigan was any less busy. A upsurge in the number of consumer bankruptcy filings that began almost as soon as the code went into effect but that escalated sharply in the late 1990s, the departure of most of the district's judges early in the 2000s, and a major change in the Bankruptcy Code in 2005 made the first decade of the twenty-first century a very eventful one in the history of the court.

11

BANKRUPTCY IN THE NORTHERN DIVISION

Although Congress divided the Eastern District of Michigan into Northern and Southern divisions in 1894, the Northern Division did not have its own distinct existence until the 1960s (although Frank Picard maintained his home in Saginaw and presided over the division's docket—together with a full Detroit caseload—after his appointment in 1939). The bankruptcy court, however, had a regular referee assigned to Bay City beginning in 1905, when Judge Swan appointed Lee Joslyn as referee-in-bankruptcy, until 1919, when Arthur Tuttle created the system in which the referees were based in Detroit but shared concurrent jurisdiction throughout the district.

That arrangement remained in place until 1961, when the Federal Judicial Conference authorized a fourth referee for the Eastern District. The district judges used the opportunity to establish a dedicated judgeship for the Northern Division. They selected Flint attorney Harold Bobier for the new spot. Although Bobier officially shared district-wide concurrent jurisdiction with the exiting referees, he presided almost exclusively over cases in the Northern Division, and by the time he was formally reappointed in 1967 his office was officially designated as such.

A native of St. Ignace, Bobier began practicing law in 1943 and was employed for a time prior to his appointment as referee-in-bankruptcy as the Genesee County Circuit Court's assignment clerk. Many attorneys remember Bobier as a fair and courteous judge.[1] He was also a prolific opinion writer. Twenty-five of Bobier's decisions were published in the *Bankruptcy Reporter* between 1979 and his retirement in 1982.[2]

By 1977, the district court appointed a longtime Saginaw lawyer, sixty-four-year-old Harvey Walker, to the combined post of bankruptcy judge and U.S. magistrate for Bay City.[3] Walker's appointment effectively split the district into three parts, with Walker hearing all of the cases on the Bay City docket, Bobier (and later Stanley Bernstein) those in Flint, and the remaining three judges dividing up the large Detroit docket. By 1983, however, a number of events transpired that would lead to a single judgeship for the Northern Division. First, the Administrative Office for the U.S. Courts decided to eliminate the few remaining part-time judgeships around the country. This in turn spurred Judge Walker, who was nearing seventy years of age and reaching the end of the first term of his appointment, to retire.[4] At the same time, George Woods was nominated to replace Judge Patricia Boyle, who had won election to the Michigan Supreme Court. The district bench decided to move Bobier's successor, Stanley Bernstein, down from Flint to fill Woods's vacated seat.

SPECTOR'S APPOINTMENT AND THE BANKRUPTCY "CRISIS"

With both Flint and Bay City bankruptcy judgeships open, the district court decided to designate a single person to fill both spots. After a delay of several months, thirty-four-year-old Arthur J. Spector was sworn in as the district's new bankruptcy judge on March 29, 1984. Spector was a New York native and former prosecutor who had practiced in Bay City since 1976. Even though he had won approval of the judicial merit selection panel "with flying colors," it was not at all clear that his appointment would last for as long as a few weeks, or perhaps even days. This is because of the crisis precipitated by the Supreme Court's decision in the *Northern Pipeline v. Marathon Pipeline* case.

The Chief Justice of the United States, Warren Burger, was one of the most vocal opponents to granting bankruptcy judges Article III status, lobbying both Congress and President Jimmy Carter to block the change.

Although he was unsuccessful, his opposition and that of others led Congress to create a unique hybrid status for the bankruptcy bench in which those judges were formally designated as Article I judges without the life tenure or salary protection enjoyed by their Article III counterparts but with most of the broad powers exercised by those Article III jurists.[5]

The new scheme came under attack shortly after it went into effect. Northern Pipeline Construction Company filed an adversary proceeding against Marathon Pipeline in the bankruptcy court for the District of Minnesota in March 1980, alleging breach of contract and other state law claims. The Justice Department intervened in the case. The bankruptcy judge found the new statute constitutional but was reversed by the district court. The Justice Department sought, and was granted, a direct appeal to the Supreme Court.

On June 28, 1982, the Supreme Court, in a highly splintered decision (there were four opinions, none of which gained a majority of five votes), agreed with the district court, finding that bankruptcy judges could not exercise Article III powers without having full Article III status.[6] As a result, the new code was held to be unconstitutional.[7]

The Supreme Court stayed its decision until October 4, 1982, to give Congress time to remedy the constitutional infirmity. However, the issue proved difficult to resolve, causing the Court to twice stay the effect of its ruling. Those orders expired without a congressional resolution, leading the Judicial Conference of the United States to promulgate an interim rule, which was adopted by each federal district including the Eastern District of Michigan. That rule placed the bankruptcy courts back within the authority of the district courts but allowed the district judges to delegate most of their authority in bankruptcy cases to the bankruptcy courts. The crisis was finally resolved in 1984, when Congress enacted new legislation that essentially made permanent the administrative order.[8]

In retrospect, the crisis does not seem like much of a crisis at all. Because of the stays issued by the Supreme Court and the Judicial Conference's interim rule, cases proceeded without interruption. Lawyers and parties might not have noticed any difference in the day-to-day operation of the courts. Internally, however, Congress's inability to resolve these issues led to intermittent bouts of high anxiety. Once such incident involved the swearing in of Arthur Spector. Having successfully been selected as the new Northern Division judge, Spector was scheduled to take the judicial oath on March 29, 1984. Both the House and Senate had by that time passed their own version of a new bankruptcy law, but a joint conference committee had not been able to resolve differences in the two bills. With the existing authorizations set to expire on March 31, Spector faced the possibility of having one of the shortest judgeships ever, two days. However, Congress finally reached an agreement on amendments, and Spector's position was secured when President Reagan signed the Bankruptcy Amendments and Federal Judgeship Act into law on July 10, 1984. Court clerk David Sherwood turned philosophical in response to the uncertainty caused by Congress's repeated delays, stating, "One of the neater things about the Western world is this construction of a notion of faith. So in times like these, when the body gets infirm, you construct a notion of faith. That's what we're doing."[9]

Arthur Spector was a busy judge. He routinely held hearings on reaffirmations of consumer debt,[10] long after such proceedings had ceased being mandated by the bankruptcy rules, and at times he made extensive objections of his own to disclosure statements and plans in Chapter 11 cases. He was also a frequent opinion writer. Many of those decisions were of far-reaching or precedential importance. In *In re Gilbert*,[11] Spector ruled that a clerical error resulting in the omission of a secured creditor did not render the lender's security interest to attack by a Chapter 7 trustee, where the lien was properly applied for and the omission of the lender's name on the title was wholly the fault of the clerk. In another case, *In re Spradlin*,[12] Spector made a narrow, textual interpretation of Michigan's individual retirement account exemption to block a debtor's attempt to exempt multiple accounts. That case still stands as the definitive interpretation of the exemption statute and survived its amendment in 2012. Another of Spector's oft-cited opinions was in the case of *Winom Tool & Die*.[13] There, to the chagrin of many Chapter 7 trustees, he ruled that property of the estate that vested in a debtor upon confirmation of its Chapter 11 plan of reorganization did not become part of the estate when the debtor's case was subsequently converted to Chapter 7 in the absence of plan language specifically providing as such. However, of all the cases over which Spector presided, none was more important (and arguably none was more important up to that time in the history of the Eastern District) than that of Dow Corning.

As noted in the preceding chapter, the majority of major corporate reorganization cases are filed in the Southern District of New York or, to a lesser extent, in Delaware. Therefore, it was a surprise to many court observers when a team of lawyers appeared at the clerk's office in Bay City on May 15, 1995, to file a new Chapter 11 case on behalf of Dow Corning, a multibillion-dollar company headquartered in Midland, Michigan, but doing business throughout the United States and the world.

THE DOW CORNING CASE

Dow Corning Corporation was once the world's major manufacturer and supplier of silicone breast implants. Beginning in the early 1960s, the company supplied implants to over one million women. By the 1990s, it held 50 percent of the international market for the implants. Other manufacturers and suppliers included Dow Corning's two corporate parents, Dow Chemical Co. and Corning, Inc., as well as the 3M Company and Bristol-Myers Squibb.

However, as early as the 1970s, some women claimed that the silicone implants caused them to suffer from auto-immune disorders, connective tissue diseases, chronic fatigue, muscle pain, joint pain, headaches, and dizziness. Despite early federal Food & Drug Administration approval of the implants and the lack of authoritative research linking their disorders to the implants, women began to file and win suits against Dow Corning and the other manufacturers and suppliers.[14] Dow Corning (and the other manufacturers) stopped making silicone breast implants in 1992 when the FDA banned them. By then, tens of thousands of women claimed that they had been injured by reactions to their implants; twenty thousand suits were filed against Dow Corning alone (some with multiple defendants); many were filed against the other companies as well.

By the early 1990s, federal judges were actively seeking ways to manage the thousands of tort claims flooding their docket. These included not only the breast implant cases but litigation involving asbestos and other medical devices as well. On June 25, 1992, the Federal Judicial Panel on Multidistrict Litigation consolidated all of the breast implant cases then pending in the federal courts, ordering them transferred to Judge Sam Pointer of the U.S. District Court for the Northern District of Alabama. The order effectively moved the cases along. On September 1, 1994,

Judge Pointer approved a global settlement agreement creating a $4.25 billion settlement fund for payment of breast implant claims. Under the terms of the agreement, Dow Corning was to have contributed half of the settlement amount based on its market share.

However, the breadth of the settlement proved to be its undoing. It left unresolved the question of what kinds of injuries and illnesses would be eligible for reimbursement from the fund. Approximately 410,000 women sought recovery from the fund, apparently far more than Dow Corning or the other defendants had anticipated. In addition, Dow Corning's various insurers balked at providing about $1 billion in coverage against the claims. From Dow Corning's perspective, the global settlement agreement had failed. By early May 1995, the company acknowledged both publicly and privately that it was contemplating a Chapter 11 filing.[15]

Dow Corning filed for reorganization under Chapter 11 in Bay City on May 15, 1995. Unlike most debtors, the company was not insolvent, nor did it have a cash flow problem. Dow Corning was a very successful, highly profitable company. Breast implants, and more generally medical products, were a relatively small part of its business, accounting for about 10 percent of sales. Instead, the bankruptcy filing was a response to the potential harm posed by the thousands of claims asserted against the company. The filing had the immediate benefit of staying two hundred cases that were scheduled to go to trial by year's end. In the long term, bankruptcy held the promise of allowing Dow Corning to resolve the breast implant cases using techniques developed in other mass tort cases.

The strategy contemplated by Dow Corning was to use Chapter 11 to establish a claims trust that would, upon confirmation of a plan of reorganization, become the sole source of recovery for women asserting injuries from its implants. In that sense, the bankruptcy was much like the global settlement. However, earlier Chapter 11 cases filed by mass tort defendants like Johns-Manville and A. H. Robins suggested that such companies could find added benefits in bankruptcy. As Vairo explains: "The bankruptcy system seeks to provide equality of distribution to creditors in a proceeding that encompasses the interests of all parties while mitigating the effect that a huge mass tort liability may have on the worth of a business. Because of its jurisdictional reach, bankruptcy provides an important vehicle to resolve mass tort liabilities" (Vairo 2004, 98).

Dow Corning's anticipated use of Chapter 11 followed the tactic successfully developed by Johns-Manville in the 1980s. Manville was the world's largest asbestos producer and one of the largest manufacturers of asbestos products. Research began connecting asbestos to various lung ailments in the 1960s (unlike the case with silicone breast implants, researchers were able to tie asbestos to a number of serious and even fatal lung diseases). Faced with a growing number of lawsuits and potential liability in the billions, Johns-Manville sought bankruptcy protection in 1982. Like Dow Corning, Johns-Manville was by no measure insolvent when it filed bankruptcy. Rather, the move was triggered by concerns of its potential liability, a special concern in the case of asbestos, which has a latency period of several decades.

Four years of negotiation between Johns-Manville and its creditors resulted in the confirmation in 1986 of a plan of reorganization that included an innovative claims trust. The trust included two key parts. The first was the creation of an Asbestos Health Trust. The trust would compensate all existing and future asbestos claims against the company (for compensatory but not punitive damages). In order to establish the amount of each claim, claimants were required to first engage in mandatory settlement negotiations with the trust. If the claim was not resolved in that manner, claimants could proceed by mediation, binding arbitration, or traditional tort litigation.

The second key part of the settlement was the bankruptcy court's injunction against all current and future claims against Johns-Manville for recovery outside of the trust. Therefore, tort claimants were barred from suit even if they did not yet know they had a claim, and notwithstanding the fact that as a result they had no right to vote on the plan. Moreover, suit was barred not against Johns-Manville but against its various subsidiaries and operating entities, insurers, and certain other parties.

Other companies facing mass tort claims for allegedly defective products soon thereafter sought relief in Chapter 11, modeling their cases on the Johns-Manville claims trust. The debtors included other asbestos manufacturers and A. H. Robins, the manufacturer of the Dalkon Shield contraceptive device. Congress considered the tactic so successful that it codified it (although only for asbestos-related cases) in 11 U.S.C. §524(g) in the 1994 Bankruptcy Amendments. Therefore, by 1995, the use of Chapter 11 to create claims trusts to resolve mass tort claims was well settled. The controversy for Dow Corning would come from its efforts to extend the benefits of the trust to its non-bankruptcy parent, Dow Chemical Company.

Shortly after filing, Dow Corning filed a motion to transfer all of the lawsuits pending with "opt-out" plaintiffs.[16] However, it asked the district court for the Eastern District of Michigan to assert jurisdiction not only over cases in which the debtor was a defendant but also over cases in which either of its parent companies, Dow Chemical and Corning, were defendants as well, regardless of whether Dow Corning was also a party in those suits.[17]

Dow Corning's attempted use of the bankruptcy jurisdictional statutes (28 USC §157(b)(5) [18] and 28 U.S.C. §1334)[19] to benefit its corporate parents provoked strenuous opposition from the plaintiffs, who at this point were looking to maximize the number of parties available to satisfy their claims. The plaintiffs were on legally sound footing as well. Case law under the relevant jurisdictional statute limited the court's ability to assert jurisdiction over cases not involving the debtor to those involving "unusual circumstances." Moreover, those cases made clear that a court's assertion of jurisdiction based on a finding of such circumstances should be exceedingly rare.

And so the district court ruled here. On September 12, 1995, Judge Denise Page Hood ordered that all of the cases pending against the debtor, Dow Corning, be transferred to the Eastern District of Michigan.[20] Judge Hood, however, denied the motion with respect to the two non-debtor defendants, Dow Chemical and Corning, finding insufficient grounds to permit such an order under §1334.

While the plaintiffs were elated by the decision, the two Dow companies sought an immediate appeal to the Sixth Circuit. In April 1996, the Sixth Circuit entered an order reversing the district court, finding sufficient room in §1334(b) to permit the district court to exercise "related to" jurisdiction over the non-debtor defendants. The court concluded that many claims against the non-debtor parents had a conceivable impact on the estate because they would probably lead to claims by those entities for contribution and indemnification against Dow Corning, and that the value of the joint insurance policies of debtor and its non-debtor parents might be diminished if litigation pending against the parents were permitted to proceed separately from debtor.[21] However, the Sixth Circuit also remanded the case to Judge Hood with instructions to determine whether the mandatory abstention provisions of §157 or the discretionary ones of §1334 applied in this case. The directions for remand specified that abstention should be determined on a case-by-case basis and stated other limits to be followed on remand.

The Sixth Circuit's decision was undoubtedly and admittedly an expansive reading of the jurisdictional statutes. However, on remand, Judge Hood gave the two statutes a limited reading to conclude that both mandatory and discretionary abstention applied to the non-debtor lawsuits. This set up yet another appeal to the Sixth Circuit, which made no effort to hide its frustration at seeing the case again. Responding to Judge Hood's finding in favor of mandatory abstention, Sixth Circuit Judge Boyce Martin, writing for a unanimous panel, stated in reversing Judge Hood, "Despite our clear articulation of the risks to Dow Corning's estate [if litigation proceeded separately against Dow Chemical and Corning] and our call for individualized abstention determinations, the district court, without benefit of a hearing and without analysis of any individual claim, globally abstained from the cases against the shareholders."[22]

The tenor of the opinion suggests that the appellate panel was intent on pushing the law in a new direction unconstrained by a more conservative approach. This created tension between the panel and Judge Hood that played out over a brief and highly charged time period. Communications between appellate and lower courts are often incomplete and inefficient, relying as they do on written opinions. These effects are magnified when the higher court takes the law in bold new directions in one or a few opinions. As a result, lower court judges are left to rule with uncertainty. The appellate panel, however, characterized that tension between the courts as insubordination on the part of Judge Hood, using terms that remain surprising to read almost twenty years after the fact. It described her rulings as being "fraught with clear error," "inadequate," and "troubling"[23] and cast the interplay between the two courts as one of high conflict: "We nevertheless find that our prior examination of the record was correct and that the district court's determinations are without support. Thus, because the district court clearly erred in making its abstention determinations, issuance of a writ of mandamus is appropriate in this case."[24] In short, the Sixth Circuit panel strongly wanted all of the various lawsuits to be resolved in a single court, and it would and did emphatically reject any efforts by Judge Hood to interfere with that goal.

The legal merits aside, the Sixth Circuit's decision did move the case toward a conclusion. With the jurisdictional and venue issues resolved, Dow Corning was able to move forward with its plan of reorganization, which had actually been filed with the court late in 1996. Under Dow Corning's proposed plan, creditors were divided broadly into two groups, commercial claimants and tort claimants. Creditors in the former group would receive their share of $1 billion. The tort claimants were further divided into settling and litigating groups. The settlors would share in a $600 million Settlement Trust Fund. The litigants, if successful in pursuing their cases, would be paid from a $1.4 billion Litigation Trust Fund. While each of the litigants would be required to separately prove their own damages, the issue of causation would be determined in a single trial.

Negotiations led to increases in the amount of the tort funds to a total of about $3.2 billion. According to the settlement, plaintiffs could receive from $12,000 to $300,000, with additional sums available for plaintiffs who had experienced ruptured implants and wanted their implants removed. Characteristic of class tort settlements, even women who had no claimed no illness but still filed claims could settle for $2,000. The increases were sufficient to win the support of most of the tort claimants, and the amended plan of reorganization was confirmed in December 1999, with one key exception.

Consistent with the earlier jurisdictional litigation, Dow Corning proposed to extend the post-discharge injunction under 11 U.S.C. 524 to the non-debtor tort defendants, particularly Dow Chemical and Corning. However, relying on the Supreme Court's recent decision in *Grupo Mexicano de Desarrollo v. Alliance Bond Fund, Inc.*,[25] bankruptcy judge Arthur Spector ruled that the court lacked the authority to extend the post-discharge injunction against non-consenting plaintiffs, finding that "absent creditor consent, such an injunction is tantamount to forcing that creditor to accept terms that she considers to be unacceptable."[26] However, Judge Spector did not believe that his conclusion barred confirmation of the plan, finding that the provisions could be reasonably construed to apply only to consenting creditors.[27]

Of course, confirmation of Dow Corning's plan led to several appeals to Judge Hood, the most important of which was an appeal of Judge

Spector's decision not to extend the post-discharge injunction to the non-bankrupt defendants. This time, Judge Hood's decision was more responsive to the circuit court's earlier rulings. Quoting directly from the circuit court's earlier opinion, Judge Hood wrote:

> There is no dispute that this case "is one of the world's largest mass tort litigations, and the threatened consequences of the thousands of product liability claims arising from its manufacture and sale of silicone breast implants and silicone gel, [is the reason] Dow Corning filed a petition for reorganization...." In re Dow Corning, 86 F.3d at 485. "The potential for Dow Corning's being held liable to the nondebtors in claims for contribution and indemnification, or vice versa, suffices to establish a conceivable impact on the estate in bankruptcy. Claims for indemnification and contribution, whether asserted against or by Dow Corning, obviously would affect the size of the estate and the length of time the bankruptcy proceedings will be pending, as well as Dow Corning's ability to resolve its liabilities and proceed with reorganization." Id. at 494. Pursuant to the Sixth Circuit's mandate, all the claims against the Shareholders were transferred to this District. To date, there are approximately 14,795 cases filed with this Court against the Shareholders. The cost to defend these number of cases by the Shareholders would have a substantial affect [sic] on the insurance policies shared with the Debtor. Id. at 494–95. Any indemnification and contribution sought by the Shareholders against the Debtor relating to the manufacture of the breast implants would also substantially affect the Debtor's estate. The bankruptcy action before this Court is an unusual case. The Bankruptcy Court erred in its conclusion of law that the bankruptcy court has no authority, statutory or otherwise, to issue a non-consensual permanent injunction in favor of non-debtor parties.[28]

More appeals were made to the Sixth Circuit, which largely agreed with Judge Hood but found that the record was lacking in a finding of the unusual circumstances necessary to support a non-debtor post-discharge injunction. Accordingly, the case was remanded to the district court with instructions to determine whether such special circumstances existed,[29] and on remand, the district found that they, in fact, did.[30]

With that, the case moved to an inevitable, if slow, conclusion. Various appeals were resolved, settled, or withdrawn. Finally, in June 2004, nine years after Dow Corning filed Chapter 11, the company indicated that it would begin making distributions under the plan to the holders of settlement claims.

The Dow Corning Chapter 11 was the most significant bankruptcy case ever filed in the Eastern District of Michigan (with the possible exception of Detroit's municipal bankruptcy filing in 2013). For one thing, the sheer enormity of the case sets it apart from the others. While small compared to modern Chapter 11 behemoths like Lehman Brothers and General Motors, the case was huge by the standards of the time and remains so by any ordinary criteria, both in terms of the number of contested claims and the potential liability of the company had it been found responsible for the women's illnesses.

For another, Dow Corning's unprecedented use of the Bankruptcy Code to directly protect the shareholder entities Dow Chemical and Corning was revolutionary. The main purpose of the corporate form is to insulate owners from the affairs of their companies. In bankruptcy cases, efforts to disregard this boundary are rare and are ordinarily seen in two contexts, one offensive and one defensive. Creditors or trustees use the tactic offensively to "pierce the corporate veil" so that they can pursue claims against shareholders and related companies who have failed to adequately distinguish corporate and personal affairs, assets, and obligations. The defensive use is usually seen in the case of small, closely held companies that seek to extend the automatic stay to their manager-owners, usually on the grounds that the distraction of litigation would interfere with the manager's ability to effectively oversee the debtor's reorganization. In the Dow Corning case, the courts, specifically the Sixth Circuit, used the close connections between the parent and subsidiary companies as a basis to extend to non-debtors the most important benefits offered in bankruptcy, a permanent injunction against future litigation and an effective discharge beyond their contribution to the settlement trust. Dow Corning opened the door to a more expansive notion of Chapter 11 than had been previously (or at least not successfully) contemplated.[31]

The Northern Division returned to a more normal pace as the Dow Corning case wound its way to its conclusion. However, the court would soon again be disrupted. Arthur Spector had always had a difficult relationship with the local bar. Notwithstanding his intellect, many considered him fickle and unpredictable; others faulted his demeanor on the bench and thought him uncivil and even demeaning. When Spector came up for reappointment in 2002, the local bar mounted an organized campaign against him. It would seem that they found their mark. Although the Sixth Circuit's merit selection panel did not disclose its reason for doing so, it denied Spector reappointment to another term.[32] Regardless, under Arthur Spector, the Northern Division became a court in its own right and not just an adjunct of the Southern Division. During his eighteen years on the bench, both the Bay City and the Flint bankruptcy courts moved into their own, brand-new courthouses. Spector was also the first Northern Division judge to be the chief judge of the Eastern District. However, more than anything else, it was Spector's prodigiously intellectual approach to judging that gave the court its own distinct identity. Spector would go on to have a successful career in private practice in south Florida.

Spector's place in the Northern Division was taken for a long period of time by the newly "retired" Southern Division judge, Walter Shapero. In fact, almost four years passed before a new judge was selected for the court. Thirty-four applicants sought the position. The Sixth Circuit chose forty-nine-year-old Midland attorney Daniel Opperman for the Bay City/Flint seat in 2006.

12

THE COURT IN
THE CONSUMER
BANKRUPTCY ERA

For bankruptcy officials and practitioners, one of the many successful effects of the Bankruptcy Code was a dramatic improvement in the general and professional image of the bankruptcy courts. This was particularly important in the Eastern District of Michigan, where it may have helped offset the stigma of the scandals of the early 1980s. The local media lost interest in the court once August and Bogoff were sent to prison. To the extent the court drew attention at all, it was because of cases of some public importance like that of McLouth Steel or those involving famous debtors, like DeLorean Motors, and not because of the misdeeds of its own officials.

Nonetheless, the scandal was such a traumatic event in the history of the court that some observers saw its lingering influence on court operations well into the next two decades. One such matter was in the continued choice of the Eastern District's federal judges not to participate in the Sixth Circuit's Bankruptcy Appellate Panel. The Sixth Circuit is one of five federal judicial circuits to establish a bankruptcy appellate panel (commonly called a BAP). These panels consist of three bankruptcy judges from within the circuit who hear appeals from bankruptcy court decisions. The idea is to have bankruptcy appeals heard by specialized judges rather than generalists. Therefore, BAP appeals take the place of appeals to the district courts and may themselves be appealed directly to the circuit courts of appeal.

Participation by a bankruptcy court in the BAP is rather convoluted, as are most matters related to bankruptcy jurisdiction. Congress authorized the panels in the 1978 and 1994 bankruptcy laws. However, the actual creation of and participation in the panels are optional at every level. The federal circuits, through their individual judicial conferences, may opt out of creating bankruptcy appellate panels.[1] Only five circuits have elected to create BAPs to date. Beyond that, each district within the circuit, through the district judges, must agree to participate in the BAP.[2] Finally, even in districts that participate in the BAP, any party may elect to have the appeal heard by the district court.

Currently, the district courts for the Eastern District of Kentucky, the Western District of Michigan, the Northern and Southern districts of Ohio, and the Middle and Western districts of Tennessee participate in the Sixth Circuit Bankruptcy Appellate Panel. However, while many of the Eastern District of Michigan's bankruptcy judges hear BAP appeals and have even served as the panel's chief judge, the district judges have never authorized the district to allow bankruptcy appeals to be heard by the BAP. The Eastern District is not unique in its non-participation, even within the Sixth Circuit; neither the Western District of Kentucky nor the Eastern District of Tennessee participates in the BAP.

Some attorneys and longtime court observers believed that the district court's reluctance to authorize BAP participation derived from the judges' uneasiness with giving the bankruptcy bench too much independence that dated back to the scandals of the early 1980s. However, given the fact that district judges in many jurisdictions throughout the country also rejected BAP participation, it seems too easy to conclude that the Eastern District's judges' rationale for doing so could be so neatly contained. An institutional commitment to independent review on appeal might offer one explanation. Some judges might also have taken a professional interest in retaining bankruptcy appeals; both Eastern District Bankruptcy Judge Steven Rhodes and longtime federal District Judge Avern Cohn[3] suggested in interviews that many of the district's federal judges actually enjoyed hearing bankruptcy appeals, as those cases provided them with a unique departure from their usual judicial duties.[4] The many reasons that district judges might retain their authority to hear bankruptcy appeals and the fact that they chose to do so in several jurisdictions besides cautions against assigning specific motives to the Eastern District judges for doing so.

Issues like BAP participation tend to generate some amount of discussion within the local bankruptcy community but have little effect outside it. That was not true of two series of events that would profoundly affect the court in the first decade of the twenty-first century. Those were the departure and replacement of three of the district's bankruptcy judges and the dramatic rise in the number of consumer bankruptcy cases, both nationally and in the Eastern District, culminating in the passage of the Bankruptcy Abuse Prevention and Consumer Protection Act (BAP-CPA) in 2005.

Judge Walter Shapero's retirement in 2002 was both anticipated and planned for; moreover, while Shapero formally retired on July 14, 2002, he immediately assumed "recall" status, taking over the Bay City branch of the court in place of the departed Arthur Spector.[5] On the other hand, the Sixth Circuit's denial of Spector's reappointment surprised many court observers. Even though some attorneys had mounted a campaign to block the judge's appointment to another term, complaints by lawyers about judges are common, and Spector was nonetheless widely respected throughout the bankruptcy community for his legal acumen.

The departure in 2001–2 of Ray Reynolds Graves was even more surprising. Graves was appointed to the bench in 1981 to replace the retiring David Patton. The thirty-five-year-old son of a Detroit dentist and a graduate of Trinity College (Connecticut) and Wayne State University Law School, Graves was the youngest judge and first African American appointed to the court since Harry Hackett took the bench in 1957. Despite his relatively young age and the fact that he had not previously practiced much before the bankruptcy court, Graves quickly gained a reputation for taking on some of the district's most difficult cases. Those cases included Nu-Trax (Chatham stores), Salem Mortgage (a 1983 case involving a local mortgage broker that utilized dubious business practices and was accused of bilking borrowers and investors alike in ways that somewhat foreshadowed the build-up and collapse of the home-lending business in the 2000s), and the *DeLorean* case, of which Graves reportedly said, "Some of these motions seem simple, but then, nothing in this case is ever simple."

Moreover, some of Graves's early opinions, coming as they did in the infancy of the Bankruptcy Code, established important parameters that have structured bankruptcy practice ever since. These included *In re James*,[6] in which he ruled that a bankruptcy filing does not stay the running of the redemption period following foreclosure, and *In re Great Northwest Development Corporation*,[7] where he held that Michigan corporations law does not permit a corporate officer to authorize a bankruptcy filing without shareholder approval.[8]

Graves had served on the court for eighteen years when it came time for his reappointment in 2000.[9] Though the judge had been the target of his share of grumbling by attorneys over the years (no judge is exempt from this), his reappointment was widely expected within the bankruptcy community. Therefore, many people were surprised when the Sixth Circuit declined to reappoint him to another fourteen-year term. The circuit's judicial selection committee had uncovered certain irregularities in Graves's personal finances during its review process, including unfiled tax returns. The panel contended that it gave the judge an opportunity to rectify these problems but denied his reappointment when he failed to do so in a timely manner. Graves's account differed; he contended that the circuit had already granted him reappointment before the financial problems were uncovered and that he was entitled to his job. Graves took the extraordinary action of filing suit to retain his position against the Sixth Circuit Court of Appeals and its chief judge; the dispute was quickly resolved when Graves was appointed for one year to sit as a judge in Flint with limited duties.

The departure of Judges Spector and Graves so close together placed new strains on the court. Not only did it have two fewer judges, but its caseload had grown to the point that Congress had authorized the creation of another judgeship for the district. The gap was filled with visiting judges drawn from the circuit's other districts. These judges performed yeoman's work, traveling to hear cases in the Eastern District while maintaining their own dockets at home. The added strain was resolved in March 2003 when three new judges took their places in the court's Southern Division. They included Marci McIvor, an assistant Michigan

attorney general; Phillip Shefferley, a local business reorganization lawyer; and Thomas Tucker, a litigator from Toledo, Ohio. A permanent
replacement for Arthur Spector was not selected until 2006, when Daniel
Opperman was appointed to sit in Bay City and Flint.

These new judges joined the bench during a period in which the
court faced a new kind of challenge; while the big Chapter 11 cases had
in large measure disappeared (as discussed in chapter 10), the filings of
new consumer Chapter 7 and Chapter 13 cases reached unprecedented
high levels. By the early 2000s, consumer cases had come to dominate
the judges' attention.

After a small decline in the mid-1980s, consumer bankruptcy filings in the Eastern District climbed to previously unthinkable levels.
Although new case filings had come close to the 10,000 mark in the
early 1980s, they did not top that threshold until 1988, when they totaled
10,294. Filings increased 78 percent to 18,348 by 1992 and reached 20,048
in 1996 before receding slightly and then rising to 30,345 in 2001.[10]

This phenomenon was not limited to the Eastern District of Michigan. The nationwide escalation of consumer borrowing, both through
credit card purchases and through new forms of mortgage refinancing,
was generally considered the main factor contributing to the increase
in consumer bankruptcy filings. Congress was sufficiently alarmed by
the increase to create a new bankruptcy review commission in 1996 to
consider changes to the Bankruptcy Code. Like the panels established
in the 1930s and 1970s, the new commission was dominated by bankruptcy scholars and professionals associated with the National Bankruptcy Conference.

However, unlike those earlier review commissions, the new group
worked in an ideological atmosphere sharply divided over who should
bear the greater share of responsibility for the increase in bankruptcy
filings. On one side of that divide were those from the bankruptcy establishment who saw the rise in filings as the result of careless lending practices. They saw little need for new legislation that would deviate from
American bankruptcy law's traditional emphasis on providing debtors
with a fresh start. On the other side of the debate were those who believed
that both the code and consumers themselves had become too lax; they
saw the problem as one of moral hazard, that easily obtained bankruptcy
discharges encouraged irresponsible consumer borrowing. Those in the

latter group favored amendments that would make it more difficult for consumers to file bankruptcy and obtain a discharge.

A new National Bankruptcy Review Commission was appointed by Congress in 1994 with a limited mandate to make recommendations without disturbing "the fundamental tenets of current law."[11] The commission accordingly recommended only small adjustments to the code when it issued its report in 1996. Congressional Republicans (who had gained leadership of the House of Representatives in 1995) and many Democrats immediately rejected this approach in favor of more stringent limitations on consumer debtors. However, the traditional view of bankruptcy had some staying power. It would take eight years for the more restrictive measures, known as the Bankruptcy Abuse Prevention and Consumer Protection Act, to finally become law.

The most important and most controversial parts of the new law were qualifying provisions intended to limit debtors at the beginning of consumer cases. The most controversial addition, means testing, conditioned individual filers' election of the quicker, less burdensome Chapter 7 proceedings over Chapter 13 on their qualification under a complex income and expense analysis derived from IRS collection procedures. Debtors with specified net cash flow, identified in the law as "disposable income," would be compelled to repay at least a portion of their debts to creditors under a Chapter 13 plan of three to five years. New filers who passed the means test were not automatically in the clear. Their cases might still be subject to dismissal if a judge concluded that the filing was for an improper purpose that was an "abuse" of the terms and protections of the Bankruptcy Code (11 U.S.C. §707(b)).

Other parts of BAPCPA, while still controversial, drew less attention than the means test. All consumer filers were required to attend a debtor education class before seeking bankruptcy relief. In addition, the new law imposed an obligation on attorneys to independently verify the accuracy of the information contained in their debtor clients' schedules of assets and liabilities and statements of financial affairs, documents that require a detailed analysis of a filer's financial circumstances. Corresponding changes in Chapter 13 cases were intended to maximize repayment to creditors. One uncontroversial provision placed restrictions on serial filers, who, for example, filed bankruptcy to stop foreclosure on their homes but otherwise did nothing until their cases were dismissed and then filed again when foreclosure proceedings were restarted against them.

Fears over the BAPCPA's restrictions led to a spike in consumer case filings in the period leading up to its October 2005 effective date. Nationally, case filings increased from about 1.6 million in 2004 to more than 2 million in 2005. The same pattern held true in the Eastern District of Michigan, as the number of new cases rose from 44,803 in 2004 to 55,326 in 2005 (see chart 12.1). However, the rush of filings quickly receded once BAPCPA went into effect. In the opinion of most observers, this had little to do with the new law but instead was the result of the pool of potential filers being drained in a rush to avoid the new law. Nationally, new case filings in 2006, the first year after the law's enactment, barely exceeded 617,000, while in the Eastern District of Michigan they dropped to about 40,000. However, case-filing rates began to turn upward by 2008, in part due to normalization after two years of dramatic swings but mostly because of the impact of the approaching recession. Michigan never fully bounced back after the relatively small economic downturn in 2001–2. The state's unemployment rate hovered at around 7 percent in the middle of the decade but quickly jumped to 10.6 percent by the end of 2008 as manufacturers and suppliers closed or made substantial cutbacks.[12] The unemployment rate topped out at 14 percent a year later and remained in double digits until the end of 2011.

The rate at which new consumer bankruptcy cases are filed tends to follow the unemployment rate (see chart 12.2). This held true in Michigan in the late 2000s, as filing rates began to increase after 2007, which saw 33,799 new cases filed. Filings exceeded 41,000 the next year and 51,000 the year after that, topping out at 53,218 in 2010. National filing rates followed a similar pattern. Both the intentions of BAPCPA's supporters and the fears of its opponents were overwhelmed by the effects of the Great Recession in the years immediately following the law's enactment. This makes some intuitive sense: as employment rates and wages declined, many consumer debtors lost the ability to repay loans they were previously able to afford. Means testing became a formality for many filers who had lost all or a substantial part of their income.

However, the volume of new case filings dropped substantially as the U.S. economy began to recover. National filing rates dropped 24.5 percent between 2011 and 2012 (fiscal year), while filings in the Eastern

District of Michigan declined 30.4 percent in the same period. More-over, a smaller number of the new cases were filed under Chapter 13 than before the recession. The filings decline correlates with a few specific fac-tors. National credit card default rates decreased from a high of 6.78 per-cent in the second quarter of 2009 to 2.45 percent in the third quarter of 2013.[13] Moreover, outstanding revolving consumer credit in the United States decreased from just over $1 trillion in 2008 to $847 billion in the third quarter of 2013, a decline of 15.3 percent. In other words, both the amounts consumers were charging on their credit cards and their account balances were reduced significantly in the period following the Great Recession as compared to the early and mid-2000s.[14]

The decline in Chapter 13 filings, in both real and relative terms, was attributable in large part to two factors. The first is that post-recession U.S. incomes rose very little in actual or adjusted terms.[15] Consumer prices grew steadily (if unspectacularly) over the same period,[16] indicating that borrow-ers had less disposable income to fund a Chapter 13 plan. The other factor was the decline in foreclosures. Both the availability of the automatic stay and the ability to cure mortgage deficiencies through a plan made Chapter 13 an alternative remedy for many borrowers facing foreclosure. However, mortgage foreclosures declined to their lowest level in years by the end of 2013.[17] With fewer mortgages in default, fewer homeowners were com-pelled to seek bankruptcy relief to save their homes.

The reduced caseloads and the increased portion of consumer cases did not necessarily mean that the Eastern District's judges were less busy. The meaning and application of several of the 2005 amendments were litigated. Legislative efforts to limit serial re-filers were tested in *In re Sanders*,[18] where the Sixth Circuit Court of Appeals ultimately ruled that the four-year limitation in 11 U.S.C. §1328(f)(1) on filing a new Chapter 13 case after previously receiving a discharge in Chapter 7 started when the previous petition was filed, not on the date of discharge. Another Chapter 13 case, *Baud v. Carroll*,[19] required that the circuit court resolve a conflict between two new code provisions that appeared to mandate two different periods for the required length of a Chapter 13 plan. Citing congressional intent, among other factors, the court resolved the conflict in favor of the interpretation that provided for the longer plan length, which in turn maximized the amount contributed by the debtor toward repayment of creditors.

However, the most unusual case was technically not a bankruptcy case at all but a suit filed by the IRS against the district's Chapter 13 trustees, seeking to be excused from any obligation to turn over debtors' annual tax refunds to the trustees for distribution through a confirmed plan. In 2008, the Eastern District's bankruptcy judges, recognizing the low percentage of Chapter 13 cases in the district that were actually completed, began to enter orders confirming plans that required the IRS to turn over debtors' tax refunds to the trustees.[20] After about a year of operating under the orders, the IRS brought a legal action seeking to be excused from complying with them in existing cases and blocking their entry in future ones.[21]

However, rather than taking the conventional route of seeking appeal of such orders in one or more cases in which they were entered, the government took the unusual action of filing suit in district court against all of the district's Chapter 13 trustees individually but in their official capacities, seeking a declaratory judgment preventing the trustees from enforcing the existing refund-redirection provisions and a writ of mandamus prohibiting the bankruptcy court from including these provisions in future Chapter 13 plans.[22] In effect, one branch of the federal government was suing another, as the Department of Justice's United States Trustee Program supervises the Chapter 13 trustees. Moreover, since the relief sought was in effect an unorthodox challenge to an order of the Eastern District's bankruptcy judges, they, too, collectively participated in the cases as amici curiae.

Judge Denise Page Hood granted summary judgment in favor of the IRS, and the trustees appealed. On appeal, Judge Jeffrey Sutton of the Sixth Circuit Court of Appeals, writing on behalf of a united panel, reversed. Citing the unusual posture of the case, the panel held that the IRS lacked standing to sue the trustees, ruling in effect that the government had gone after the wrong parties:

> The government sued a group of bankruptcy trustees, but the harm it suffered—administrative costs associated with processing tax refunds—flows not from the trustees' actions but from the bankruptcy court's orders. When an entity does not like a court order, the answer is not to sue the lawyer or party who recommended the order; it is to appeal the order or, if utterly

necessary, to sue the court. Bankruptcy trustees do not control bankruptcy courts. . . . Even if the trustees have a role in enforcing these [refund redirection] orders, that does not mean a judgment against the trustees will eliminate the problem. Trustees are not the only parties to Chapter 13 bankruptcies. Other parties, including the debtor and creditors, have an interest in ensuring that tax refunds make their way to the trustees. Nothing prevents these entities from asking the bankruptcy court to issue the same order. No less importantly, nothing prevents the bankruptcy court from doing the same on its own, exercising its equitable powers over the bankruptcy process to fashion an equivalent order. The Bankruptcy Code authorizes just such authority, and that indeed is how these orders originated in the first place.[23]

The Sixth Circuit's decision in favor of the trustees did not end the matter, however. The IRS again challenged the redirection orders in consolidated appeals from several cases and reached a settlement that addressed the issue administratively.

By July 2013, consumer filings dominated the Eastern District of Michigan's bankruptcy caseload. For the twelve-month period ending on June 30, only 349 of the court's 34,371 new filings were business cases.[24] Neither consumer cases nor the courts that hear them gain much attention, and that was true of the Eastern District's bankruptcy court. The

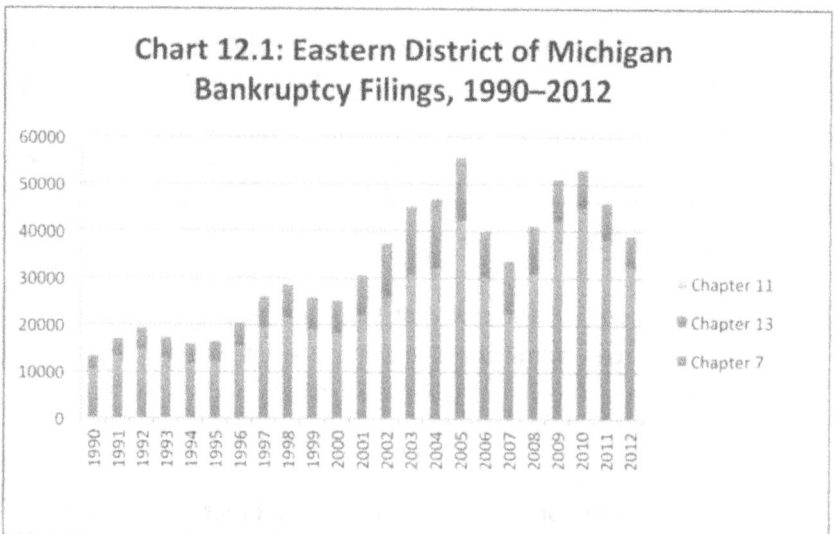

Chart 12.1: Eastern District of Michigan Bankruptcy Filings, 1990–2012

Chart 12.2: Comparison of Eastern District of Michigan Bankruptcy Filings with U.S. Bankruptcy Filings and Michigan Unemployment, 2003–2012

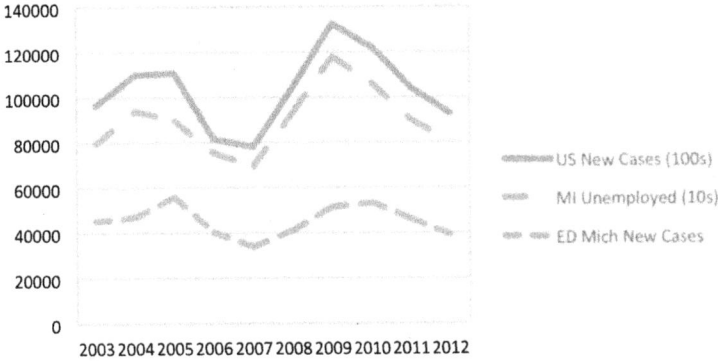

Detroit Free Press, one of the city's two main papers, did not make even a single mention of the court in the same twelve-month period. That would all change, however, on July 18, when Detroit became the largest city in American history to seek protection in a U.S. bankruptcy court.

13

THE CITY OF DETROIT
BANKRUPTCY CASE

It can be said without hyperbole that no American city ever rose so high or fell so far as Detroit. At the beginning of the nineteenth century, Detroit was the thirteenth largest city in the United States with almost 286,000 residents.[1] Its primary businesses were the manufacturing of stoves, railroad cars, pharmaceuticals, and cigars. However, within a few short years, it was the fastest-growing city in America and on its way to becoming one of its wealthiest, as it became the center of the country's automobile industry. By 1910, its population had grown to 466,000. European immigrants, southern migrants, rural farmers, and men simply looking to make a decent wage flocked to Detroit to make cars, especially after Ford Motor Company raised its wage for factory workers to $5 per day in 1914. Detroit effectively became a one-industry town as the national demand for automobiles exploded.

By 1920, 933,000 residents lived within the city of Detroit, making it America's fourth largest city. After Americans bought more than 5 million vehicles in 1928, motor vehicle sales stalled and then plummeted during the Great Depression. Sales remained low during the 1930s, but Detroit's auto factories were revived by the mobilization effort for World

War II, when Detroit earned the nickname the "Arsenal of Democracy" and its 1.6 million residents enjoyed full employment.

When the war ended, auto manufacturing quickly returned to its pre-Depression production levels and continued to grow. Car sales quickly returned to their pre-Depression levels to meet the demands of an American public made wealthier by the G.I. Bill. Sales reached 5.3 million in 1948, 6.6 million in 1949, and more than 8 million in 1950.

This success caused fundamental changes in the ways that Detroiters lived and worked. By 1950, 1.8 million residents were crammed into Detroit's 139 square miles. With their increased affluence, Detroiters sought modern homes on larger lots, moving first to the edges of the city and then beyond them, creating new suburbs. The people who made the cars fueled the exodus to the suburbs. This included not just management but line workers as well. The UAW had successfully gained better wages and benefits for its employees, providing them with the wealth necessary to buy new cars and suburban homes. By 1960, Detroit's population had decreased by 200,000 while the population of its suburbs increased by that much and more.

This trend continued unabated throughout the 1960s and increased after Detroit's 1967 riots, which exacerbated longstanding racial tensions in the city and contributed to the phenomenon called white flight, as most of the residents leaving Detroit for the suburbs were white and their exit extended the city's existing racial divisions across its borders. By 1970, 4.8 million people lived in metropolitan Detroit, but only 1.5 million of them resided within the city itself. While the metropolitan area's population remained relatively stable throughout the rest of the century, Detroit's continued to decline. By 2000, the city's population dropped below 1 million, and by 2010 Detroit had barely 700,000 residents.

As Detroiters moved to the suburbs, the automobile industry was decentralizing, shifting their manufacturing operations away from the Motor City. Detroit's automakers, the Big Three, faced an increasingly competitive and difficult business environment by the early 1970s. Imports from Japan drew sales away from the American manufacturers, beginning in the 1970s when the Arab oil embargo led to sharp increases in gasoline prices. The imported cars were not only more fuel efficient than those built by Ford, GM, and Chrysler but less expensive and perceived by many consumers to be of higher quality as well. Vehicles produced by Japanese manufacturers like Honda and Toyota became part of the American automotive landscape. Eventually those companies would build their own factories in the United States but not in Detroit. Seeking to maintain their price advantage over the Big Three, the foreign manufacturers located their new plants in places where support for labor unions was weak and the prevailing wages much lower than in Michigan.

With a need to compete on costs, and concluding that labor contracts prevented them from doing so in Michigan, the Big Three moved their operations to other locations throughout the United States and into Canada.[2] Moreover, by the 1990s, automation, rather than decentralization, became the dominant factor in the declining need for local automobile workers as machines took over much of the work on assembly lines.

In an investigative report published after the city filed bankruptcy,[3] the *Detroit Free Press* concluded that while suburbanization and the decentralization of the automobile industry were the basic causes underlying Detroit's financial downfall, the actions or inaction of city officials exacerbated its descent. Despite the continuous decline of the city's population, Detroit officials for too long failed to sufficiently downsize its workforce. Even though its population declined by more than 50 percent, Detroit had reduced its workforce by only 28 percent by 2004. According to one telling statistic, there was one city worker for every 51 residents in Detroit in the early 2000s.

Instead of cutting payroll, Detroit officials increased taxes; when that was insufficient, they took on additional debt. Both actions were counterproductive. Despite a series of tax increases, the city's revenues fell 40 percent from 1962 to 2012. The taxes made the city a more expensive place in which to live and do business, discouraging both residents and companies from remaining or relocating in Detroit.

Moreover, the oversized payrolls ultimately led to oversized retiree obligations. According to the *Free Press*, the expense of retiree pensions and health care increased 46 percent from 2000 to 2012 while revenues fell by 20 percent. In 2000, the city spent $99 million on retiree health care benefits. By 2012, it was spending $145 million.

The city's growing pension debt was worsened by a dubious practice of the pension funds known as the "thirteenth check." Beginning around 1985, while the pension funds were still healthy, the city began to issue retirees an additional check at year end, a kind of holiday bonus. The extra payment was wholly discretionary and not part of the pension plan. The payments hastened the depletion of the pension funds but continued even as pension revenues sharply declined.

Detroit's declining tax base could not generate the revenues necessary to support its financial obligations, so city officials regularly resorted to borrowing to fill the gap. In 1960, Detroit's revenues totaled $2 billion while total accumulated debt exceeded $3 billion (adjusted 2013 dollars). Although revenues stabilized and debt actually declined under Mayor Coleman Young, they returned to their slow decline in the 1990s and 2000s while debt climbed precipitously. A pattern emerged: whenever Detroit's finances improved, its bond rating would also improve. City officials would then borrow more, the city's debt burden would increase, the city's financial health would continue to deteriorate, and its debt would be downgraded again. Revenues barely cleared $1 billion in 2013, while accumulated debt, exclusive of future accrued pension, health care, and interest liabilities, reached $8 billion. In 1985, the city's debt-to-revenue ratio was 0.66. By 2013, that ratio was 7.1.

What would turn out to be the final straw for Detroit was a transaction that became known as the COPS and swaps deal.[4] In 2005, Mayor Kwame Kilpatrick's administration negotiated a complicated $1.44 billion deal to fund Detroit's pension liabilities. Although lauded by Wall Street at the time,[5] the deal was in many ways characteristic of the transactions that led to the 2008 financial collapse and ultimately became its prime cause. Under the complex structure of the deal, Detroit sold pension obligation certificates of participation to investors, using the money to shore up its pension funds. The certificates bore variable rates of interest. In order to protect the city against dramatic rate increases, it bought instruments called interest rate swaps, which allowed it to lock in interest rates at about 6 percent but which required substantial termination payments from the city to avoid default if rates dropped too precipitously. The parties' use of multiple financial devices and its complex structure provided two benefits to the Kilpatrick administration: it allowed Detroit to borrow an enormous sum of money that would not have been available to it in a conventional transaction, and it allowed it to avoid borrowing limitations imposed by state law. However, it also carried great risks; the city would incur huge penalties if certain events occurred, including a sharp drop in interest rates.

That is exactly what happened in 2008. The nation's financial crisis precipitated historic interest rate reductions and triggered Detroit's obligation to pay between $35 and $45 million[6] to the swaps parties, UBS and Bank of America (which had purchased Merrill Lynch), each year for ten years, the remaining term of the agreements. That Detroit lacked the wherewithal to make such payments was well understood, certainly by the swaps creditors. The swaps agreements were renegotiated in June 2009, with one of the city's few lucrative revenue streams, its tax collections from its three casinos, used as collateral.

Regardless, the deal proved too costly to Detroit. By June 2013, the city was underwater on the swaps deal by almost $300 million, a sum it would owe as a termination fee if the swaps creditors canceled the contracts. By July, that amount was reduced to $220 million because of negotiations and rate fluctuations. It was still too much; by 2013, the COPS and swaps deal accounted for 20 percent of the city's financial obligations and had brought the city to the brink of bankruptcy.

THE EMERGENCY MANAGER

By the end of 2011, Detroit's political instability and its deepening fiscal woes led Michigan's treasurer, Andy Dillon, to conduct a preliminary review of the city's finances. He issued a report on December 21, 2011, concluding that Detroit was in "probable financial stress," and recommended the appointment of a financial review team. Included among the treasurer's findings were the following:

- The city ran a $58 million budget deficit for the 2010 fiscal year. The report predicted that the deficit could increase to as much as $97 million in the next fiscal year.
- Detroit's long-term debt exceeded $8 billion, with 2010 debt-service costs alone costing the city $597 million.
- The city's unfunded pension liabilities exceeded $5.5 million.
- The city had rapidly declining cash revenues.
- The city had made little or no progress in developing or implementing a realistic restructuring plan.

- The city had a "BBB" long-term fund rating (i.e., junk status).[7]

The ten-member state financial review team issued its report on March 26, 2012, detailing a worsening financial picture even grimmer than the one described by the treasurer and concluding that Detroit was in "severe financial distress." Under Michigan law, that finding would support Governor Rick Snyder's appointment of an emergency financial manager for the city. However, with strong opposition to such a move within the city of Detroit and limited support within the state legislature, Snyder instead opted to enter into a consent agreement with the city on April 5, 2012. The agreement provided for the creation of a nine-member Financial Advisory Board, which was given oversight responsibilities for the city's financial operations but had limited authority to develop or enact reforms.

The advisory board was unable to effect any meaningful changes without such authority. The governor's financial review team continued to monitor the situation throughout 2012 and early 2013 and found the city's finances to be in deepening chaos. In its February 19, 2013, report to the governor, the review team concluded that "a local government financial emergency exists within the City of Detroit because no satisfactory plan exists to resolve a serious financial problem."[8] According to the review team, Detroit's budgets routinely overstated the city's revenues and understated its expenditures. The city's books and records were likewise replete with errors and inaccuracies.

The financial review team found that the city's long-term liabilities, mostly pension obligations, actually exceeded *$14 billion*, not the $5.5 billion identified in the treasurer's report, with almost $2 billion of that amount coming due in the next five years. The review team also found that the city's general fund was $326 million in the red, and predicted that its current budget deficit would reach $100 million by June. Finally, the team concluded that, notwithstanding the input of the advisory board, both the mayor and the city council had failed to effectively address the crisis.

APPOINTMENT OF AN EMERGENCY FINANCIAL MANAGER

The financial review team's findings left Governor Snyder with only one realistic option. On March 1, 2013, he found that Detroit was in a financial emergency under state law and on March 14, 2014, he sought the appointment of an emergency financial manager for the city. Under

Michigan law, an emergency financial manager is effectively a municipal receiver who acts in the stead of local officials on matters necessary "to rectify the financial emergency and to assure the fiscal accountability of the local government and the local government's capacity to provide or cause to be provided necessary governmental services essential to the public health, safety, and welfare."[9] Some people, especially critics, would come to describe the manager as a financial czar.

Kevyn Orr, a fifty-five-year old attorney from the Washington, D.C., office of the international law firm Jones Day, was appointed as Detroit's emergency financial manager on March 15, 2013. Orr was a graduate of the University of Michigan and was the former acting director of the Executive Office for United States Trustees in the Department of Justice. At Jones Day, he was part of the team that ushered Chrysler through its lightning-quick reorganization in 2009. However, notwithstanding Orr's qualifications, his appointment provoked controversy on two interrelated fronts. One was public displeasure, especially among residents of Detroit, over the displacement of democratically elected local officials with a state appointee. The other was the perceived legitimacy of the move, which grew out of the convoluted history of Michigan's emergency financial manager law.

Michigan's original emergency financial manager law, Public Act 72, was enacted in 1990. Utilized in a handful of small to midsized cities, the law was often criticized as a usurpation of local control. Nevertheless, in 2011, the Michigan legislature revamped the law, now designated Public Act 4. Michigan voters rejected that law in a statewide referendum in November 2012. The legislature responded by passing yet another emergency financial manager law, Public Act 436,[10] in December 2012. That law had an effective date of March 28, 2013. Supporters of the use of emergency manager, including state officials, claimed that the voters' repeal of P.A. 4 merely revived the law it replaced, P.A. 72, which would apply in fiscal crises until the new law went into effect.

While the three laws were basically similar, their shifting status added a high degree of complexity and uncertainty to Detroit's rapidly declining financial situation and provided opponents legal grounds to challenge Orr's appointment. That opposition came on multiple fronts. Municipal employees unions opposed the plan because the EFM ostensibly had the power to cancel collective bargaining agreements. Local officials and many residents opposed as undemocratic the displacement of elected officials with one appointed by the governor. Interestingly, this position cut across ideological categories and found support from both political liberals and small-government conservatives. Inevitably, given Detroit's history of racially charged politics, a small but influential group voiced their opposition as a matter of civil rights. This group included some members of Detroit's city council, longtime Detroit congressman John Conyers, local civil rights activists, and the Reverend Jesse Jackson, who summarized the views of this group at one rally, stating, "We marched too long and bled too much and died too young for the right to vote to have a governor . . . take away the impact of our vote."[11]

Orr nevertheless took office on March 25, 2013 (three days before the effective date of the new emergency financial manger law), and immediately set about appointing a staff and delving into Detroit's finances. On June 14, 2013, he met with approximately 150 creditors to present his initial restructuring plan. Aside from making basic changes to increase revenues, Orr proposed to spin off the Detroit Water and Sewerage Department to a new metropolitan water authority, distribute $2 billion in notes pro rata to the city's unsecured creditors, including pension creditors, and set aside $1.25 billion over ten years to invest in basic city services.

Orr invited the creditors to meet for subsequent discussions, and in fact Orr's staff held various meetings with creditors over the next month. Generally speaking, however, these meetings were more in the nature of presentations than negotiations. By mid-July, Orr had made no progress in achieving agreement on a plan to address Detroit's fiscal crisis.

Orr could not be held solely responsible for this lack of progress. Detroit's retirees' employee pension plans collectively constituted its largest group of creditors; Orr and his staff had determined that Detroit's pension debt totaled about $17 billion. The pension plans were resistant to any reduction in retirees' benefits and quickly organized to oppose such action or anything that could lead to such action, including a Chapter 9 filing. They believed that their opposition was firmly supported by the Michigan Constitution, which they argued prohibited the reduction of accrued public pension benefits: "The accrued financial benefits of each pension plan and retirement system of the state and its political subdivisions shall be a contractual obligation thereof which shall not be diminished or impaired thereby."[12] The pension plans, together with Detroit's employees' unions and its retiree groups, argued that this provision not only barred the emergency financial manager from reducing benefits but prevented the governor from authorizing a Chapter 9 since the bulk of indebtedness that would be addressed in a bankruptcy case was pension debt.

Not wanting to wait for Orr's next move, the unions and pension groups filed separate suits against Governor Snyder and state treasurer Andy Dillon on July 3 and July 17, 2014.[13] The suits sought a declaratory judgment that P.A. 436 violated the Michigan Constitution to the extent that it purported to authorize Chapter 9 proceedings in which vested pension benefits might be impaired. They also sought an injunction preventing the defendants from authorizing any Chapter 9 proceeding for the city in which vested pension benefits might be impaired. The cases were assigned to Ingham County Circuit Judge Rosemarie Aquilina.

However, by the time the suits were filed, Orr had concluded that a Chapter 9 filing was his only viable option to reorganize Detroit's finances. The city was facing numerous lawsuits in addition to the ones filed for the pensioners, and attempts at negotiation were returning little result. According Orr asked the governor for permission to put the city in bankruptcy, as required by bankruptcy law. That permission was given to him on the morning of July 18, and by midafternoon, Detroit's bankruptcy lawyers at Jones Day began filing the city's bankruptcy petition. In times past, that would have meant physically taking a large stack of documents to the court to be received and docketed by a court clerk. However, in 2013, filing was accomplished by uploading the documents to the court's electronic case-filing system, known as PACER. The filing went as expected until 3:36 p.m., when PACER went down.

Unbeknownst to Orr and his attorneys, a separate drama was developing in the Ingham County Circuit Court. With rumors of an imminent bankruptcy filing swirling in the Detroit media, attorneys for the state court plaintiffs filed an emergency motion to block the bankruptcy filing. They reached the courthouse with their emergency motion at 3:37 p.m., and obtained a hearing before Judge Aquilina to begin at 4:00 p.m. However, the judge delayed the beginning of the hearing by fifteen minutes to give an attorney for the state time to appear.[14]

If the plaintiffs were seeking a favorable forum to address their concerns, they found one in the state court. With little argument from counsel and taking no evidence, Judge Aquilina quickly ruled P.A. 436 to be unconstitutional "to the extent it permits the Governor to authorize an emergency manager to proceed under Chapter 9 in any manner which threatens to diminish or impair accrued pension benefits."[15] Judge Aquilina's order went on to enjoin Governor Snyder from authorizing the emergency financial manager from proceeding under Chapter 9 "in a manner which threatens to diminish or impair accrued pension benefits." Her order also included the unusual provision, apparently added by hand by the judge herself, that a copy of her order be "transmitted to President Obama."

Despite the breadth of Judge Aquilina's decision, it was for naught. PACER was up and running again, and the Chapter 9 case was officially filed at 4:06 p.m., nine minutes before the start of the state court hearing. It appears that the plaintiffs' attorneys were aware of this and duly notified the judge of the filing. The judge nonetheless elected to proceed, but to no effect, as the bankruptcy court would ultimately find that her ruling violated the automatic stay of proceedings that went into effect immediately upon the filing of the Chapter 9 petition. Both Judge Rhodes and the Michigan Court of Appeals issued stays of the Ingham circuit court case shortly after the bankruptcy filing, but Judge Aquilina's ruling would nonetheless cause confusion among the media and the general public during the early days of the case.

MUNICIPAL BANKRUPTCY

Municipal bankruptcy was originally added to the Bankruptcy Act in the 1930s, and it was later incorporated into the Bankruptcy Code as Chapter 9. Such cases are unusual. About six hundred local governments had invoked the provision before 2013, none of them similar in size to Detroit. Operationally, Chapter 9 most closely resembles Chapter 11. As in Chapter 11, a municipality restructures its financial affairs while under court protection. Unlike Chapter 11, however, a Chapter 9 debtor cannot be ordered to liquidate property; the court's authority is limited to adjusting debts.[16] Hence, a Chapter 9 debtor's plan is called a plan of adjustment, although the procedures for voting and court approval of the plan are the same as those in Chapter 11.

The other major differences concern eligibility. First, a municipality can only seek relief under Chapter 9 if authorized to do so under state law. Michigan law required that the municipality first obtain permission from the governor, as Kevyn Orr did before authorizing his attorneys to file Detroit's Chapter 9 petition. Second, unlike other voluntary bankruptcy cases, where the filing is presumed to be valid and eligibility is rarely challenged, Chapter 9 requires a formal determination of eligibility by the bankruptcy court upon a finding that specific statutory criteria have been met. The determination of whether Detroit was eligible for Chapter 9 would be made by the Eastern District's veteran bankruptcy judge, Steven W. Rhodes.

ELIGIBILITY

Unlike other bankruptcy cases, where judges are assigned to cases by random draw, the chief judge of the circuit court appoints the judge to preside over a Chapter 9 case.[17] The Eastern District's bankruptcy judges and its district judges both unanimously recommended that the appointment go to longtime bankruptcy judge Steven W. Rhodes. When Chief District Judge Gerald Rosen contacted the Sixth Circuit's chief judge, Alice Batchelder (who was traveling in Scotland), to advise her of the recommendations, she told him that Judge Rhodes was the unanimous choice of the circuit bench as well.[18]

Steven Rhodes was born in 1948. Although he trained to be an engineer at Purdue University, graduating in 1970, he decided to become a lawyer and attended law school at the University of Michigan. After graduating in 1972, he clerked for U.S. District Judge John Feikens of the Eastern District of Michigan and served as an assistant U.S. attorney and then as a magistrate judge prior to his appointment to the bankruptcy bench in 1985 as Judge Stanley Bernstein's replacement.

The twenty-eight-year veteran of the bench had presided over some of the biggest Chapter 11 cases in the court's recent history, including those of automotive suppliers Key Plastics and Collins and Aikman. Rhodes was the Eastern District's chief bankruptcy judge from 2002 until 2009, and he served on the Sixth Circuit Court of Appeals' Bankruptcy Appellate Panel from 1997 until 2004 and again from 2008 until 2011 (and served as its chief judge from 2002 until 2004). Rhodes was also the only judge in the district with Chapter 9 experience, having once presided over the case of a small public hospital. He was known as being fair and smart but also stern. He had a reputation for not tolerating what he perceived as nonsense in his courtroom, and observers expected that he would maintain control over the high-profile case. Moreover, although Judge Rhodes was a frequent speaker at professional conferences, he tended to avoid publicity. He even refused to allow news photographers to take a new picture of him to use in media reports on the case; newspapers and websites resorted to using an old file photo.[19] Rhodes had already announced his plan to retire from the bench at the end of 2013, but he suspended that plan when he was formally recalled to take on the Detroit case.

Some media outlets portrayed Detroit's slow decline as a cautionary tale for the rest of the country, and it is not surprising that the case drew an enormous amount of national attention. However, notwithstanding that publicity, relatively little happened between the time the case was filed and the start of the eligibility trial in October. Two events from that period nevertheless stand out. In August, Rhodes made several appointments, including that of a committee to represent Detroit's retirees and another for a fee examiner. However, the most important would be his decision to appoint Chief District Judge Gerald Rosen as his chief mediator in the case. According to Rhodes, he was acting on the advice of judges in other Chapter 9 cases who had stressed to him the importance of mediation in municipal bankruptcy cases.[20] It would turn out to be one of the most significant decisions in the case.

One of the most unique and compelling events in the case happened in mid-September, when Judge Rhodes provided an opportunity for forty-five of the city's residents and retirees to have their day in court.[21] One woman, the widow of a Detroit police officer, described the challenge facing retirees and their families in stark terms: "The bankruptcy could take me and my daughter's pension away and we would be thrown directly to the welfare rolls." A retiree from Detroit's water and sewerage department explained how, in his thirty-five years with the city, he "worked in human waste with my fellow employees, working to serve the city of Detroit. My fellow employees and I are entitled to a pension. I pray that your Honor objects to this bankruptcy."

From a legal standpoint, the issues raised by the testimony of those forty-five people would be absorbed into the larger issues of eligibility.[22] However, they placed the case in human terms in a way that rarely happens in large bankruptcy cases, where the challenges facing real people are usually reduced to classes and claims. Judge Rhodes, who described the hearing as a "truly exceptional session of the court," said, "Everyone who has a stake in the outcome of this case should take the time to listen to this," describing the statements as "moving, thoughtful, and passionate."[23] After the conclusion of the case, he told an interviewer that the hearings "had an impact on me. Hearing from these people directly, their anger, and their mistrust, and their feelings, had an impact on how I dealt with the case from beginning to end."[24]

The eligibility trial began on October 22, 2013. Battle lines between the city and its creditors were quickly drawn in opening arguments. Attorneys for the city maintained that its financial problems were so enormous that Chapter 9 was a fiscal inevitability. Union and retiree lawyers, as expected, challenged the "good faith" of the city's filing, arguing that it was a predetermined effort by the governor to wrest control of the city from its elected officials, or at least that the city rushed to file its Chapter 9 case without seriously pursuing other alternatives.

The city called to the witness stand several city officials, its finance expert, Ken Buckfire, and ultimately Kevyn Orr. Together, these witnesses presented a grim picture of the city and a compelling case for bankruptcy. In terms of numbers, the city's witnesses testified that Detroit's total indebtedness as of the filing was $18.3 billion, which included $6.4 billion in secured debt and $11.9 million in unsecured debt. The unsecured debt included $5.7 billion in retiree benefits and $3.5 billion in unfunded pension obligations; $1.9 billion arose from Detroit's failed efforts to control its pension debt, and another $950 million was owed on account of general obligation bonds and employee and operating expense liabilities. Just as had happened during the August hearing, the testimony went beyond the numbers to convey in very human terms the impact such large debt had on the city's 700,000 residents. Orr testified that he "knew things were bad, but it was somewhat shocking just how dire it was." He described a city so lacking in resources to protect the public's safety that children fought their way to school and that crews could not repair many of the city's electrical grids because they were in places workers could not access safely.[25] In separate testimony, the chief of police described conditions within the department as "deplorable," saying that the morale among police officers was the lowest he had never seen in his career.[26]

While the union and retiree groups did make some effort to challenge the city's financial data, the major thrust of their efforts was to attack the legitimacy of the bankruptcy case itself. The various arguments raised included the following:

- federal constitutional challenges to Chapter 9 based on the Tenth Amendment[27]
- challenges to Michigan's emergency financial manager law, both as enacted and as applied in the case
- challenges to the authority of the emergency financial manager
- challenges to the applicability of Chapter 9 to retiree pensions
- challenges to the good faith of the governor and the EFM at various points in the filing and the events leading to it

The most prominent argument raised by the creditors was the one they had prevailed on in the state court hearing, that the protections afforded pensions in the state constitution directly or indirectly barred the city from seeking relief under Chapter 9. Judge Rhodes queried whether such objections were premature, since the city had yet to file any proposed plan of adjustment, let alone one that proposed pension cuts. Claude Montgomery, the attorney for the official retirees committee, responded that a proposal to cut pensions had in fact been made at one of the pre-filing meetings between creditor groups and the emergency financial manager, and argued that Rhodes in any event had authority to preclude pension cuts without waiting for a formal plan.[28]

The other legitimacy challenge raised by the unions and retirees was that the emergency manager law ran afoul of the state constitution, not least because, they alleged, it violated concepts of local sovereignty, in particular as expressed in constitutional provisions for municipal "home rule." "The breadth of the powers granted the emergency manager is inappropriate. It doesn't allow the wholesale takeover of the city," one union attorney told Judge Rhodes.[29]

Attorneys for the unions and retirees also argued that the efforts by Kevyn Orr to resolve Detroit's financial problems were perfunctory at best. Under the Bankruptcy Code, a Chapter 9 debtor must show either that it negotiated in good faith for a resolution with creditors before filing bankruptcy or that such negotiations are impracticable.[30] The creditors characterized the emergency financial manager's position as one of take-it-or-leave-it, telling Judge Rhodes that "the city announced at that meeting that these were not negotiations" and that Orr and his representatives provided them with insufficient information on which to base an assessment of their proposal. Bruce Bennett, the city's lead attorney at the trial, countered that trying to negotiate settlements with Detroit's vast number of bondholders would have been "pointless" and that Orr's early attempts to discuss concessions with unions and retirees were flatly rejected. "We received no concrete proposal or feedback. What we got was 'no,'" he said of the meeting.[31]

One of the eligibility trial's most notable moments came when the UAW's lawyers called Governor Rick Snyder to the witness stand. It was the first time that a sitting Michigan governor had ever appeared as a witness in any kind of trial. The governor testified that the decision to put Detroit into Chapter 9 was a tremendously difficult one to make, but the right one. He said that he had no preconceived plan to put Detroit in Chapter 9 and that he decided to appoint an emergency manager only after the city defaulted on the April 2012 consent agreement that left the mayor and city council in control of the city's affairs.

Ultimately, Governor Snyder's background in finance kept him in good stead on the witness stand, and creditors' lawyers made no headway against the state's justification for bankruptcy. Moreover, Snyder rejected efforts to be pinned down on the impact the bankruptcy could have on pensioners, simply responding that any plan would have to be "a legal one."[32]

The eligibility trial concluded on November 8, 2013, and Judge Rhodes announced from the bench his decision finding Detroit eligible for relief under Chapter 9 on December 2, 2013. Beyond determining eligibility, however, the decision would turn out to be a pivotal one because Rhodes also affirmed the authority of the emergency financial manager and rejected all of the arguments advanced by the unions and the retirees. That would force them to the negotiating table, an essential step in the expeditious resolution of the case.

Among the arguments raised by the union and retiree groups were their objections to the filing on federal constitutional grounds. The retirees' argument, as summarized by Judge Rhodes, was that "if chapter 9 permits the State of Michigan to authorize a city to file a petition for chapter 9 relief without explicitly providing for the protection of accrued pension benefits, the Tenth Amendment is violated."[33] This argument garnered a great deal of attention in pre-trial media coverage of the case and even in legal circles. It was, in fact, essentially the grounds on which the state judge relied when she issued her injunction against the governor in the Ingham County Circuit Court.

Judge Rhodes rejected the retirees' argument in a succinct and straightforward analysis. First, the judge referenced longstanding case law finding constitutional support for the impairment of contracts in bankruptcy cases, noting in any event that the Constitution's ban on contract impairment limits the states but not the federal government.[34] Second, Rhodes looked at both the history of the adoption of the Michigan Constitution's clause protecting contracts and state Supreme Court case law to find that Michigan law unequivocally defines pension rights as contract rights. Accordingly, Rhodes wrote: "Because under the Michigan Constitution, pension rights are contractual rights, they are subject to impairment in a federal bankruptcy proceeding. Moreover, when, as here, the state consents, that impairment does not violate the Tenth Amendment. Therefore, as applied in this case, chapter 9 is not unconstitutional."[35]

In a post-confirmation interview, Rhodes suggested that the decision was not a complicated one: "I have to say from a legal perspective, it was not a particularly difficult decision. I looked at the Michigan law, the case law, the Michigan Supreme court case law says that pensions are contracts, pension obligations are contract obligations and we impair contract obligations all the time in bankruptcy, that's what we do."[36]

Rhodes similarly dismissed the argument that the emergency financial manager law violated city residents' right of self-governance. The pension groups argued that the city of Detroit was effectively insulated from state management because of home rule provisions in the Michigan constitution.[37] However, the pension groups' arguments failed to recognize the longstanding rule that municipal corporations like the city of Detroit are creations of the state and ultimately derive their powers from the state.[38] Judge Rhodes noted that such limitations are specifically included in the Michigan Constitution and recognized in the city's charter, and he relied on a long line of cases affirming that authority in rejecting the pensioners' home rule arguments.

Once Judge Rhodes resolved the retiree groups' legal challenges to the filing, he disposed of questions on the effect of the Ingham County

Circuit Court decision in a similarly definitive manner. This was another issue treated by the media with more concern than it was given by bankruptcy professionals. Despite the efforts by plaintiffs' attorneys to file their emergency motion in the circuit court before the bankruptcy filing, and notwithstanding the technical delays encountered with PACER, Detroit's attorneys filed the city's petition some nine minutes before the start of the state court hearing. That nine minutes made all the difference.

Judge Rhodes noted that federal law[39] gives the bankruptcy courts exclusive jurisdiction over a debtor's affairs once its case is filed. He found that this includes issues related to Chapter 9 eligibility.[40] Therefore, to the extent that the circuit court might ever have been able to claim jurisdiction over the issue, it lost it the moment the bankruptcy case was filed. Moreover, Judge Rhodes found in any event that the state order was void because it violated the automatic stay, which halts all litigation against the debtor once its bankruptcy case is filed, without the need for any order and without notice to any affected parties.[41] Any actions taken that violate the stay are void and of no effect. Therefore, Rhodes ruled that the order had no bearing on the city's bankruptcy case, notwithstanding the fact that the city was not a defendant in the circuit court case, finding that "the suit was clearly an act to exercise control over the city's property."[42]

Judge Rhodes then found that Detroit did, in fact, meet the criteria to be eligible for relief under Chapter 9. He described as "overwhelming" the evidence of the city's inability to pay its debts as they came due,[43] but he made special mention of what had been described by several witnesses as the city's "service delivery insolvency," that is, its ability to pay for all costs of providing services at the level and quality that are required for the health, safety, and welfare of the community. Of this, the judge wrote: "While the City's tumbling credit rating, its utter lack of liquidity, and the disastrous COPs and swaps deal might more neatly establish the City's 'insolvency' under 11 U.S.C. §101(32)(C), it is the City's service delivery insolvency that the Court finds most strikingly disturbing in this case."[44]

Rhodes likewise resolved in short order the issue of whether the city intended in good faith to propose a plan of adjustment, indicating that Kevyn Orr had already circulated a plan and that the various objections claiming that Orr did not intend in good faith to submit a plan were essentially objections to his anticipated treatment of retiree pensions.[45]

Of the remaining issues, the one that appeared to pose the most trouble for the city in the opinion of many pre-trial analysts was the question of whether Orr had sufficiently attempted to reach a negotiated settlement with the city's creditors before filing bankruptcy. In this respect, Rhodes found the emergency manager's efforts to be lacking, calling the June 14, 2013, proposal "vague" and agreeing with the creditors' contention that Orr had failed to provide them with "sufficient information to make meaningful counter-proposals."[46]

However, given the large number of creditors, the intractability of key creditor groups, and the precipitous drop in the city's liquidity, Rhodes found that pre-filing negotiations were "impracticable," excusing the absence of a good faith effort to negotiate as permitted by 11 U.S.C. §109. Therefore, after resolving a handful of other various objections, Judge Rhodes found that Detroit was eligible to be a debtor under Chapter 9.

Given its breadth, the eligibility decision had a major impact beyond just the issue of eligibility. Judge Rhodes resolved questions about the legitimacy of the emergency financial manager law. In broader national terms, Rhodes's resolution of the question of whether municipalities could use Chapter 9 to reduce their outstanding pension obligations notwithstanding conflicting protections provided by state law was a precedent for financially troubled cities in states with similar statutes. Finally, although they sought an appeal, the decision forced the city's largest creditor groups to the bargaining table and thus provided the starting point for resolving Detroit's financial troubles.

SAVING THE DETROIT INSTITUTE OF ARTS: THE GRAND BARGAIN

The Detroit Institute of Arts (DIA) is one of the foremost art museums in the United States. Its collection includes well-known paintings by Van Gogh, Rembrandt, Breugel, and many other artists of note. However, unlike other major American art museums, the DIA was municipally owned. In and out of its own financial difficulties for much of its existence, ownership of the DIA was transferred to the city in 1919 in an effort to save it from closing. Despite its sizable funding from devoted patrons, the museum was temporarily shuttered in 1973 and thereafter relied extensively on a combination of state and local funding to stay open. A 1997 agreement transferred operation of the museum to its nonprofit Founders' Society, but ownership of the collection itself remained with the city. In 2012, the DIA was saved from shutdown again when voters in Wayne, Oakland, and Macomb counties approved a dedicated tax increase providing the museum with ten years of funding for operations at the rate of about $22 million per year. Given the unique connection between the museum and local government, forged through debt, it perhaps should not have been surprising that the idea of using the DIA's art collection to satisfy some of the city's financial difficulties was in the air in early 2013 as a Detroit bankruptcy filing was seen as increasingly inevitable.

The talk became real in the spring of 2013 as Kevyn Orr indicated both in his public comments and privately through his lawyers and financial advisors that the DIA's collection would need to be accounted for in any plan to resolve the city's debts. The notion was formally broached with the DIA in April in a conference call between Orr's lawyers and the DIA's leaders, and in a second meeting in May where Orr's team proposed that the museum would need to raise and contribute as much as $400 million over twenty years to prevent its art from being sold.

The proposal staggered museum officials. Its donors had only recently pledged $330 million to the museum, which was also committed to adding $250 million to its endowment by the early 2020s. However, the sale of even a few items from its collection was even more unthinkable. Such action would jeopardize most of the DIA's donor contributions as well as further funding from the 2012 millage. Seemingly without any good options, DIA officials dug in for what they anticipated would be a long and difficult battle.

After Judge Rhodes was appointed in the case, he sought the advice of judges from around the country who had handled some of the more significant Chapter 9 cases. One of the most important suggestions that he received was to hire a strong mediator. To that end, Rhodes appointed Gerald Rosen, chief judge of the United States District Court for the Eastern District of Michigan, as his chief mediator. He would later describe that move as "the smartest thing I did in the case."[47] Rosen, who was appointed to the bench by President George Bush in 1990, had been a litigator with the Detroit firm of Miller, Canfield, Paddock & Stone. Rosen set to work assembling a team of mediators.[48]

At the same time, Rosen was considering the plight of the DIA, outlining a plan in which ownership of the museum could somehow be transferred from the city to some other entity, with the infusion of new cash into a plan of adjustment for the city. However, finding sufficient funds from normal sources to satisfy creditors and the court was the difficulty; state officials were unsupportive when Rosen raised the idea with them. Moreover, the DIA was likewise reluctant to take up Rosen's proposal, bolstered by an opinion from Michigan's attorney general, Bill Schuette, that the DIA was held by the city in a charitable trust and could not be sold to pay creditors.

Rosen, however, was not quick to abandon his idea. A path to a solution emerged when Rosen, at lunch in a downtown Detroit deli in September, bumped into Mariam Noland, the president of the Community Foundation of Southeast Michigan. Rosen took Noland up on her offer of help after a brief conversation about the bankruptcy case. Drawing on her extensive contacts within the local and national philanthropic communities, Noland set up a meeting in Detroit on November 5 between Rosen and the leaders of some of America's largest charitable foundations, including the Ford and Knight foundations, the Kresge Foundation, and the Flint-based Mott Foundation. The basic plan devised at that meeting, building on Judge Rosen's idea, provided for the foundations to donate a large sum of money that would be dedicated to the payment of Detroit retiree pensions in exchange for making the DIA off-limits in the bankruptcy case by transferring it out of city ownership to a private nonprofit entity.

Rosen and the foundations faced multiple challenges. The idea of bringing nonprofit donors into a case to resolve a major dispute was unprecedented both in and outside of bankruptcy. None of the foundations had an official connection to the case or the city of Detroit, although several of them had roots in the city's past. Both the Ford and Mott foundations owed their beginnings to auto fortunes. The Knight family had long owned the *Free Press*, Detroit's morning daily newspaper. Only the Kresge Foundation, started by Detroit retailing magnate S. S. Kresge in the 1920s, had been actively involved in funding recent efforts to revitalize the city.

These potential hurdles were offset by the threat to the DIA, the plight of the city, and the persuasiveness of Judge Rosen. Darren Walker, head of the Ford Foundation, lobbied his colleagues with the argument that it would be "philanthropic malfeasance" not to pursue the plan. By early December, the foundations had committed over $250 million to the plan. That sum would increase to more than $300 million by the end of January 2014 as other philanthropists were drawn to the project. As word of the plan became public in early December, an article in the *Detroit Free Press* dubbed the plan the "Grand Bargain."[49] It would be known by that name ever afterward, in media coverage and in court papers.

However, philanthropic contributions were only part of the Grand Bargain. The success of the plan would ultimately depend on substantial funding from the State of Michigan and the DIA itself, as well as on the agreement of the unions and retirees. Although they were more optimistic than they had been when they first met with the emergency financial manager, museum officials still approached negotiations about the DIA's role in the Grand Bargain with caution. They refused to make a specific offer in discussions with Kevyn Orr in early January 2014, even though they were prepared to commit $50 million to the plan. However, both Orr and Governor Snyder had already concluded that that amount would be insufficient, both because the museum's fundraising capacity appeared to support a greater contribution and because the museum would need a stronger commitment to draw support for the plan from state lawmakers.

The governor decided to get directly involved in discussions with the DIA. He met in late January with Eugene Gargaro, the chairman of the museum's board of directors. Rejecting Gargaro's offer of $50 million from the DIA, the governor told him that $100 million would be needed to "solve the problem."[50] At a meeting five days later, the museum's board followed Snyder's recommendation and agreed to make a $100 million contribution to the Grand Bargain.

The last piece on the funding side of the Grand Bargain was the state's contribution. Addressing Detroit's insolvency had mostly been Governor Snyder's project. Michigan's legislature was dominated by outstate Republicans, many of whom carried with them the region's historic antipathy toward the city of Detroit. As a result, they were reluctant to make any financial contribution to the city. "No way, no how," House Speaker Jase Bolger was reported as saying. "We're not going to write another check to continue business as usual."[51]

Despite such opposition, a bipartisan coalition formed in support of the Grand Bargain after intense lobbying by the governor and his staff. Legislators were concerned that the state might wind up bearing the financial burden of newly impoverished retirees. However, it was a contribution to the plan from the UAW that clinched support from legislative Republicans, who blamed unions for many of the city's woes. Legislation committing $195 million to the Grand Bargain passed the state House on May 22, 2014, and was approved by the Senate and signed by the governor on June 3. Although much of the victory could be attributed to Snyder's lobbying effort, he said after the victory, "This shows the spirit of people trying to solve the problem statewide, because everyone rallied. This is something we should really be proud of."[52]

The unprecedented nature of Detroit's bankruptcy case and the seriousness of Detroit's financial problems called for new ideas. The Grand Bargain was the first in a series of innovative outcomes that would be essential to the resolution of the Chapter 9 case. Judge Rhodes would later describe the Grand Bargain as the "key and crucial settlement in the case," adding that it was "unprecedented, as far as I know, for a mediator to go outside of a case to find money."[53]

RESOLVING THE "COPS AND SWAPS" PROBLEM

By late January, then, two of the most substantial barriers to confirming a plan of adjustment had been removed from the case with Judge Rhodes's ruling on the restructuring of pension obligations and the commitments for funds to save the DIA from the auction block. A third challenge was removed in January when Rhodes took a hard line against the settlement of claims by UBS and Bank of America arising out of the complicated plan brokered by Detroit mayor Kwame Kilpatrick in 2005 to shore up the city's ailing pension funds known as the COPS and swaps deal.

The COPS and swaps deal came before Judge Rhodes indirectly, when Kevyn Orr petitioned the court to approve a $285 million loan from Barclays. Of that amount, $165 million was earmarked for termination of the swaps agreements in a deal mediated by Judge Rosen on December 23 and 24, 2013, when Judge Rhodes had sent the parties back to the drawing board after he effectively rejected a deal that would have allowed Detroit to terminate the swaps agreement for $230 million. Both Orr and Judge

Rosen concluded that the additional $55 million reduction was as much of a concession as they were going to get from UBS and Bank of America short of litigation. Judge Rosen took to the bench on Christmas Eve to publicly announce the settlement.

Judge Rhodes, however, was not nearly as sanguine about the settlement. Stating that "if it were close, the court would approve it, but by any rational analysis, it's not close," he rejected the settlement when it came before him for approval on January 16, 2014. Rhodes took the additional step of opining that he thought it reasonably likely that Detroit would prevail if it sued UBS and Bank of America to void the swaps agreement.[54] As he later explained, "I came to the conclusion that the city had a very strong likelihood of prevailing [if it brought suit to challenge the deal]. I also concluded . . . it might have a very strong counterclaim to recover the money it had paid. . . . The whole transaction was a sham. . . . It enabled the city to evade the state law limits on municipal debt."[55] Backed by Judge Rhodes's critical assessment, Orr sued the swaps creditors a few weeks later. They quickly agreed to settle for $85 million.

Judge Rhodes approved the swaps settlement in April 2014. Referring to the emergency manager's plan to exit bankruptcy by autumn, Rhodes said, "The settlement agreement is quite likely to be the fastest, surest and least costly way for the city to achieve that goal."[56] That remark might have referred to more than the $155 million Detroit saved in the settlement. Besides accepting the reduced termination fee, Bank of America and UBS also agreed to support the city's plan of adjustment. That agreement in turn created a major strategic advantage for the city in its effort to exit bankruptcy. In Chapter 9, as in Chapter 11, creditors are segregated into classes for treatment under, and approval of, the plan. The claims of creditors within a class must be of similar type and must be treated the same under the plan, that is, they must receive a proportionate distribution relative to the size of their claims. Additionally, creditors vote as a class to approve the plan; if a majority of the voting creditors within a class approve the plan, that class approves the plan. However, that same "majority rule" principle does not necessarily apply to the final approval of the plan. The Bankruptcy Code entrusts that decision to the judge, who may approve the plan over the votes of dissenting creditors, so long as one impaired class (i.e., one receiving less than full payment) approves the plan.

This procedure, known as "cramdown," provides debtors with a major advantage in the plan confirmation process. Debtors are given the primary choice of placing creditors in particular classes. The courts give deference to the debtor's creditor placements so long as they meet the "similarly situated" standard. While debtors cannot gerrymander classes by anticipated votes, they can rely on small distinctions to segregate certain creditors from a larger group, increasing the likelihood of gaining at least one consenting class.

Detroit could justifiably place the swaps creditors in their own voting class by virtue of the unique nature of their claims. Their agreement to support the city's proposed plan therefore provided the means to invoke the cramdown provisions of the Bankruptcy Code. Moreover, the possibility of cramdown generally encourages other creditors to reach their own settlements with the debtor, lest they be left behind at confirmation. However, while the threat of cramdown moved some creditor groups to negotiate in earnest, others dug in for a hard fight.

SYNCORA

Once the Grand Bargain was reached, most of Detroit's other creditors signed on to its proposed plan of adjustment. Retirees, once seen as the biggest obstacle to Detroit's restructuring, overwhelmingly supported the city's plan after Shirley Lightsey, president of the Detroit Retired City Employees Association, urged them to support it, saying, "You can't eat principles and uncertainty doesn't pay the bills."[57]

A handful of creditors nevertheless stood in opposition to the plan, none of them more significant than two of the city's bond insurers, Syncora Guarantee, Inc. and Fidelity Guarantee Insurance Co. (FGIC). Syncora was owed $400,000, FGIC over $1 billion. Like the retirees, the bond insurers were unsecured creditors. However, under the city's plan of adjustment, the two groups were separated into different classes for purposes of voting and distribution. While Detroiters lauded the announcement of the Grand Bargain, the bondholders' attorneys argued that the plan should be rejected unless their clients received similar treatment to that of the retirees. Syncora was an especially vocal opponent of the deal. "We think this is about us getting as much recovery as we can and getting similar recovery to other similarly situated creditors like the pensioners and retirees," said James Sprayregen, Syncora's counsel. "But from the get-go for whatever reason, we have been vilified as the big bad Wall Street creditor against the little people. And we think that's very inappropriate and unfair."[58]

Attorneys and officials for the city's emergency financial manager described Syncora in less charitable terms. A spokesman for Kevyn Orr said, "It's safe to say they have employed a kitchen sink strategy with all of their objections. All that does is add more work for the judge and more delay for the confirmation of the plan." Attorneys for the city described Syncora's tactics in the case as a "scorched earth litigation strategy" and a "carpet-bombing approach."[59]

Regardless of Syncora's motivations, its aggressive tactics led it to overreach and draw the ire of the court. Syncora took aim at the Grand Bargain in its objections to the city's proposed plan of adjustment. It argued that the plan violated the Bankruptcy Code's requirement for equal treatment of similarly situated creditors. According to Syncora, the Grand Bargain effectively discriminated between creditors by providing retirees a far greater portion of their pension claims than would be received by bondholders and bond insurers. Going beyond its legal arguments, however, Syncora challenged the integrity of the negotiation process leading to the Grand Bargain by attacking the impartiality of the chief mediator, Judge Gerald Rosen, and his chief deputy, prominent Detroit attorney Eugene Driker.

In their objection, Syncora's lawyers alleged that the Grand Bargain was "the product of agenda-driven conflicted mediators who colluded with certain interested parties to benefit select favored creditors to the gross detriment of disfavored creditors and, remarkably, the city itself." The attorneys acknowledged that they had no direct evidence of collusion or even of mishandling of the Grand Bargain negotiations. Instead, they cited some of Rosen's public statements about the deal: "Regrettably, but truly, it could not be clearer that the mediators—rather than mediating discrete disputes—designed and later executed a transaction in furtherance of their own personal vision of what was important to protect and for whom."[60]

Syncora's attack on Driker was based on the fact that his wife, Elaine, was a former member of the art museum's board of directors. Syncora cited this as evidence of an improper conflict of interest and claimed that the relationship had been hidden from its lawyers. The city sought sanctions against Syncora, calling its allegations "false and defamatory," "sensationalized," and "designed to generate maximum press coverage."[61]

Judge Rhodes held a hearing on the city's motion on August 27, 2014, and found Syncora's charges against Judge Rosen and the Drikers to be entirely without merit. He found not only that Elaine Driker's relationship to the DIA had been disclosed to Syncora but also that there was no basis for the allegations of favoritism on the part of either mediator. Rhodes said that Rosen and Driker "were in no position to 'collude' with anyone, to 'orchestrate' or 'engineer' anything. . . . The mediators' record of accomplishment in this case establishes but one plan, one agenda, one bias—to settle as much of the case as they can and to do so tirelessly and selflessly." The judge ordered that the allegations against Rosen be stricken from the record, stating that they were "legally and factually unwarranted, unprofessional, and unjust." Finally, he ordered Syncora's lawyers to show cause why they should not be sanctioned for the statements and suggested on the record that they owed an apology to Judge Rosen, Eugene Driker, and Elaine Driker.[62]

When the trial on confirmation of Detroit's proposed plan of adjustment began on September 2, 2014, the claims of both Syncora and FGIC were unresolved. With the most at stake of the holdout creditors, the bond insurers took the lead in opposing confirmation of the plan. However, negotiations between Detroit and the insurers continued, and on September 9, Syncora and the city announced that they had reached a settlement. Under the deal, Syncora would gain a twenty-year extension of its operating lease on the "Detroit side" of the Detroit-Windsor tunnel, the connection between the city and Windsor, Ontario, that runs below the Detroit River. Syncora had gained its existing tunnel lease in partial satisfaction of its claim in an unrelated bankruptcy case. The bond insurer would also receive a portion of the real estate adjacent to the tunnel's U.S. entrance, control of a parking garage beneath the city's Grand Circus Park, a $6.25 million credit to bid on any city property put up for sale, and cash distributions from the plan of $48 million. In all, Syncora would receive cash, property, and interests equal to nearly 25 percent of its claim.

Moreover, Syncora's lawyers did provide the apology to Judge Rosen and Eugene and Elaine Driker that Judge Rhodes had urged them to make. In a filing made on September 15, 2014, titled "Corrected Syncora Guarantee Inc., and Syncora Capital Assurance, Inc.'s Notice of Settlement in Principle," the lawyers wrote:

[Syncora's objection to the debtor's plan] should not have said or implied that there was a failure to disclose that Mr. Driker's wife had an association with the Detroit Institute of Arts. In fact, Chief Judge Rosen himself had arranged for the disclosure of that information in an email that he (through his clerk) had sent us and other counsel in these proceedings on September 9, 2013. While we have already privately conveyed our apologies to Judge Rosen and the Drikers, the public nature of the mistaken claim demands both a formal withdrawal of that claim and, just as importantly, a public apology. We are deeply sorry for the mistake we made and for any unfounded aspersions it may have cast on Chief Judge Rosen and the Drikers.

FINANCIAL GUARANTY INSURANCE COMPANY

Once Syncora settled, it seemed to observers that it would be only a matter of time before Detroit reached a deal with the other major holdout, Fidelity Guaranty Insurance Company. However, FGIC was owed more than $1 billion, and it seemed willing to leverage its isolation to its maximum advantage. Another court-ordered round of mediation did not bring a deal, so by the time Kevyn Orr took the stand in early October, FGIC effectively stood alone in its opposition to the court's approval of the city's plan of adjustment.

Financial Guaranty's lawyers kept Orr on the stand for more than three days to challenge key parts of the 1,111-page plan of adjustment. Sparring with Orr, Ed Spoto, FGIC's counsel, advanced FGIC's argument that the DIA's art collection should be "monetized" through the sale, lease, or collateralization of many of its individual pieces and that the Grand Bargain was made at the expense of bondholders like itself.

However, with Syncora out of the picture, those arguments lacked the weight they might otherwise have carried, and in any event FGIC was generally considered to be angling for a better settlement in its ongoing negotiations. Indeed, on October 16, attorneys for the city and FGIC announced that they had resolved the bondholder's claims. FGIC would be granted rights to build a hotel, retail, and condominium complex on the riverfront site of the Joe Louis Arena once it was vacated by the city's NHL franchise, the Red Wings (which had plans to move to a new arena). In addition, the company would receive $20 million in credits that FGIC could use to bid on other city property and notes valued at about $146 million.

Rhodes would later describe the Syncora and FGIC settlements as "groundbreaking."[63] He elaborated in a radio interview: "In the long-term, it's a win-win. The whole concept of giving creditors a stake in the outcome of a municipality in this very direct way is unprecedented. . . . The development opportunities that these creditors have will accelerate the city's revitalization so I think that in the long term the price the city paid by giving up these properties will be more than outweighed by the benefit it will obtain from this accelerated revitalization."[64]

THE CONFIRMATION TRIAL

With the objection of the major creditors resolved, confirmation of the city's plan of adjustment was in little doubt. The only open question was whether Detroit's plan was feasible, as required under Chapter 9.[65] Questions about the feasibility of Detroit's plan of adjustment had effectively been resolved in July when Martha Kopacz, Judge Rhodes's own appointed expert, filed her report concluding that the proposed plan was feasible, albeit with reservations. Kopacz was concerned not only about the financial aspects of the plan but also about Detroit's leadership and bureaucracy.

> Current human resources are lacking and senior leadership, while generally capable is not plentiful. To meet the projections in the POA, the City will need to recruit a significant number of employees with improved skill level and continue to change the culture of performance and accountability, I believe that the City has identified human capital as an issue and is addressing this both formally and informally. I am relying on Mayor Duggan, CFO John Hill, and the other capable executives I have met at the City to execute effectively on the human capital strategy. (Kopacz 2014, 210)

However, by the time that Kopacz, the last witness to take the stand, testified at trial, she indicated she had more reason to feel optimistic about the city's future. "There is a genuine desire to right the ship," she stated.

"There is a significant level of enthusiasm among the mayor [and] his direct reports."[66]

That optimism was shared throughout metropolitan Detroit. The city's November 2013 general election had brought into office a new wave of public officials committed to revitalizing the city, including Mike Duggan, who was elected mayor. Combining federal and state funds with private foundation contributions, significant resources were devoted to the removal of the city's more than seventy thousand abandoned buildings. Street lamps that hadn't worked for years were being repaired or replaced, as were many of Detroit's old and malfunctioning police cars, and ambulances and fire trucks were purchased with donations from several of the city's most prominent corporations.

People and business were finding opportunities in Detroit. Local financier Dan Gilbert, the owner of Quicken Loans and the NBA's Cleveland Cavaliers, invested heavily in the city's downtown, spending over $1 billion to acquire more than three million square feet of office space in the city. Artists and entrepreneurs, likewise captivated by Detroit's cheap real estate prices, began to relocate to the city. Shinola, a maker of high-priced watches, bicycles, and luxury goods, located its operations in the city's Midtown area near Wayne State University. So did many new residents, driving rental housing in the city's core to near full occupancy.

On November 7, 2014, Judge Rhodes took the bench to announce his approval of Detroit's plan of adjustment, just sixteen months after the case began. The plan eliminated $7 billion of city debt, some of that from the bond insurers but much from the retirees, who, as part of the Grand Bargain, agreed to accept smaller benefits going forward. Retired general municipal workers' monthly payments would be reduced by 4.5 percent. They would also see an end to cost-of-living adjustments and would bear a higher share of their health care costs. Moreover, the retirees would forfeit the year-end "thirteenth check" payments that had deepened Detroit's pension liabilities.

Besides adjusting past debts, the plan had forward-looking components as well. It provided for $1.7 billion to be set aside over the next decade to continue the removal of abandoned and blighted buildings, to purchase new fire trucks and ambulances, and to upgrade the city's hopelessly outdated computer systems. In addition, the plan established, at the insistence of the state in return for its contribution to the Grand Bargain, an appointed board to oversee the city's finances.

Only two smaller classes of unsecured creditors voted to reject the plan of adjustment. Although it was well within Judge Rhodes's authority to confirm the plan over those objections, he used them to expand on one of the key concerns he had addressed throughout the case: the sorry condition of the city that was a daily fact of life for its residents:

> A large number of people in this City are suffering hardship because of what we have antiseptically called service delivery insolvency. What this means is that the City is unable to provide basic municipal services such as police, fire, and EMS services to protect the health and safety of the people here. Detroit's inability to provide adequate municipal services runs deep and has for years. It is inhumane and intolerable, and it must be fixed. This plan can fix these problems and the City is committed to it. So if to fix this problem, the Court must require these few creditors that rejected the plan to nevertheless share in the sacrifice that the other creditors have agreed to endure, then so be it.[67]

Detroit's Chapter 9 case was already considered a landmark in municipal bankruptcy law by the time of confirmation. Judge Rhodes was lauded for his handling of the case, which was predicted to last years but instead was resolved in only sixteen months. His decision on the adjustment of public pensions in Chapter 9 was already being cited as a model for other distressed local governments. However, for all the attention the threatened sale of the DIA's collection had received, it had not yet come directly before Judge Rhodes for review.

The judge used his decision approving the plan to express his view that the art was not and could not be liquidated, as part of the bankruptcy case or otherwise:

> No provision of law allows the creditors to access the DIA art to satisfy their claims, whether in bankruptcy or outside of bankruptcy. The market value of the art, therefore, is irrelevant in this case. A judgment creditors' sole remedy is a court-ordered property

tax assessment process under Michigan's Revised Judicature Act. Michigan law prohibits execution on municipal property.

Some creditors argue that the best interest test in chapter 9 requires this Court's full consideration of all of the City's assets, including the art, even if the assets would not be accessible to unsecured creditors outside of bankruptcy.

The Court also rejects the argument. The legal limitations on the collection of judgments that apply outside of bankruptcy also constrain the best interests of creditors test in bankruptcy. Neither the bankruptcy code nor case law suggests otherwise.[68]

In addition to the legal issues it addressed, Detroit's bankruptcy case was notable for its demonstration of how such cases offered a platform for the resolution of disputes between competing and compelling interests when ordinary political processes have failed. As Judge Rhodes stated from the bench, "The settlements that the mediators assembled in this case are extraordinary and unprecedented. Never before have bankruptcy mediators proactively sought to marshal the community's financial resources to solve a community problem. Most importantly, they knew that their work was not simply about resolving a bankruptcy case. It was about fixing a broken city."[69]

However, Judge Rhodes understood that the recovery of that "broken city" was ultimately dependent on the political process. He used the closing portions of his opinion to address his concerns and hopes, directing his remarks first to the State of Michigan and its elected officials:

History will judge the correctness of this finding, and it will judge that this finding was correct only if what happened to Detroit never happens again. The State of Michigan can sustain that finding in history only by fulfilling its constitutional, legal and moral obligation to assure that the municipalities in this state adequately fund their pension obligations. If the state fails, history will judge that this Court's approval of that settlement was a massive failure.[70]

Then to the city's residents he said, "I urge you not to forget your anger. Your enduring and collective memory of what happened here, and your memory of your anger about it, will be exactly what will prevent this from ever happening again. It must never happen again."[71] Rhodes closed with a final appeal:

> We have used the phrase, the grand bargain, to describe the group of agreements that will fix the City's pension problem. That description is entirely fitting. In our nation, we join together in the promise and in the ideal of a much grander bargain. It is the bargain by which we interact with each other and with our government. It is now time to restore democracy to the people of the City of Detroit. I urge you to participate in it. And I hope that you will soon realize its full potential.[72]

Judge Rhodes issued his written decision on confirmation on December 31, 2014.[73] He continued to preside over the case until February 2015, when he finally began his retirement.[74] Kevyn Orr stepped down in December 2014, although his return of authority to city officials had actually begun in September. Confirmation was achieved in the largest case in the court's history and the largest municipal case in the history of American bankruptcy law. With the entire nation watching, the Eastern District court played a central role in saving a major American city and offered guidance to other cities in similar circumstances through innovative public-private partnerships like the Grand Bargain and the Syncora and FGIC settlements. Ultimately, the most notable lesson from Detroit's case was not in how the court was used to resolve legal disputes but rather in how it demonstrated that the bankruptcy courts could provide a platform to resolve difficult public problems when they no longer can be addressed through the ordinary political processes.

CONCLUSION

As explained in the introduction to this book, the title, *Adversity and Justice*, is meant to capture the dual nature of American bankruptcy law and the particular way in which those concepts played out in the bankruptcy court for the Eastern District of Michigan. Every bankruptcy proceeding originates in the financial adversity of the debtor, whether it is the city of Detroit's Chapter 9 filing, McLouth Steel's attempts to survive in a shifting business environment, or the case of an individual with tens of thousands of dollars in medical bills she cannot afford. Justice is inherently part of every case, too. The moral disapprobation once shown toward debtors is a distant part of America's legal past, replaced by the principle of the fresh start.

In that sense, adversity and justice are not unique to the Eastern District of Michigan. Generally speaking, their application is much the same there as it is in every one of the other federal districts throughout the United States. However, as this book demonstrates, these concepts have played a particular role in the history of the Eastern District court. The court twice faced adversity in the form of internal crises that threatened its integrity as a dispenser of justice.

In the first, in 1919, Judge Tuttle's swift action in removing Lee Joslyn kept the crisis from expanding. Tuttle's appointment of Paul King to replace Joslyn became one of the signal moments in the history of the court. As described in chapter 4, King worked tirelessly to maintain strong relations with Judge Tuttle and with the bankruptcy bar. Moreover, King did more than anyone, in the Eastern District or elsewhere prior to the adoption of the Bankruptcy Code in 1978, to elevate the level of officiating in bankruptcy cases through his efforts to create the National Association of Referees in Bankruptcy and his advocacy for better case administration. In a system of laws, judicial process is the cornerstone of justice. Paul King's efforts to improve the administration of bankruptcy cases put the Eastern District of Michigan in the vanguard of justice in the first half of the twentieth century.

The second incident, in the early 1980s, was the court scandal described in chapters 8 and 9. This time the district court did not take action, allowing corruption and cronyism to fester for years until they were revealed in a series of media exposés. The pervasiveness of the problems and the public manner by which they were exposed ensured that the court would have a longer road to recovering its reputation than it did in 1919. Although its actions would continue to be scrutinized for years, not least by the district judges, the court was restored to respectability, initially through the efforts of Judge George Woods and chief clerk David Sherwood and then through the judges that followed. The corrupt image of the court was replaced by a reputation for integrity and justice that it has maintained to the present, culminating in the widespread acclaim given to Judge Steven Rhodes's handling of Detroit's bankruptcy case.

However, the court also proved to be a leader in using bankruptcy to address broader public adversity. In the 1930s, Paul King provided national leadership in amending the bankruptcy laws to adapt them to the public adversity of the Great Depression. More recently, the court directly engaged major public policy questions in the Detroit case. The extensive use of mediation, the resolution of disputes over municipal debt through the creation of public-private partnerships, and Judge Rhodes's ruling on the adjustment of retiree pensions are certain to serve as a model for other local governments as they search for ways to address their intractable financial deficits.

Therefore, these dual themes have played out in the history of the court in ways both large and small, and they have brought out the strength of the institution. The final words on the subject can be those of Judge Rhodes:

> The most interesting thing about bankruptcy in particular, is that every case is interesting from a human perspective: how people get into financial trouble, how they try to work their own way out, the difficulties they have. And every case was interesting on a human perspective. . . . The same is true in business cases, even the larger business cases that I have because they're all run by people and they make mistakes and they have bad luck and the question is what can we do in the bankruptcy system to help them.[75]

APPENDIX 1

Referees and Judges of the Court

HARLOW P. DAVOCK (1898–1910)

Davock was born in Buffalo, New York, in 1848. He graduated from the University of Michigan in 1870 with degrees in both civil engineering and the humanities. Davock read for the law in the office of a Detroit law firm, passing the bar in 1878. He was appointed referee in 1898 and was the Eastern District of Michigan's only referee until Lee Joslyn's appointment in 1904. Davock died in New Hampshire while on vacation in 1910.

LEE E. JOSLYN (1905–19)

Joslyn was born in New York State in 1864 but grew up around Dryden and Lapeer, Michigan. He attended neither college nor law school and instead read for the law, thereafter establishing a law practice in Bay City. He was first appointed referee-in-bankruptcy for the court's Northern Division in 1905. Joslyn transferred to Detroit in 1910 upon Harlow Davock's unexpected death and served there until he resigned in 1919. Joslyn thereafter taught at the Detroit College of Law and maintained a prominent law practice in Detroit until his death in 1936.

GEORGE E. MARSTON (1910–37)

Marston was born in Bay City in 1873. He received a bachelor of laws degree from the University of Michigan in 1896. He was the United States Commissioner in Bay City from 1908 until he succeeded Lee Joslyn as the Northern Division's referee-in-bankruptcy in 1910. He relocated to Detroit in 1919. Marston took a leave of absence from the court for health reasons in 1953 and formally retired from the bench in 1947. He died in Arcadia, California, in 1953.

PAUL H. KING (1919–42)

King was born in Nebraska in 1879. He was admitted to practice law in Michigan in 1904 after reading for the bar. King was appointed by District Judge Arthur Tuttle to replace Lee Joslyn in 1919. He organized the National Association of Referees in Bankruptcy in 1926 and served as its first president. Throughout the 1930s, he led efforts that resulted in major revisions to the Bankruptcy Act in 1938 as well as the formation of the National Bankruptcy Conference. King died in Detroit in 1942.

WALTER I. MCKENZIE (1943–60)

McKenzie was born in Muskegon, Michigan, on February 9, 1888. He graduated from the University of Michigan with a bachelor of laws degree in 1915. He was appointed referee-in-bankruptcy in 1943 by Judge Arthur Tuttle. McKenzie took a leave of absence from the bench to serve as a U.S. prosecutor in the Far East war crimes trials during 1946–47. He served as president of the National Association of Referees in Bankruptcy in 1953. McKenzie retired from the bench in 1960 and died in Arizona in 1962.

ARCHIE KATCHER (1946–47, 1948–56)

Katcher was born in North Dakota in 1914. He graduated from the Detroit College of Law in 1940. He was appointed to the bench in 1946 on a temporary basis while Walter McKenzie was on leave and again in 1948 to fill the spot formerly occupied by George Marston. After Katcher resigned in 1956, he had a prominent career as a private attorney. He died in Royal Oak, Michigan, in 1974.

JOSEPH MURPHY (1956–64)

Murphy was born in Milwaukee in 1907. He graduated from the University of Detroit Law School in 1930. He was active in state Democratic politics throughout the 1940s. Murphy served as interim U.S. Attorney for the Eastern District of Michigan in 1949 and 1951. He resigned his position on the bankruptcy bench in 1964 and died in 1987.

HARRY G. HACKETT (1957–81)

Hackett was born in Cedar Bluff, Arkansas, in 1923. He graduated from Wayne State University Law School in 1952. He was appointed as a referee-in-bankruptcy in 1957 to fill a newly created position. Hackett resigned in 1981 and died in Ann Arbor in 1987.

GEORGE BRODY (1960–88)

Brody was born in Brooklyn, New York, in 1913. He graduated from the University of Michigan Law School in 1947. He was appointed referee-in-bankruptcy in 1960 to succeed Walter McKenzie. Brody served as the district's chief bankruptcy judge during 1981–88. He resigned in 1988, although he continued to serve as a visiting judge in various jurisdictions, primarily the Southern District of California. Brody died in 2007.

HAROLD BOBIER (1961–82)

Bobier was born in St. Ignace, Michigan, in 1909. He began practicing law in 1943 but never attended law school. According to some accounts, he is the last federal judge not to have a formal legal education. In 1961 Bobier was appointed to a newly created position. He primarily sat in Flint, Michigan. He retired in 1982 and died in 1985.

DAVID PATTON (1965–82)

Patton was born in Pennsylvania in 1912. He graduated from the University of Illinois law school in 1939. He served as a naval intelligence officer in World War II. Patton was appointed to the bankruptcy bench in 1965 to replace Joseph Murphy. He retired from the bench in 1982. Patton died in Ann Arbor in 1993.

HARVEY D. WALKER (1977–83)

Walker was born in 1913. He graduated from the Detroit College of Law in 1940. He had a six-year dual appointment as a federal magistrate judge and a bankruptcy judge from 1977 until part-time positions were eliminated in 1983. Walker died in 2003.

GEORGE E. WOODS JR. (1981–83)

Woods was born in 1923 in Cleveland. He graduated from the Detroit College of Law in 1949. He was appointed to succeed Harry Hackett following his resignation in 1981. Woods resigned from the bankruptcy bench to accept an appointment and a U.S. District Court judgeship in Detroit in 1983, in which capacity he served until his retirement in 2004. He died in 2007 in Waterford, Michigan.

STANLEY BERNSTEIN (1982–84)

Bernstein was born in 1941. He graduated from Rutgers Law School in 1970. He was appointed to succeed Harold Bobier in 1982 and subsequently transferred to Detroit to succeed George Woods in 1983. Bernstein resigned from the bench in 1984 and subsequently served as a bankruptcy judge in the Eastern District of New York from 1996 until 2007.

RAY REYNOLDS GRAVES (1982–2001)

Graves was born in Tuscumbia, Alabama, in 1946. He graduated from Wayne State University Law School in 1970. He was appointed to the Eastern District of Michigan bankruptcy bench to succeed David Patton in 1982. Graves left the bench in 2001.

ARTHUR J. SPECTOR (1984–2002)

Spector was born in New York City in 1974. He graduated from the Boston University School of Law in 1984. He was appointed to succeed Harvey D. Walker and to replace Stanley Bernstein in the court's Northern Division in 1984. Spector served as the court's chief judge during 1989–90. He left the bench in 2002 (his appointment was not renewed). He currently practices law in Florida.

STEVEN W. RHODES (1985–2015)

Rhodes was born in New York City in 1948. He graduated from the University of Michigan Law School in 1972. He was appointed to succeed Stanley Bernstein in 1985. Rhodes served as chief judge in 1990–91 and 2002–9. He took senior status in 2013 and was recalled to preside over the city of Detroit Chapter 9 case in 2013. Rhodes retired in 2015.

WALTER SHAPERO (1988–PRESENT)

Shapero was born in Detroit in 1930. He graduated from the University of Virginia Law School in 1954. He was appointed to the bench in 1988 to succeed George Brody. Shapero retired in 2002 but immediately assumed recall status, serving first in Bay City and then Detroit. He continues to serve in that status as of 2015.

PHILLIP J. SHEFFERLEY (2003–PRESENT)

Shefferley received his law degree from Wayne State University in 1979. He was engaged in private practice with a specialization in business reorganizations and Chapter 11 bankruptcy until appointed in the bench in 2003 to fill the spot vacated by Judge Walter Shapero. Shefferley is currently the chief judge of the court.

MARCI B. MCIVOR (2003–PRESENT)

McIvor graduated from Wayne State University Law School in 1988. She was an assistant attorney general for the State of Michigan prior to her appointment to the bench. She was appointed to the bench to fill a newly created position in 2003.

THOMAS J. TUCKER (2003–PRESENT)

Tucker received his law degree from Harvard University. He was a commercial litigator prior to taking the bench. He was appointed in 2003 to succeed Ray Reynolds Graves.

DANIEL J. OPPERMAN (2006–PRESENT)

Opperman was born in Millington, Michigan. He received his law degree from Wayne State University in 1981. Prior to taking the bench, he practiced with Braun Kendrick Finkbeiner, PLC, in Saginaw, Michigan, concentrating in litigation, bankruptcy, and real estate. Opperman was appointed to the bench in 2006. He currently sits in Bay City and Flint.

MARK A. RANDON (2014–PRESENT)

Randon received his law degree from the University of Michigan in 1992. He was appointed to the Michigan 36th District Court in 2001 and as a U.S. magistrate judge in 2009. He succeeded Steven Rhodes on the Eastern District of Michigan bankruptcy court in 2014.

APPENDIX 2

Places of Court

The various divisions of the United States Bankruptcy Court for the Eastern District of Michigan have had several different homes over the court's long history. The position of referee-in-bankruptcy was originally conceived as a part-time position. Referees commonly had law practices or other businesses in addition to their appointed duties. Moreover, they were responsible for securing and furnishing their own offices and courtrooms. In addition, the Bankruptcy Act required that court be conducted in the county of the debtor's residence and place of business, although this rule was not always strictly followed. This brief essay describes some of the court's more significant locations.

DETROIT

Harlow P. Davock, the court's first referee, had his offices in various locations in downtown Detroit, eventually locating in Detroit's Trussed Concrete Building, a landmark structure located at the northeast corner of West Lafayette and what is now Washington Boulevard, across from the present Theodore Levin U.S. Courthouse. Completed in 1907, the Trussed Concrete Building (later called the Owen Building) was designed by Detroit architect Albert Kahn and was notable as the city's first concrete office building. Joslyn took over this office when he succeeded Joslyn in 1910, and remained there throughout his tenure as referee.

However, the Owen Building was inadequate for two referees, and so in 1919 Paul King and George Marston established new offices for the court in the Gray Estate Building at 117 West Fort Street.[1] They moved the court three more times over the next six years, first to 419 W. Fort St,[2] and then in 1923 to the Majestic Building, a fourteen-story beaux-arts structure located at the intersection of Michigan and Woodward avenues on the north side of Campus Martius.[3] The court moved again in 1925, this time to the sixth floor of the then new Buhl Building at the corner of Griswold and Congress streets in 1925. The twenty-six-story Buhl Building was, and remains today, one of Detroit's most prominent and most beautiful office buildings.

The bankruptcy court remained in the Buhl Building for nine years until it moved to the tenth floor of the newly completed U.S. Post Office and Federal Building at 231 W. Lafayette Street in May 1935. At the time, it was unusual for bankruptcy courts to be within a federal courthouse, and the new location undoubtedly added to the courts prestige. The bankruptcy court would eventually expand to take over half of the federal building's tenth floor, which served as the court's home until the late 1990s.

The increase in case filings over the course of the 1990s necessitated a move to larger space in an office building across the street from the federal courthouse at 211 W. Fort Street. There, the court occupied several floors of the twenty-seven-story structure. Built in 1963, 211 W. Fort Street was once the headquarters of Comerica Bank. In addition to the bankruptcy court, the building contains the offices of the United States Attorney and the Detroit office of the United States Trustee.

BAY CITY AND FLINT

George Marston, individually and then after 1919 jointly with Paul King, maintained an office for the bankruptcy court in Bay City's Shearer Building at 315 Center Avenue. The arrangement instituted by Judge Arthur Tuttle by which case assignments were made jointly to all of the district's bankruptcy judges prevailed until the early 1960s, but it still was not until 1977, when Harvey Walker received his joint appointment as both bankruptcy and magistrate judge, that the division had its own judge. This arrangement discouraged the court from gaining a permanent home in the Northern Division. The bankruptcy court was for many years located within the U.S. Post Office and Courthouse at 1000 Washington Avenue in Bay City, which had been completed in 1933. However, the space allotted the court there was never adequate. The office space was small, and the bankruptcy court shared a courtroom with the district court. In 1995, the court moved to its current stand-alone location at 111 First Street on Bay City's riverfront, where it had sufficient space and facilities to address the challenges of full time twenty-first century bankruptcy administration.

Unlike Bay City, Flint was considered to be a branch of the Southern Division. The bankruptcy court did not have a dedicated facility there until the 1960s. Instead, space was rented as needed in a variety of locales. Hearings were sometimes held, for example, in the Flint city council chambers. However, Harold Bobier sat regularly in Flint following his appointment in 1961. The bankruptcy court at that point met in the Federal Building and U.S. Courthouse at 600 Church Street. Like Bay City, the facilities were small and shared with the district court. However, the Flint bankruptcy court also gained its own facility in the mid-1990s, when it moved to its present location 226 W. Second Street.

NOTES

INTRODUCTION

1. This is described in chapter 3.

2. As is described in this book, bankruptcy judges were formally identified as referees until the early 1970s. Again, this book will identify the officials in their historical context.

3. Paul King's story is contained in chapter 4.

4. 292 U.S. 234, 245 (1934). The notion has biblical roots: "Every seventh year you shall grant a remission of debts. And this is the manner of the remission: every creditor shall remit the claim that is held against a neighbor, not exacting it of a neighbor who is a member of the community, because the Lord's remission has been proclaimed." Deut. 15:1–3 (NRSV).

5. The story of the events of 1919 is contained in chapter 2. The latter events are described in chapters 8 and 9.

6. This chapter describes the state of the law as it existed in the middle of the second decade of the twenty-first century. Readers should bear in mind that America's bankruptcy laws have been revised several times. Some of those revisions are part of the court's history and are recounted here. Other differences are explained within the text when necessary to promote the reader's understanding.

7. Other forms of bankruptcy include Chapter 9 (municipalities) and Chapter 12 (family farmers). Chapter 9 is discussed in the last chapter of this book.

8. Administrative Office of the United States Courts, *2010 Report of Statistics Required by the Bankruptcy Abuse Prevention and Consumer Protection Act of 2005* (Washington, DC: GPO, 2011).

9. For example, a lender that repossesses a motor vehicle from the debtor after bankruptcy without first obtaining court approval will have to return the vehicle to the debtor.

10. Administrative Office of the U.S. Courts, www.uscourts.gov/Statistics/BankruptcyStatistics.

11. Ibid.

CHAPTER 1

1. "Hovey K. Clarke," *Detroit Free Press*, July 23, 1889, p. 5.

2. *New York Times*, November 19, 1880.

3. "The National Bankruptcy Bill," *Detroit Free Press*, June 23, 1898, p. 4.

4. "Fosters Big Risks," *Detroit Free Press*, July 28, 1898, p. 8.

CHAPTER 2

1. The Trussed Concrete Building itself was quite innovative, as it was the first concrete office building built in Detroit. Kahn, who would go on to design many Detroit landmarks like the Fisher Building, the General Motors Building, and the Ford Rouge Assembly Plant, kept his own offices in the building, as did his brother Julius, who invented the use of steel reinforcement for concrete.

2. *Detroit Free Press*, August 20, 1899, p. 6.

3. Creditors filed involuntary petitions against bankrupts much more often in the early decades of practice under the Bankruptcy Act than they do now under the modern code.

4. The Currie cases were notorious and much reported on at the time. Articles and legal opinions drawn on in preparing this account include the following: In re Currie, et al., 197 F. 1012 (E.D. Mich. 1910); Austin v. Hayden, et al., 171 Mich. 38, 137 N.W. 317 (1912); Austin v. Hayden, et al., 190 Mich. 528, 157 N.W. 93 (1916); "Debtors Like New Bankruptcy Law," *Detroit Free Press*, August 20, 1899, p. 6; "Defects in the Bankruptcy Law," *Detroit Free Press*, August 20, 1899, A4; "Detroiter Chosen," *Detroit Free Press*, August 30, 1901, p. 9; "Plea for English Bankruptcy Law," *Detroit Free Press*, October 23, 1904, p. 9; "Currie Creditors to Meet," *Detroit Free Press*, September 30, 1908, p. 5; "Davock Gives Austin Control," *Detroit Free Press*, October 19, 1908, p. 1; "Knappen Affirms Currie Ruling," *Detroit Free Press*, November 14, 1908, p. 12; "Currie Says Case Led Big Brokers' Firm to Failure," *Detroit Free Press*, December 16, 1908, p. 1; "Currie and Case Friends," *Detroit Free Press*, December 17, 1908, p. 8; "No Discharge for Currie and Case," *Detroit Free Press*, March 11, 1910, p. 7; "Compromise Is Offered in Currie Bankruptcy Case," *Detroit Free Press*, June 21, 1914, p. 20; and *New-York Daily Tribune*, July 19, 1908, p. 14.

5. Austin v. Hayden, 171 Mich. 38, 56, 137 N.W. 317 (1912).

6. Ibid., 137 N.W. at 324.

7. *Detroit Free Press*, March 11, 1910, p. 7.

8. Ibid.

9. Although the University of Michigan's law school was established in 1859, legal education in Michigan was just coming into its own. The Detroit College of Law was founded in 1891, and the University of Detroit's law school would not open until 1912. Most lawyers at the end of the nineteenth century still "read for the law," clerking for lawyers and studying under their direction until they passed the state bar examination and set up their own practices. In a letter to a law firm in East Saginaw asking for a clerking position, Joslyn wrote, "I am without much capital and what I want, is to save enough [in] three or four years work to purchase a small library, when I shall begin for myself." Lee Joslyn to Hon. T. E. Tarsney, July 18, 1884, courtesy of Robert Joslyn.

10. In fact, Joslyn was the only Democrat to be appointed a referee in the Eastern District of Michigan until Walter McKenzie's appointment in 1942.

11. The information about Lee Joslyn and Oscar Baker is taken from Gansser 1905; Oscar W. Baker, announcement of association with Lee E. Joslyn, July 1, 1902, courtesy of Robert Joslyn; and Oscar W. Baker to Mrs. Lee E. Joslyn, July 2, 1948, courtesy of Robert Joslyn.

12. Attorney General of the United States, *Annual Reports* (Washington, DC: GPO, 1913–19).

13. Today $263,023 would be worth approximately $360,000 using CPI methods of calculating relative value, while $9,907 would be equivalent to $115,000 in today's dollars.

14. Joslyn 1925, vi; emphasis in original.

15. "Attack Made on Bankruptcy Law," *Detroit Free Press*, June 7, 1916, p. 16.

16. Ibid.

17. Lee E. Joslyn to Arthur J. Tuttle, March 18, 1916, Arthur J. Tuttle Papers, Bentley Historical Library, University of Michigan (hereafter AJT Papers).

18. Arthur J. Tuttle to Lee E. Joslyn, January 16, 1919, AJT Papers.

19. Report of Special Agent Cole to Chief, Bureau of Investigation, Department of Justice, June 23, 1919, AJT Papers.

20. Ibid.

21. This was not a bankruptcy matter.

22. Joslyn to J. W. Gardner of the Department of Justice, January 16, 1920; Tuttle to LaRue Brown, September 29, 1919, both in AJT Papers.

23. Tuttle to Joslyn, January 16, 1919, AJT Papers.

24. Joslyn to Gardner, January 16, 1920.

25. Tuttle to Thomas Gregory, February 5, 1919, AJT Papers.

26. LaRue Brown to Tuttle, February 15, 1919, AJT Papers.

27. Tuttle to Joslyn, March 16, 1919, AJT Papers.

28. Joslyn to Tuttle, April 1, 1919, AJT Papers.

29. "Federal Bankruptcy Referee Resigns," *Detroit Free Press*, April 3, 1919.

30. Tuttle to Attorney General Mitchell Palmer, April 3, 1919, AJT Papers.

31. Cole Report.

32. Arthur J. Tuttle to Attorney General Mitchell Palmer, February 3, 1920, AJT Papers.

33. Joslyn to Tuttle, April 1, 1919.

CHAPTER 3

1. *Detroit Free Press*, September 18, 1914.

2. The act did not allow involuntary bankrupts to convert their cases to a different chapter, as might happen today; as explained earlier, the act did not include any provisions for corporate reorganization until 1933. Moreover, the act as constituted in 1914 did not permit corporations to voluntarily file bankruptcy.

3. *Detroit Free Press*, September 24, 1914.

4. Warren was one of the original fifty investors who brought Lozier to Detroit (Davis 1988, 75). A partner in the firm of Warren, Cady, Ladd & Hill, he was one of Detroit's most prominent lawyers. He would serve as the U.S. ambassador to Japan in 1921–22 and as ambassador to Mexico in 1924.

5. *Detroit Free Press*, November 24, 1914.

6. 11 U.S.C. §303(h).

7. Farmers or wage earners were exempted from being subject to involuntary filings. On the other hand, corporations were not permitted to file voluntary petitions but were subject to involuntary ones. See 1898 Act §4.

8. 1898 Act §3. These five acts of bankruptcy were half the number of acts under the 1867 law.

9. Simons was a prominent member of the Detroit legal community, not least because of his frequent representation of the Detroit Trust Company (now Comerica Bank). He joined Tuttle as a judge in the Eastern District in 1923; his appointment made him Michigan's first Jewish federal judge.

10. *Detroit Free Press*, February 4, 1915.

11. *Detroit Free Press*, October 18, 1914.

12. *Detroit Free Press*, February 5, 1915.

13. *Detroit Free Press*, March 7, 1915.

14. The new investors were not associated with the bankrupt company (*Detroit Free Press*, April 11, 1915).

15. *Detroit Free Press*, October 28, 1915.

16. Exits from the local industry kept pace, reaching similar numbers during the same period (Davis 1988, 86).

17. Chrysler is now a brand name of FCA US, LLC.

18. The recession was triggered by the demobilization following the armistice in November 1918 and was at first relatively mild. A brief recovery in 1920 was followed by a deeper recession in 1920–21. Bankruptcy filings in the Eastern District of Michigan reflected these conditions. The number of new cases filed held fairly steady in 1917, 1918, and 1919, with new filings of 392, 429, and 356, respectively. Filings dropped by almost half, to 200, in 1920, before doubling to 399 in 1921 and again to 761 in 1922 (Attorney General of the United States, *Annual Reports*, 1917–22).

19. Hyde 2003, 21–22. Compare this amount with the few millions that put Lozier into bankruptcy just six years earlier.

20. *Detroit Free Press*, August 11, 1920.

21. Ibid.

22. Compare this to Lozier, which could not raise $2 million six years earlier.

23. *Detroit Free Press*, April 10, 1921, p. 1.

24. Ibid.

25. *Detroit Free Press*, May 18, 1921.

26. *New York Times*, February 6, 1922.

27. The relationship between Emmons and the Lelands apparently developed during World War I, when Emmons oversaw production of aircraft engines, including Lincoln's Liberty engines, for the Army Signal Corps.

28. *New York Times*, January 12, 1922.

29. *New York Times*, February 5, 1922.

30. *Detroit Free Press*, November 9, 1921.

31. *New York Times*, January 11, 1936.

CHAPTER 4

1. The information in this section is drawn from obituaries for Paul H. King that appeared in the *Journal of the National Association of Referees in Bankruptcy* 16, no. 4 (July 1942): 115, and in the *New York Times*, May 19, 1942. Additional material is taken from Andrews 1928 and J. H. Newmark, "Paul H. King: The Story of a Man Who Delivered the Goods," *Detroit Free Press*, June 6, 1915.

2. Except as otherwise noted, the information in this section is from Dunbar and May 1995; Ervin 1935; and several articles appearing in the *New York Times* between January 27, 1920, and January 10, 1922.

3. *New York Times*, January 27, 1920.

4. King's debilitation, whatever its nature, appears to have been quite real. In a letter to Judge Tuttle dated September 30, 1920 (AJT Papers), Marston

explained King's extended absence from the bench as "on account of ill health."

5. *New York Times*, March 22, 1920.

6. Newberry v. United States, 256 U.S. 232, 41 S.Ct. 469, 65 L.Ed. 913 (1921).

7. Tuttle to King, January 29, 1920, AJT Papers.

8. Tuttle to USDOJ, July 9, 1920, AJT Papers.

9. However, the case remained sufficiently notorious in 1945 that mention of it appeared in the headline of Truman Newberry's *New York Times* obituary on October 4, 1945.

10. Tuttle to J. S. Hurd, April 14, 1919, AJT Papers.

11. Tuttle to Clyde Webster, April 14, 1919, AJT Papers.

12. *New York Times*, February 11, 1923.

13. Tuttle to King, April 20, 1940, AJT Papers.

14. The fees and costs arising from the court's administration of cases as compared to the sums distributed to creditors in those cases were the seventeenth lowest of the country's eighty-four judicial districts.

15. *New York Times*, June 16, 1939.

16. *New York Times*, August 23, 1938.

17. King to Tuttle, June 13, 1939, AJT Papers.

18. King to Attorney General Frank Murphy, April 13, 1939, AJT Papers.

19. King's role in creating Easter Seals is documented at the organization's website, easterseals.org, and a Rotary website, rotary100.org.

20. Tuttle to King, June 15, 1939, AJT Papers.

21. King to Tuttle, August 14, 1939, AJT Papers.

22. "Paul H. King, 1879–1942," *Journal of National Association of Referees in Bankruptcy*, no. 4 (July 1942): 116.

23. Ibid.

CHAPTER 5

1. Edmund Shepherd to Tuttle, August 10, 1942, AJT Papers.

2. Tuttle to Edmund Shepherd, October 28, 1942, AJT Papers.

3. Archie Katcher to McKenzie, July 3, 1946, Walter McKenzie files, box 3, Bentley Historical Library, University of Michigan, Ann Arbor (hereafter McKenzie files).

4. George Read to McKenzie, July 25, 1946, ibid.

5. Marston was the first referee in the district to actually retire from his position, as Davock and King died while holding office, and Joslyn was forced to resign by Judge Tuttle.

6. The system was similar to the one currently employed to compensate Chapter 13 trustees.

7. McKenzie to Judge Tuttle, January 15, 1944, McKenzie files, box 1.

8. Catherine P. Waddle, "The Civil Service Retirement Act," *Journal of the National Association of Referees in Bankruptcy* 20, no. 1 (1946): 16–17.

9. McKenzie diary, March 29, 1919, reference number 85307.0002.001, McKenzie files.

10. According to McKenzie's obituary, he was wounded in battle while in Russia. However, according to his diary, he broke or probably sprained his ankle in what he described as a "sham battle" on September 16, 1918: "Walter McKenzie Dies; Ex-Head of Goodfellows," *Detroit News*, May 13, 1962. McKenzie's own diary entry indicates that the sham battle was a training exercise and not actual combat. McKenzie diary, September 16, 1918, reference number 85307.0002.001.

11. George W. Stark, "Biggest Customer: Old Newsboys Spend $125,000 with Santa," *Detroit News*, December 9, 1936; "Walt's Santa for 60,000 Needy Kids," *Detroit News*, December 14, 1959.

12. McKenzie to Tuttle, January 15, 1944, McKenzie files, box 1.

13. McKenzie files; McKenzie 1947.

14. Aside from his article recounting his experiences on the war crimes tribunal, McKenzie contributed two articles to the journal (McKenzie 1951a; McKenzie 1951b).

15. C. G. Bunting to C. Judge Arthur Lederle, April 24, 1957, McKenzie files, box 3.

16. Earl Warren to McKenzie, May 11, 1957, McKenzie files, box 3.

17. Archie Katcher, Application for Registration, State Bar of Michigan, May 24, 1940.

18. Marquis Who's Who (compiler's copy, provided to the author by Jonathan Katcher).

19. Recall that Katcher had applied in 1942 to succeed Paul King.

20. "Murphy Gets 6-Year Term as Bankruptcy Referee," *Detroit News*, April 26, 1956. The maximum amount authorized by Congress for referees' salaries was $12,500, but that amount increased to $15,000 by the end of that year. Covey 1958.

21. Katcher was briefly replaced after his retirement by David E. Nims Jr., a referee-in-bankruptcy in the Western District of Michigan. Nims was first appointed referee in the Western District in 1954. He served in the Eastern District in January and February 1956 and again from September 1956 until March 1957. He was on the bench in the Western District until 1992.

22. National Association of Referees in Bankruptcy, "Referee Archie Katcher Resigns," *Journal of the National Association of Referees in Bankruptcy* 30, no. 3 (April 1956): 54.

23. National Association of Referees in Bankruptcy, "Joseph C. Murphy Replaces Referee Katcher," *Journal of the National Association of Referees in Bankruptcy* 30, no. 4 (July 1956): 78.

24. Unless otherwise noted, details about Joseph Murphy's early life are taken from Parker 2009, 203–4.

25. "Joseph C. Murphy," *Detroit News*, November 13, 1932.

26. "Bill Providing Branding of Crash Cars Offered," *Detroit News*, May 8, 1935.

27. Except where otherwise noted, details about Hackett's early life are from "Janitor Work Helps Gain $15,000 U.S. Job," *Detroit Free Press*, February 8, 1957.

28. Now known as Wayne State University.

29. See chapter 8.

CHAPTER 6

1. United States Bankruptcy Court, Eastern District Court case filing data, provided to the author by the Clerk of Court.

2. Some sources indicate that Brody was born in 1918. However, a careful examination of the evidence indicates that the earlier date is the correct one.

3. Adam Bernstein, "ADL Lobbyist David A. Brody Dies at 88," *Washington Post*, June 30, 2004.

4. Douglas Martin, "David A. Brody, 88, a Lobbyist for Jewish Causes," *New York Times*, June 30, 2004.

5. But ironically not bankruptcy or courses related to it like contracts, property, or sales.

6. This appears to be the only time in Brody's adult life that he was not employed in academia or by the government.

7. Brody related that Judge Levin once told him "that he was impressed with my maturity. Now, where that came from, I don't know" (Brody 1996, 25). Given Brody's propensity for misstating his age, one must wonder if Judge Levin was hinting to Brody that he was on to his secret.

8. In his keynote address to the Golden Gate Law School bankruptcy symposium in 2011, Chicago bankruptcy attorney Gerald Munitz singled out Judge Brody for the effect the clarity of his opinions had on elevating bankruptcy practice (Munitz 2012).

9. The National Bankruptcy Conference (NBC) claims to be the elite intellectual organization for bankruptcy policy in the United States. Membership in the group is by invitation. The NBC describes itself as "A non-profit, nonpartisan, self-supporting organization of approximately sixty lawyers, law professors and bankruptcy judges who are leading scholars and practitioners in the field of bankruptcy law. Its primary purpose is to advise Congress on

the operation of bankruptcy and related laws and any proposed changes to those laws" (www.nationalbankruptcyconference.org/history.cfm).

10. In re Hamilton Hardware, 11 BR 326, 330 fn. 1 (1981).

11. *Hamilton Hardware* at 333.

12. Eric Starkman, "Brody Teaches Lawyers Bankruptcy Law—And the Value of the Dollar," *Detroit Free Press*, May 8, 1988.

13. Discussed in chapters 8 and 9.

14. Bankruptcy referees began being identified as judges with the adoption of the Federal Rules of Bankruptcy Procedure in 1974.

15. *Hamilton Hardware* at 329.

16. August's client in fact testified in favor of the fee request.

17. "Lawyers Like Judge, But Find Pay Is a Trial," *Detroit News*, March 14, 1983.

18. Starkman, "Brody Teaches Lawyers Bankruptcy Law."

19. 43 B.R. 940, 802 F.2d 207 (Bkrtcy., E.D. Mich. 1982); *aff'd* (6th Cir. 1986).

CHAPTER 7

1. Clerk of Court, United States Bankruptcy Court, Eastern District of Michigan (data provided August 21, 2012).

2. Numerous books and articles detail the long process that resulted in the adoption of the Bankruptcy Code in 1978. Among the most notable are Skeel 2001; Mund 2007; and Klee 1980.

3. The commission was commonly identified both in the media and by its members as the National Bankruptcy Review Commission, which is also the name given to the congressional commission formed in the 1990s to investigate and propose new bankruptcy law reforms. However, they are distinctly different entities.

4. By one count, Kennedy published 160 articles and numerous other works during his career. Macey 2002.

5. By the time Congress in the preceding term should have been ready to give the commission's bill serious consideration it was fully occupied with matters relating to Watergate and the collapse of the Nixon presidency. As a result, no action was taken on bankruptcy legislation for the remainder of that congressional term.

6. Judicial attitudes toward the referees took on petty dimensions in some jurisdictions; referees were denied reserved parking spaces at some courthouses, and others were forbidden to wear judicial robes. Some referees were barred from the judges' dining rooms (Mund 2007, 184–85). Although the district bench in the Eastern District of Michigan kept its distance from the bankruptcy judges, there is nothing to suggest that their conduct ever reached such trivial levels.

7. Mund, interview by Robert Feidler, former Assistant Counsel, Senate Judiciary Committee, August 13, 2003, in Mund 2007, 184.

8. Hearings before the Subcommittee on Improvements in Judicial Machinery on H.R. 8200 and S. 2266, comprehensive bills to recodify U.S. bankruptcy law, 32, http://congressional.proquest.com.proxy.lib.wayne.edu/congressional/ docview/t29.d30.hrg-1977-sjs-0023?accountid=14925.

9. "The effect of the changes . . . has been to usher in a dramatically new bankruptcy regime. The political balance between debtors' and creditors' interests remains intact, but the 'bankruptcy ring' has disappeared. For both better and worse, bankruptcy no longer is a mysterious process that takes place in dark rooms or behind closed doors" (Skeel 2001, 159).

10. American Bankruptcy Institute, Annual Bankruptcy Filings by District, 1980–1984, www.abiworld.org/AM/AMTemplate.cfm?Section=Home&TEMPLATE=/ CM/ContentDisplay.cfm&CONTENTID=35486; United States Bankruptcy Court, Eastern District of Michigan casefiling data provided to the author by the clerk of court.

CHAPTER 8

1. Ric Bohy, "Bankruptcy Unit Probed," *Detroit News*, December 6, 1980, 12-C.

2. Don Ball, "Lawyer Fees Too High, Bankruptcy Judge Told," *Detroit News*, January 30, 1981, 1-B.

3. August, it will be recalled, is the same attorney whose requested fees were reduced by Judge Brody in the *Hamilton Hardware* case.

4. Gene Fogel, WJR Radio Newsfile #1, February 23, 1981, Capital Cities Communications, in author's possession.

5. Don Ball, "Specter of Sex Scandal Grows at U.S. Courthouse," *Detroit News*, June 26, 1981, 1A.

6. Ibid., 2A.

7. Rod Hansen, WJR Radio Newsfile #2, February 24, 1981, Capital Cities Communications, in author's possession.

8. Dougherty either denied most of the allegations made by WJR throughout its reports or offered explanations for others. He sued WJR and its parent company, Capital Cities Communication, in 1981, claiming defamation, disparagement, invasion of privacy, and intentional infliction of emotional distress. That case, which was filed in the U.S. District Court in Detroit, was decided in favor of the defendants, largely on grounds of privilege. 631 F.Supp. 1566 (1986). However, in rendering his opinion in the case, Judge Horace Gilmore wrote, "Here, plaintiff has been unable to point to a single specific statement that was 'of and concerning him,' defamatory, or untrue. Although plaintiff painstakingly presents his version of the story behind each of the broadcasts in his appendix A to his response to defendants' motion, he does not succeed in uncovering any significant statement about him that is false." Ibid. at 1569.

9. Rod Hansen, WJR Radio Newsfile #3, February 25, 1981, Capital Cities Communications, in author's possession.

10. A later report indicated case reassignments should have been made using the blind draw system. Gene Fogel, WJR Radio Newsfile #8, March 4, 1981, Capital Cities Communications, in author's possession.

11. Gene Fogel, WJR Radio Newsfile #4, February 26, 1981, Capital Cities Communications; Rod Hansen, WJR Radio Newsfile #5, February 27, 1981, Capital Cities Communications, both in author's possession.

12. Gene Fogel, WJR Radio Newsfile #6, March 2, 1981, Capital Cities Communications, in author's possession.

13. Rod Hansen, WJR Radio Newsfile #7, March 3, 1981, Capital Cities Communications, in author's possession.

14. Approximately six thousand cases of all types were filed in Detroit during the same time period.

15. 18 USC §154.

16. Don Ball, "Bankruptcy Court Curbed," *Detroit News*, May 7, 1981, 1B.

17. Guercio v. Brody, 911 F.2d 1179, 1181 (1990).

18. Ibid.

19. Ibid.

20. Don Ball, "Bankruptcy Court Has Tough New Set of Rules," *Detroit News*, May 14, 1981, 1B.

21. Ibid., 3B.

22. David Sherwood, telephone interview with the author, December 2, 2008.

23. 18 U.S.C. §154 read, in pertinent part: "Whoever, being a custodian, trustee, marshal, or other officer of the court, knowingly purchases, directly or indirectly, any property of the estate of which he is such officer in a case under title 11 ... Shall be fined not more than $500, and shall forfeit his office, which shall thereupon become vacant." The statute had been on the books since the 1940s, long before Harper went to work at the court in 1957.

24. Don Ball, "Court Clerk Guilty of Illegal Purchases," *Detroit News*, June 13, 1981, 1B.

25. As Sherwood recalls it, Hackett gave him a resignation letter and the key to his office, suggesting that he was prepared for Edwards's decision. David Sherwood, telephone interview with the author, December 2, 2008.

CHAPTER 9

1. August's firm filed approximately half of all Chapter 11 cases in the Eastern District of Michigan in the late 1970s and early 1980s. United States v. August, 745 F.2d 400, 402 (1984).

2. 11 U.S.C. §327(a).

3. Krieger was a nationally noted criminal attorney who would later gain fame as the attorney for reputed mafiosi Joe Bonanno and John Gotti.

4. Tim Belknap, "Fraud Trial Opens; Attorney Acted in Double Role," *Detroit Free Press*, October 19, 1982.

5. In other words, the fee arrangement with House of Imports.

6. Tim Belknap, "Lawyer Cleared in Fraud Case," *Detroit Free Press*, November 5, 1982.

7. Count V of the indictment, which charged August with attempting to improperly influence Judge Hackett, was not tried with the Bogoff charges and was eventually dismissed by the government in August 1983. United States v. August, 745 F.2d 400, 401 fn. 1.

8. 11 F.2d at 403, fn. 4.

9. Technically, Brody drew eight August cases during the period, but half of them were consolidated with some of the others. However, the odds of Brody's name being drawn only eight times were still a considerable 3,685-to-1 (745 F.2d 406).

10. Tim Belknap, "Bankruptcy Lawyer, Judged Linked," *Detroit Free Press*, April 1, 1983, A3.

11. 745 F.2d at 407.

12. Tim Belknap, "'Shopping' for Judges Called Routine," *Detroit Free Press*, August 10, 1982.

13. Tim Belknap, "Court Ploy Was Legal, Lawyer Says," *Detroit Free Press*, March 23, 1983, 3A.

14. 745 F.2d at 402, fn.3.

15. Bogoff and August would eventually marry, have a child, and divorce.

16. Tim Belknap, "Clerk Tells Court She Did a Favor for U.S. Attorney," *Detroit Free Press*, April 22, 1983, 10F; Don Ball, "Bankruptcy Ex-aide Tells of Her Love," *Detroit News*, April 22, 1983, 3A.

17. Belknap, "Clerk Tells Court She Did a Favor."

18. Don Ball, "Jury Gets Bankruptcy Fee Case," *Detroit News*, April 28, 1983, 9B.

19. Tim Kiska, "Lawyer, Clerk Given Prison in Court Scam," *Detroit Free Press*, June 29, 1983, 3A.

20. Don Ball, "Bankruptcy Court Loses All Trustees," *Detroit News*, August 14, 1981, 3-A.

21. Gene Fogel, WJR Newsfile #8, March 4, 1981, Capital Cities Communication, in author's possession.

22. Dougherty v. Capital Cities Communications, Inc., 631 F.Supp. 1566, 1567 (E.D. Mich. 1986).

23. Ibid., at 1576.

24. Guercio v. Brody, 911 F.2d. 1179, 1181 (6th Cir. 1990); Solicitor General's Brief for Respondent Brody to Petition for a Writ of Certiorari to the United States Court of Appeals for the Sixth Circuit, Guercio v. Brody, Case No. 90-1027, justice.gov/osg/briefs/1990/sg90228; *cert. den.* 500 U.S. 904 (1991).

25. Tim Kiska, "Whistle Blower Is a Real Wonder," *Detroit Free Press*, November 18, 1983, 1B.

26. Helen Guercio had already received her due in one way, however. In November 1983 she received national recognition for her role in exposing corruption in the court when the Wonder Woman Foundation named her a "Woman Pursuing Truth." She was feted with an award, a $7,500 check, and a luncheon at a New York hotel. But she did not get her job back.

27. Allan Lengel, "Schools' Judge Is Tough Jurist," *Detroit News*, September 18, 1991, 5A.

28. In re U.S. Truck Co., Inc., 24 B.R. 853 (1982); NLRB v. Bildisco & Bildisco, 465 U.S. 513 (1984).

CHAPTER 10

1. 11 U.S.C. §1101 seq.

2. 11 U.S.C. §1121(b).

3. American Bankruptcy Institute, Annual U.S. Bankruptcy Filings by District, www.abiworld.org/AM/AMTemplate.cfm?Section=Home&TEMPLATE=/CM/ContentDisplay.cfm&CONTENTID=35486.

4. Michigan State Senate, U.S. Motor Vehicle Industry, www.senate.michigan.gov/sfa/ Publications/Issues/MOTORVEH/MOTORVE1.html.

5. "McLouth Steel in Chapter 11 Filing," *New York Times*, December 9, 1981.

6. Winston Williams, "A Steel Company Fights for Its Life," *New York Times*, May 2, 1982.

7. Reuters News Service, "McLouth Sets Sale of Assets to Tang," *New York Times*, August 5, 1982.

8. The purchase price reflected the weakened state of the American steel industry. The portion of the purchase price attributed to the assets was $46 million. Those assets were listed on McLouth's books at the time as having a value of $140 million and a replacement value of $1.2 billion. The purchase agreement had several clauses that would have allowed Tang to back out of the deal if he had chosen to do so; moreover, McLouth would need to negotiate a new labor contract and obtain tax concessions from local governments. Moreover, the entire purchase price was borrowed, most of it from McLouth's existing secured creditors.

9. The confirmed sale price was $81.5 million. The sale did not include McLouth's accounts receivable, which totaled approximately $40 million. Those were

earmarked for the company's secured lenders, who were owed a total of about $75 million.

10. The company itself would not file a plan of reorganization to deal with its remaining assets and obligations until September 1984.

11. Now renamed McLouth Steel Products Corporation.

12. Steven Greenhouse, "McLouth Steel Bounces Back," *New York Times*, December 10, 1983.

13. Allied's attorney was Irving August, and the judge was Harry Hackett. George Woods took over the case when he was appointed to replace Hackett.

14. See, e.g., Borman's, Inc. v. Allied Supermarkets, Inc., 706 F.2d 187 (6th Cir. 1983).

15. 11 U.S.C. §1113.

16. U.S. v. Dandy, 998 F.2d 1344 (6th Cir. 1993).

17. 998 F.2d at 1348 (6th Cir. 1993).

18. A prepackaged Chapter 11 case is one in which all or most of the details of a plan of reorganization have been worked out with creditors and new lenders or investors in advance of the filing.

19. Reuters, "Auto Parts Maker Lear Corp Files for Bankruptcy," July 7, 2009, www.reuters.com/article/2009/07/07/us-lear-idUSTRE56616220090707.

20. Not coincidentally, GM's case was filed one day after bankruptcy judge Arthur Gonzalez approved Chrysler's §363 sale.

21. 28 U.S.C. §1408.

22. Adam Levitan, "Chapter 11 Bankruptcy Venue Reform," September 5, 2011, www.creditslips.org/creditslips/2011/09/chapter-11-bankruptcy-venue-reform.html.

23. 11 U.S.C. §1408(2).

24. See generally chapter 4 in Lopucki 2005.

25. For a critique of the handling of those cases, see Zywicki 2011.

26. While the language of the section seems to give bankruptcy courts broad authority to depart from the code's express restrictions, they had in fact long been cautioned that the provision is not an open-ended grant of authority to be used to expand or contradict the specific powers given to them by the Bankruptcy Code (Norwest Bank Worthington v. Ahlers, 485 U.S. 197 (1988)).

27. Lopucki 2005, 164–67. It should be noted that in a 2005 debate, Judge Steven Rhodes of the Eastern District of Michigan challenged Lopucki's conclusions, stating, "The bottom line is that this book is an inflammatory attack on the judges in New York and Delaware." Tresa Baldas and Brent Snavely, "Judge Steven Rhodes Selected to Oversee Detroit Bankruptcy," *Detroit Free Press*, July 19, 2013, www.freep.com/article/ 20130719/NEWS01/307190070/.

28. The Kmart case had been filed in Chicago based on the location of a defunct affiliate notwithstanding the fact that Kmart's headquarters were in Troy, Michigan.

29. In re Kmart Corporation, 359 F.3d 866 (7th Cir. 2005). The disparate treatment between critical and non-critical vendors in these cases is emphasized by the fact that Kmart's unsecured creditors, including the putative critical vendors, ultimately received about 10 cents on the dollar for their claims, most of it in the form of stock in the reorganized company (Lopucki 2005, 284). In other words, had the bankruptcy court's critical vendor order been affirmed, the critical vendors would have received 1,000 percent more than their fellow unsecured trade creditors.

30. See chapters 6 and 4, respectively.

31. Indeed, the size of the fee requests made in the city of Detroit's Chapter 9 case, heard in the Eastern District of Michigan, quickly became a source of controversy. Monica Davey, "Billions in Debt, Detroit Faces Millions in Bills for Bankruptcy," *New York Times*, October 7, 2013. The fees sought by attorneys and other professionals in the Eastern District of Michigan Chapter 11 bankruptcy case of Collins & Aikman drew public scrutiny because of their size. Peter Lattman and Henny Sender, "Bankruptcy Fees Face Legal Test in Collins & Aikman Billing Case," *Wall Street Journal*, December 14, 2006, A15. Judge Rhodes appointed a special fee examiner in each case.

32. Key Plastics filed Chapter 11 again in 2008 but in Delaware.

33. Although it is not explicitly authorized in the Bankruptcy Code, the courts commonly allow debtors that cannot successfully confirm a plan of reorganization to instead wind down their affairs in the Chapter 11 case without appointing a trustee or converting the case to Chapter 7.

CHAPTER 11

1. Joseph W. Wagar, "After 21 Years, Harold Bobier Retires as Bankruptcy Judge," *Flint Journal*, October 1, 1982.

2. By comparison, fifteen decisions written by George Brody, considered by many to be the district's most scholarly judge, were published during the same time period.

3. The district judge primarily responsible for selecting Walker for the position was James Harvey. Interestingly, Harvey had defeated Walker for the Republican nomination to succeed U.S. congressman Alvin Bentley in 1960 and went on to serve six terms before being appointed to the federal bench in 1974.

4. Tom Henry, "Bankruptcy Judge Harvey Retires in October," *Bay City Times*, June 16, 1983, 1A.

5. One area in which the bankruptcy judges were decidedly unequal was salary. Bankruptcy judges earned $58,500 in 1982, while the district judges' salaries were set at $70,300.

6. Northern Pipeline Co. v. Marathon Pipeline Co., 458 U.S. 50 (1982).

7. Ironically, Chief Justice Burger, who had vigorously opposed the contested provisions when they were under congressional consideration, wrote separately in dissent to indicate his view that overturning the statute would be too disruptive.

8. In their final version, the 1984 amendments contained a number of other important changes to the 1978 law, including provisions imposing new restrictions on the ability of business debtors to use bankruptcy to reject collective bargaining agreements and an amendment intended to enhance the ability of bankruptcy judges to dismiss consumer cases for abuse. Detroit Judge George Brody took an active role in developing and lobbying for the 1984 amendments through the National Conference of Bankruptcy Judges.

9. David Holtz, "Bay City Lawyer Today to Become Bankruptcy Judge," *Flint Journal*, March 29, 1984, C10.

10. Reaffirmation is a process by which Chapter 7 consumer debtors can agree to repay debt notwithstanding discharge. See 11 U.S.C. §524(c) and (d).

11. In re Gilbert, 82 B.R. 456 (Bkrtcy., E.D. Mich. 1988).

12. In re Spradlin, 231 B.R. 254 (Bkrtcy., E.D. Mich. 1988).

13. Winom Tool & Die, 173 B.R. 613 (Bkrtcy., E.D. Mich. 1994).

14. An excellent overview of the key proceedings in the Dow Corning case as well as the major mass torts bankruptcy cases that preceded it can be found in Vairo 2004.

15. Barnaby J. Feder, "Dow Corning Ponders Filing for Bankruptcy," *New York Times*, May 5, 1995.

16. Opt-out plaintiffs were women who elected not to participate in the failed settlement but instead continued to pursue their various cases individually.

17. While Corning would benefit from any relief the courts afforded Dow Chemical in the bankruptcy case, it in fact had little stake in the outcome of this and similar efforts. A 1993 court ruling concluded that Corning had not participated in any of the decision making with regard to Dow Corning's manufacture of implants.

18. 28 USC §157(b)(5) states that "the district court shall order that personal injury tort and wrongful death claims shall be tried in the district court in which the bankruptcy case is pending, or in the district court in the district in which the claim arose, as determined by the district court in which the bankruptcy case is pending."

19. 28 U.S.C. §1334 provides as follows: "(a) Except as provided in subsection (b) of this section, the district court shall have original and exclusive jurisdiction

of all cases under title II; (b) Notwithstanding any Act of Congress that confers exclusive jurisdiction on a court or courts other than the district courts, the district courts shall have original but not exclusive jurisdiction of all civil proceedings arising under title II, or arising in or related to cases under title II."

20. Another order entered three days later provided the same thing for all of the opt-in plaintiffs as well.

21. In re Dow Corning Corporation, 86 F.3d 482, 490–95 (6th Cir. 1996).

22. In re Dow Corning Corporation, 113 F.3d 565, 568–69 (6th Cir. 1997).

23. Ibid., 569–71.

24. Ibid., 571.

25. Grupo Mexicano de Desarrollo v. Alliance Bond Fund, Inc., 527 U.S. 308 (1999).

26. In re Dow Corning, 244 B.R. 721, 744.

27. Ibid., 745.

28. In re Dow Corning, 255 B.R. 455, 481 (2000).

29. 280 F.3d 648 (2002).

30. 287 B.R. 386 (E.D. Mich. 2002).

31. Mass torts cases have become less common in the wake of statutory amendments and rules changes making it more difficult to file and maintain class action lawsuits. Moreover, not all jurisdictions that have considered the issue have followed the reasoning of the Sixth Circuit in *Dow Corning*. One important jurisdiction in particular, the District of Delaware, has specifically rejected the decision. See In re Federal-Mogul Global, Inc., 282 B.R. 301 (Bkrtcy. D.Del., 2002).

32. "Michigan Bankruptcy Judge Leaving Position," March 4, 2002, www.abiworld.org/AM/ PrinterTemplate.cfm?Section=20092& Template= /MembersOnly.cfm&ContentID=9158&NavMenuID.

CHAPTER 12

1. 28 U.S.C. §158(b)(1).

2. 28 U.S.C. §157(b)(2)(D)(6).

3. Judge Cohn is one of only two Eastern District judges active in 2014 who were serving on the court at the time of the August scandal (the other was Julian Abele Cook; both are on senior status at the time of this writing).

4. Author interview with the Honorable Steven W. Rhodes, U.S. Bankruptcy Court, Detroit, Michigan, 2008; author interview with the Honorable Avern Cohn, U.S. Courthouse, Detroit, Michigan, December 1, 2008.

5. Shapero also heard cases in Delaware between 2002 and 2005 to help the local judges with their busy Chapter 11 case docket.

6. In re James, 20 B.R. 945 (Bkrtcy., E.D. Mich. 1982).

7. In re Great Northwest Development Corporation, 28 B.R. 481 (Bkrtcy., E.D. Mich. 1983).

8. Graves gained a certain amount of notoriety soon after taking the bench when he was identified by *Esquire Magazine* as a member of "America's new leadership class," joining celebrities like Bruce Springsteen and Eddie Murphy.

9. Changes made in the judicial selection process in the 1984 amendment necessitated Graves's reappointment in 1986.

10. Data from the Clerk of the Court, United States Bankruptcy Court, Eastern District of Michigan and the Administrative Office for the U.S. Courts, www.uscourts.gov/Statistics/BankruptcyStatistics.aspx.

11. National Bankruptcy Review Commission, *Bankruptcy: The Next Twenty Years* (Washington, DC: GPO, 1997), iv, http://govinfo.library.unt.edu/nbrc/reportcont.html.

12. http://data.bls.gov/timeseries/LASST26000003.

13. www.federalreserve.gov/releases/chargeoff/ delallsa.htm.

14. www.federalreserve.gov/releases/g19/Current/.

15. Bureau of Labor Statistics, Usual Weekly Earnings Summary, January 22, 2014, www.bls.gov/news.release/wkyeng.nr0.htm.

16. Bureau of Labor Statistics, Consumer Price Index, U.S. City Average, 1913–2013, January 16, 2013, ftp://ftp.bls.gov/pub/special.requests/cpi/cpiai.txt.

17. Associated Press, "US Homes Entering Foreclosure Process Slid in 3Q to Lowest Level in 7 Years," October 10, 2013, www.foxnews.com/us/2013/10/10/us-homes-entering-foreclosure-process-slid-in-3q-to-lowest-level-in-7-years/.

18. 551 F.3d 397 (6th Cir. 2008).

19. 634 F.3d 327 (6th Cir. 2011).

20. Sixth Circuit Judge Jeffrey Sutton explained the rationale underlying these provisions thusly: "People who seek bankruptcy protection do not always pay their creditors first when they come across unanticipated disposable income. When the IRS paid these tax refunds directly to the affected taxpayers, a significant number of them put the money to their own uses, not to pay off creditors as required by the terms of their reorganization plans." U.S. v. Carroll, 667 F3d 742, 744 (2012).

21. Affected refunds apparently increased more than tenfold from 2008 to 2009, going from 401 to 4,966. Ibid.

22. Krispen S. Carroll, one of the trustees sued by the IRS (and the first-named defendant in the suit), is the wife of the author of this book.

23. U.S. v. Carroll, at 745–46.

24. Administrative Office of the United States Courts, www.uscourts.gov/Statistics/BankruptcyStatistics.aspx.

CHAPTER 13

1. All population data in this chapter are from the U.S. Census Bureau.

2. Canada's high taxes were more than offset by its national health care system, which bore the benefit costs that the companies had to pay themselves in the United States.

3. "How Detroit Went Broke," *Detroit Free Press*, September 13, 2013. Except as otherwise indicated, the financial data in this part of this chapter are taken from this article.

4. The deal became known in the bankruptcy case as the "COPS and Swaps" transaction, based on its two distinctive financing instruments, certificates of participation and credit default swaps.

5. The deal in fact earned Mayor Kilpatrick and the city the sobriquet of Midwest Regional Deal of the Year by the *Bond Buyer*, the broadsheet of the public bond industry.

6. The amount would vary as interest rates changed.

7. The details of the treasurer's report are contained in Judge Steven Rhodes's decision on the city's eligibility to file Chapter 9, located at 504 B.R. 99, 122–23 (Bkrtcy., E.D. Mich. 2013).

8. Supplemental Documentation of the Detroit Financial Review Team, as contained in In re City of Detroit Mich., 505 B.R. 99, 125 (Bkrtcy., E.D. Mich. 2013).

9. M.C.L. §141.1549(2).

10. M.C.L. §141.1541 et seq.

11. "Protesters Decry Detroit's Emergency Financial Manager," *USA Today*, March 23, 2013.

12. Mich. Const. art. IX, §24.

13. The named plaintiffs in the suits were Gracie Webster and Veronica Thomas, vested participants in the Detroit employee pension funds.

14. There appears to have been no effort made to notify either Orr or his attorneys prior to the filing the motion.

15. Quoted in In re City of Detroit, Mich., 504 B.R. 97, 164 (Bkrtcy., E.D. Mich. 2013).

16. Some creditors maintained that a municipality could nevertheless be compelled to liquidate assets as part of confirmation if the court found that the plan of adjustment would otherwise be unfair or inequitable to creditors.

17. 11 U.S.C. §929(b).

18. Judge Gerald Rosen, comments at the retirement dinner for Steven W. Rhodes, December 11, 2014; Daniel Howes, Chad Livengood, and David Shepardson, "Bankruptcy and Beyond for Detroit," *Detroit News*, November 13, 2014, www.detroitnews.com/longform/news/local/wayne-county/2014/11/13/detroit-bankruptcy-grand-bargain/18934921/.

19. According to one published account, Rhodes even refused to allow a court videographer to photograph him during an official bus tour of the city that the judge took later in the case.

20. American Bankruptcy Institute Videocast, Steven W. Rhodes interview with Lois Lupica, December 19, 2014 (hereafter ABI interview).

21. Bill Vlasic, "Residents of Detroit Go to Court for Pensions," *New York Times*, September 19, 2013.

22. In re City of Detroit, Mich., 504 B.R. 97, 129 (Bkrtcy., E.D. Mich. 2013).

23. Rhodes would also take a bus tour in August 2014 to see conditions in the city firsthand.

24. ABI interview.

25. Bill Vlasic, "In Testimony, Michigan Governor Says Bankruptcy Was Right Call for Detroit," *New York Times*, October 28, 2013.

26. Bill Vlasic, "Detroit Manager Denies Role in Bankruptcy Filing," *New York Times*, October 25, 2013.

27. "The powers not delegated to the United States by the Constitution, nor prohibited by it to the States, are reserved to the States respectively, or to the people."

28. Bill Vlasic, "Judge Hears Arguments on Legality of Detroit Bankruptcy Filing," *New York Times*, October 21, 2013.

29. Ibid.

30. II U.S.C. 109(c)(5).

31. "Heated Start in the Trial on Detroit's Fiscal Future," *New York Times*, October 21, 2013.

32. Vlasic, "In Testimony, Michigan Governor Says Bankruptcy Was Right Call for Detroit."

33. 504 B.R. 149–50.

34. 504 B.R. at 150.

35. 504 B.R. at 154.

36. WDET-FM, "Interview with Judge Steven Rhodes," *Detroit Today*, February 17, 2015, http://wdet.org/shows/detroit-today/episode/judge-rhodes-post-bankruptcy-interview-02-17-15/.

37. Home rule is legal doctrine under which state legislatures grant local governments broad authority to self-govern. In Michigan, municipalities were granted home rule through state approval of their charters by virtue of the Home Rule City Act, M.C.L. §117.1 et seq., first enacted in 1908.

38. This is commonly known as Dillon's Rule.

39. Specifically 28 U.S.C. §1334(a).

40. 504 B.R. at 165.

41. 11 U.S.C. §362.

42. 504 B.R. at 167.

43. 504 B.R. at 169.

44. 504 B.R. at 170.

45. 504 B.R. at 171–72.

46. 504 B.R. 97, 175.

47. ABI interview.

48. The mediators included Eugene Driker, one of Detroit's most prominent attorneys; retired federal judge David Coar; U.S. district judges Victoria Roberts, David Lawson, and Sean Cox from the Eastern District of Michigan, and Wiley Daniel of Colorado; U.S. bankruptcy judge Elizabeth Perris, from Oregon; and Gina Torielli, a municipal tax specialist.

49. Mark Stryker, "DIA Joins Talks to Protect Its Art in Bankruptcy," *Detroit Free Press*, December 7, 2014, A6.

50. Nathan Bomey, John Gallagher, and Mark Stryker, "How Detroit Was Reborn," *Detroit Free Press*, November 9, 2014.

51. Howes, Livengood, and Shepardson, "Bankruptcy and Beyond for Detroit."

52. Bomey, Gallagher, and Stryker, "How Detroit Was Reborn."

53. ABI interview.

54. The rejection was also a rebuff of the recommendation of Rhodes's own mediator, Judge Rosen. According to one news report, Rhodes met with creditors in a conference subsequent to the hearing where he became more deeply engaged in resolving the dispute, telling the attorneys gathered, "Guys, don't ever do that to me with Rosen again." Bomey, Gallagher, and Stryker, "How Detroit Was Reborn."

55. ABI interview.

56. Nathan Bomey and Matt Helms, "Detroit's Settlement with Banks Allows for Quicker Bankruptcy Exit," *Detroit Free Press*, April 12, 2014.

57. Bomey, Gallagher, and Stryker, "How Detroit Was Reborn."

58. "Bond Insurer Takes on Detroit," *Wall Street Journal*, July 14, 2014.

59. Ibid.

60. "Detroit Bankruptcy Judge May Consider Sanctions for Syncora Attorneys," *Detroit Free Press*, August 24, 2014.

61. "Bond Insurer Takes on Detroit."

62. Rhodes refused to order them to make such an apology, however, stating that a coerced apology would not be a genuine one.

63. ABI interview.

64. WDET-FM, "Interview with Judge Steven Rhodes."

65. 11 U.S.C. §943(b)(7).

66. "Expert Says Detroit Bankruptcy Plan Feasible," *New York Times*, October 22, 2014.

67. In re City of Detroit, Oral Opinion on the Record, November 7, 2014 (hereafter Oral Opinion), 35.

68. Oral Opinion, 22–23.

69. Ibid., 44.

70. Ibid., 42–43.

71. Ibid., 47.

72. Ibid., 47–48.

73. 524 B.R. 147 (Bkrtcy, E.D. Mich. 2015).

74. The case was reassigned to Eastern District Bankruptcy Judge Thomas Tucker.

75. WDET-FM, "Interview with Judge Steven Rhodes."

APPENDIX 2

1. Now the site of the northeast portion of the Penobscot Building. Joslyn continued to occupy the Owen Building office after he resigned.

2. Both the Trussed Concrete Building and 419 W. Fort Street are now parking lots.

3. The Majestic Building was razed in 1962 to make way for the First Federal Building, now known as 1001 Woodward Avenue.

BIBLIOGRAPHY

ARCHIVAL COLLECTIONS

Walter I. McKenzie Papers. Bentley Historical Library, University of Michigan, Ann Arbor.

Walter I. McKenzie Polar Bear Expedition Papers. Bentley Historical Library, University of Michigan, Ann Arbor.

Arthur J. Tuttle Papers. Bentley Historical Library, University of Michigan, Ann Arbor.

Papers for the Historical Society for the United States District Court for the Eastern District of Michigan.

PRIMARY SOURCES

Brody, George. Interview by Philip P. Mason, June 4, 1996. Historical Society for the U.S. District Court for the Eastern District of Michigan Oral History Project, United States District Court Library, Detroit, Michigan.

Fogel, Gene, and Rod Hansen. 1981. WJR Radio Newsfile scripts (various dates). Capital Cities Communications.

Hertzberg, Stuart. Interview by Judith Christie, June 17, 2008. Historical Society for the U.S. District Court for the Eastern District of Michigan Oral History Project, United States District Court Library, Detroit, Michigan.

Katcher, Archie. May 24, 1940. Application for Registration, State Bar of Michigan.

Kopacz, Martha E. M. July 18, 2014. Expert Report of Martha E. M. Kopacz Regarding the Feasibility of the City of Detroit Plan of Adjustment.

Rhodes, Steven W. Interview with Lois Lupica, American Bankruptcy Institute Videocast, December 19, 2014.

Subcommittee on Improvements in Judicial Machinery (1932). Hearings on H.R. 8200 and S. 2266, comprehensive bills to recodify U.S. bankruptcy law. http://congressional.proquest.com.proxy.lib.wayne.edu/congressional/docview/t29.d30.hrg-1977-sjs-0023?accountid=14925.

WDET-FM. "Interview with Judge Steven Rhodes." *Detroit Today*,
February 17, 2015. http://wdet.org/shows/detroit-today/episode/
judge-rhodes-post-bankruptcy-interview-02-17-15/.

AUTHOR INTERVIEWS

William Cohen
The Hon. Avern Cohn
Robert Joslyn
Jonathon Katcher
Martin Reisig
The Hon. Steven W. Rhodes
David Wm. Ruskin
The Hon. Walter Shapero
David Sherwood

NEWSPAPERS AND JOURNALS

Bay City Times
Detroit Free Press
Detroit News
Detroit Times
Flint Journal
Journal of the National Association of Referees in Bankruptcy
New-York Daily Tribune
New York Times
Wall Street Journal
Washington Post

BOOKS AND ARTICLES

Andrews, Roger M. 1928. "Regarding Paul King." *Credit Digest*. February.
Brody, George. 1983. "Frank R. Kennedy." *Michigan Law Review* 82:189.
Chardavoyne, David Gardner. 2012. *The United States District Court for the
Eastern District of Michigan: People, Law, and Politics*. Detroit: Wayne State
University Press.
Clive, Alan. 1979. *State of War*. Ann Arbor: University of Michigan Press.
Covey, Edwin L. 1958. "First Decade under the Salary System." *Journal of the
National Association of Referees in Bankruptcy* 32:18.
Davis, Donald Findlay. 1988. *Conspicuous Production: Automobiles and Elites in
Detroit, 1899–1933*. Philadelphia: Temple University Press.
Davock, Harlow P. 1907. "A Symposium on the Value of Humanistic, Particu-
larly Classical, Studies as a Preparation for the Study of Law, from the Point
of View of the Profession." *The School Review* 15(6):429–31.
Dunbar, Willis F., and George S. May. 1995. *Michigan: A History of the Wolverine
State. Grand Rapids, MI: Eerdmans*.

Emmons, William R. 2012. "Don't Expect Consumer Spending to Be the Engine of Economic Growth It Once Was." Federal Reserve Bank of St. Louis. www.stlouisfed.org/publications/re/articles/?id=2201.

Ervin, Spencer. 1935. Henry Ford vs. Truman H. Newberry. New York: Richard R. Smith.

Gansser, Augustus H. 1905. The History of Bay County, Michigan and Representative Citizens. Chicago: Richmond and Arnold.

Gordon, John Steele. 2005. An Empire of Wealth: The Epic History of American Economic Power. New York: Harper Perennial.

Henderson, Tom. 1992. "The Looting of Chatham." Corporate Detroit 9.7(June):12.

Honsberger, John D. 1985. The Origins of the National Bankruptcy Conference: A Hinge Point of Change, 1932–1933. National Bankruptcy Conference. nationalbankruptcyconference.org/mission.

Hunt, Reuben G. 1937a. "The Progress of the Chandler Bankruptcy Bill." Commercial Law Journal 42:195.

———. 1937b. "Summarizing the Work of the Conference." Journal of the National Association of Referees in Bankruptcy 12(October):21.

Hyde, Charles K. 2003. Riding the Roller Coaster: A History of the Chrysler Corporation. Detroit: Wayne State University Press.

Joslyn, Lee. 1925. Student's Manual of Bankruptcy Law and Practice. New York: Matthew Bender.

Katcher, Archie. 1966. "Image of the Bankruptcy Court." Journal of the National Association of Referees in Bankruptcy 40:7.

King, Paul H. 1926a. "Meeting Proceedings." Journal of the National Association of Referees in Bankruptcy 1(2).

———. 1926b. "Bankruptcy Administration Analysis." Journal of the National Association of Referees in Bankruptcy 1(2).

———. 1928. "George Marston." Credit Journal. February.

Klee, Kenneth N. 1980. "Legislative History of the New Bankruptcy Code." American Bankruptcy Law Journal 54:275.

Levitan, Adam. 2011. "Chapter 11 Bankruptcy Venue Reform." creditslips.org, September 5. www.creditslips.org /creditslips/2011/09/chapter-11-bankruptcy-venue-reform.html.

Lopucki, Lynn. 2005. Courting Failure: How Competition for Big Cases Is Corrupting the Bankruptcy Courts. Ann Arbor: University of Michigan Press.

Macey, Morris W. 2002. "A Tribute to Professor Frank R. Kennedy." Bankruptcy Developments Journal 18:231.

McKenzie, Walter I. 1947. "The Japanese War Crimes Trials." Journal of the National Association of Referees in Bankruptcy 22 (July): 103.

———. 1951a. "Allowance of Claims, Summary Proceedings and Discharge." Journal of the National Association of Referees in Bankruptcy 25:45.

———. 1951b. "Suspended or Conditional Discharges." Journal of the National Association of Referees in Bankruptcy 25:46.

Miller, Harvey R. 2002. "Chapter 11 Reorganization Cases and the Delaware Myth." *Vanderbilt Law Review 55:1987.*

Mund, Geraldine. 2007. "Appointed or Anointed: Judges, Congress, and the Passage of the Bankruptcy Act of 1978, Part Two: The Third Branch Reacts." *American Bankruptcy Law Journal* 81:165.

Munitz, Gerald F. 2012. "Keynote Address: Stories in the Development of Bankruptcy Law." *Golden Gate University Law Review* 42:539, 541. http:// digitalcommons.law. ggu.edu/ggulrev/ vol42/iss4/4.

Nevins, Allan, and Frank Ernest Hill. 1957. *Ford: Expansion and Challenge, 1915–1933.* New York: Charles Scribner's Sons.

Parker, Ross. 2009. *Carving Out the Rule of Law: The History of the United States Attorney's Office in Eastern Michigan, 1815–2008.* Bloomington, IN: AuthorHouse.

Posner, Eric A. 1997. "The Political Economy of the Bankruptcy Reform Act of 1978." *Michigan Law Review* 96:47.

Pratt, Henry J. 2004. *Churches and Urban Government in Detroit and New York, 1895–1994.* Detroit: Wayne State University Press.

Pusey, Merlo J. 1951. *Charles Evans Hughes.* New York: Macmillan.

Remini, Robert. 1997. *Daniel Webster: His Life and Times.* New York: Norton.

Skeel, David. 2001. *Debt's Dominion: A History of Bankruptcy Law in America.* Princeton: Princeton University Press.

Stanley, David T., and Marjorie Girth. 1971. *Bankruptcy: Problems, Process, and Reform. Washington, DC: Brookings Institution.*

Tabb, Charles Jordon. 1999. "A Century of Regress or Progress? A Political History of Bankruptcy Legislation in 1898 and 1998." *Bankruptcy Developments Journal* 15:343.

Vairo, Georgene. 2004. "Mass Torts Bankruptcies: The Who, the Why, and the How." *American Bankruptcy Law Journal* 78:93–152.

Warren, Charles. 1935, 1999. *Bankruptcy in United States History. Washington, DC: Beard Books.*

Warren, Elizabeth. 1993. "Bankruptcy Policymaking in an Imperfect World." *Michigan Law Review 92:336.*

Warren, Elizabeth, and Jay Westbrook. 2009. "The Success of Chapter 11: A Challenge to the Critics." *Michigan Law Review* 107(February):603–42.

Yanik, Anthony J. 2009. *Maxwell Motor and the Making of the Chrysler Corporation.* Detroit: Wayne State University Press.

Zelenko, Benjamin L. 1969. "The Role of the Referee in the Legislative Reform of the Bankruptcy Act." *Journal of the National Conference of Referees in Bankruptcy* 43:103.

Zywicki, Todd. 2011. "The Auto Bailout and the Rule of Law." *National Affairs* 7(Spring):66–80.

CASES

Austin v. Hayden, et al., 171 Mich. 38, 137 N.W. 317 (1912).

Austin v. Hayden, et al., 190 Mich. 528, 157 N.W. 93 (1916).

In re City of Detroit, 504 B.R. 97 (Bkrtcy., E.D. Mich. 2013).

In re City of Detroit, Oral Opinion on the Record of Steven W. Rhodes, November 7, 2014.

In re City of Detroit, 524 B.R. 147 (Bkrtcy., E.D. Mich. 2015).

In re Currie, et al., 197 F. 1012 (E.D. Mich. 1910).

Dougherty v. Capital Cities Communications, 631 F.Supp. 1566 (E.D. Mich. 1986).

In re Dow Corning Corporation, 86 F.3d 482 (6th Cir. 1996).

In re Dow Corning Corporation, 113 F.3d 565 (6th Cir. 1997).

In re Dow Corning, 244 B.R. 721 (Bkrtcy., E.D. Mich. 1999).

In re Dow Corning, 255 B.R. 455, 481 (E.D. Mich. 2000).

In re Dow Corning, 280 F.3d 648 (6th Cir. 2002).

In re Dow Corning, 287 B.R. 386 (E.D. Mich. 2002).

In re Federal-Mogul Global, Inc., 282 B.R. 301 (Bkrtcy., D.Del., 2002).

In re Gilbert, 82 B.R. 456 (Bkrtcy., E.D. Mich. 1988).

In re Great Northwest Development Corporation, 28 B.R. 481 (Bkrtcy., E.D. Mich. 1983).

Grupo Mexicano de Desarrollo v. Alliance Bond Fund, Inc., 527 U.S. 308, 119 U.S. 1961, 144 L.Ed.2d 319 (1999).

Guercio v. Brody, 911 F.2d 1179 (6th Cir. 1990).

In re Hamilton Hardware, 11 BR 326, 330 (Bkrtcy., E.D. Mich. 1981).

In re James, 20 B.R. 945 (Bkrtcy., E.D. Mich. 1982).

In re Kmart Corporation, 359 F.3d 866 (7th Cir. 2005).

Local Loan Company v. Hunt, 292 U.S. 234, 54 S.Ct. 695, 78 L.Ed. 1230 (1934).

Newberry v. United States, 256 U.S. 232, 41 S.Ct. 469, 65 L.Ed. 913 (1921).

Northern Pipeline Co. v. Marathon Pipeline Co., 458 U.S. 50, 102 S.Ct. 2858, 73 L.Ed.2d 598 (1982).

Norwest Bank Worthington v. Ahlers, 485 U.S. 197, 108 S.Ct. 163, 99 L.Ed.2d 169 (1988).

In re Spradlin, 231 B.R. 254 (Bkrtcy., E.D. Mich. 1988).

United States v. August, 745 F.2d 400, 402 (6th Cir. 1984).

U.S. V. Carroll, 667 F3d 742, 744 (6th Cir. 2012).

U.S. v. Dandy, 998 F.2d 1344 (6th Cir. 1993).

In re U.S. Truck Co., Inc., 24 B.R. 853 (Bktcy., E.D. Mich. 1982).

In re Winom Tool & Die, 173 B.R. 613 (Bkrtcy., E.D. Mich. 1994).

DATA SOURCES

Administrative Office of the United States Courts (uscourts.gov).

American Bankruptcy Institute (abiworld.org).

Attorney General of the United States (1899–1930). *Annual Reports.* Washington, DC: GPO.

Bureau of Labor Statistics.

Clerk of the Court, United States Bankruptcy Court, Eastern District of Michigan.

Federal Reserve Board.

Michigan State Senate.

INDEX

www.ingramcontent.com/pod-product-compliance
Lightning Source LLC
Chambersburg PA
CBHW070438100426
42812CB00031B/3332/J